Humbling and Humility

Rian Nejar

Anasim Books

Humbling and Humility is a work of fiction. Names, characters, places, and events are either the product of the author's imagination or are employed fictitiously. Any resemblance to actual events, locales, or persons, living or dead, is coincidental.

Humbling and Humility.
Nejar, Rian

ISBN–10: 0–9908035–4–6
ISBN–13: 978–0–9908035–4–6

Published by *Anasim Books*, 3838 E Encinas Ave, Gilbert, AZ 85234.
     October 15, 2014, in *print* and *e-book* formats. **Small Print** edition.
     Updated: July 15, 2018.

Written, edited, and proofed in the **United States of America** and **Canada**.

Acknowledgment: Assistance by **Diana Maryon**, author of *O Love How Deep* **(2017)**, in editing this updated version, is gratefully acknowledged by the author. Her insightful comments and suggestions have lent this work clarity and brightness.

Library of Congress Cataloging-in-Publication Data
On order.

To my children:

May truth and integrity guide you into peace and happiness.

Prologue

Education is the inculcation of the incomprehensible in the indifferent by the incompetent.
— John Maynard Keynes

Walking in, on a pleasant southwest December afternoon, to my court-ordered intervention program, I harbored much resentment for what was to come, and little hope of learning anything useful. This program was the remedy prescribed by a seemingly uncaring judicial system, the great American system of justice, which I fell afoul of by disorderly conduct. It was either this, paid for in addition to court fees and fines, or six months' residence in a notorious correctional system of the state. That really wasn't much of a choice. State hospitality in germ-infected facilities, tent camps in the hot desert with rattlesnakes and scorpions for company, and pink underwear designed to attract attention—this could be my lot under Wariduna Sheriff Waspoia's eminently questionable rules of incarceration. A lose-lose situation, or so I thought, steeling myself to face the re-education mandated.

Being a forty-something first generation immigrant from enchanting India, the largest and most complex democracy by population, where culture and education are given high priority in one's growth into adulthood, made this unsought inculcation all the more fun.

But that was almost five years ago. Though I'd decided then to document every aspect of that experience, my urge to write remained muted—until the recent arrest and prosecution of another, from my land of origin, by the American justice system. This event awoke buried memories; it also made all the news. The US secretary of state and the Indian prime minister commented on it. Ministers declared procedural war upon American embassy and consular officials in India. The Indian media was agog with this event in America and its public backlash at home.

The arrest and strip-search in New York of an Indian consular officer, a young mother, for alleged offenses of providing false visa information and underpayment of her domestic employee, inflamed her family and countrymen. The event incurred immediate public retaliation in large, vociferous demonstrations in her nation. Priyavani Cobraghatta's modesty had been outraged, her consular status disrespected, and America had greatly overstepped its authority, or so claimed her supporters. There was indeed something deeply disturbing about events relating to her arrest. My memories could now no longer be denied expression.

I recall my own deplorable journey through the American justice system. An inexplicable arrest at night, in my minimal house-wear, a harrowing day in state holding, and a struggle to regain my freedom. This was followed by prosecution by an adversarial district attorney's office, and a defense, of sorts, by Mindy Castle, a lump-sum-fee local lawyer. Priyavani on the other hand was prosecuted by a prominent man of the law, Veer Batata, an immigrant hailing from the same land as us, famous for prosecuting and jailing many a captain of industry here. She was represented by a New York lawyer, and a good few Indian ministers and politicians spoke for her through the raucous Indian media and communication channels between the two administrations. There could, surely, be no similarity in how she and I journeyed through our legal processes.

But did either of us learn something, anything, from all that transpired? There is one thing vividly common: all I wanted to do, when subjected to the system and its processes, was surrender my citizenship and leave, and I imagine all she desired was to be relieved of her assignment and official role here in America, and leave. But there ends any such parallel. Priyavani did leave in short order, free from prosecution or accountability for her actions in this land. I, on the other hand, continued with the process in this large and powerful democracy of the world.

It is harder yet to bring up memories of my crime that led to a most unpleasant encounter with the system here. I was accused of assault and disorderly conduct with no specifics on what constituted 'assault' on my part. But that is how this system works, as I discovered in due course in my prosecution and re-education. An unwanted contact, a pull of the arm, even a poke with a finger can be termed *assault* by the honorable enforcers of the law, as Officer Gormon Grigorevic of the town of Dilbut did with me. They will then search high and low for any evidence they can employ to buttress such a charge.

Does truth really matter to such enforcers in these strange circumstances? Do they pause to consider the devastating impact their actions may have on a person and a family's future? I hoped to discover empathy as I went through the process—and perhaps also comprehend some of my failings. A sense of outrage, much like that expressed by so many supporters of Priyavani, had welled up within me then.

My attempts to talk to those involved in the process seemed of no avail. I felt then, overwhelmingly, that this legal system condemned me as a criminal and cared only to dispose of me. I would only be another conviction the state won against undesirable elements falling into its grasp. It had been a most turbulent period in life for me. As I resigned myself to the system and its cursory resolution, I did accept that my actions expressed a disturbance within. And that I had indeed behaved in an ungentlemanly manner.

• • •

In a small office, at the entrance of a drab and nondescript intervention center, I wrote my responses, to queries in an intake form, for the domestic violence program. It was clear that the form was meant to be broadly inclusive with decidedly explicit questions. Did I practise violence during sex with my partner? Did violence occur during disagreements? Did I employ violence to obtain obedience? Did I beat, shove, or slap my partner around? Did I use threats of violence with weapons? Coming from a culture of non-violence, despite a rough childhood and adolescence, I recall these questions making me cringe at their offensive nature.

There were some questions about self-esteem as well. Did others like me? Did I think others liked me? Did I desire that others like me? Did others enjoy my company? I suppose the questions had some introspective and probative value, and could help counselors develop a model of participant personality, but *did* they really care?

My intake counselor was personable enough. He asked me to describe the series of events which led me to this private establishment that employed him. Uncomfortable over answering the questionnaire, I described events as briefly as I could—a domestic argument with my spouse that became somewhat physical—and asked him instead why anger is something the state appears to require suppression of, while not providing any remedies for circumstances that lead to anger. **Sid**—the counselor—pointed out that anger leads to violence, and that then becomes a matter for the state.

"Don't get mad, get even—isn't this a common saying here in the west?" I asked. "What do you think will happen, in crowded nations like India, if everyone worked to get even instead of getting mad and venting out anger?"

"There would be chaos," replied Sid, giving me a curious look. "But conditions here are different. We have courts to help us resolve disagreements."

"What is the membership of the group I am to join?"

He figured out my oblique question. "All male. Women have separate counseling groups."

"What about the root causes for such domestic disagreements?" I dug deeper into what he helped with. "How do you address the free mingling of sexes in the typical workplace, and the resulting infidelity?"

Sid spoke with a bluntness that caught me unawares: "You are a root cause. These sessions are to address what you can do to change."

"The state requires a license to begin a family, but does not prosecute infidelity that often destroys a family," I persisted. "Is this of no concern to the state at all?"

"Some states do that..." he said, with some hesitation.

That was a revelation to me. So the law varied, state by state? How did this come about? I knew that taxes varied, but the law? How are people across the nation equal, if laws do not apply uniformly? Clearly, something new to learn.

"Isn't it futile to beat on me, a victim?" I asked, continuing my unrelenting drive to question the state's processes. "One who, despite obvious harm caused by a partner's infidelity, is trying to bring about a good end result? Is this process just to satisfy the state?"

"It is ninety percent that. You finish the course, and go beat the snot out of your partner—the state can say that they made you go through the course, at least! Cover their behind, in other words."

Sid seemed in a hurry to finish with me. He explained that he had another appointment to prepare for, a group to counsel. He asked me to meet his colleague, Dave, for an initial orientation, after which I could choose my counseling group and sessions. I sensed that he wasn't altogether comfortable with having me in his group.

I met with Dave, who explained to me that almost any form of domestic disagreement in Wariduna could be classified under domestic violence, or DV. He added further that it is not a shame or blame game, but is meant to be didactic and educational, whatever that meant. He waxed eloquent about how happiness must trickle down in families from parents, who must first be happy with each other before they can make children happy. And that feelings come from within us. Dave was an overly happy sort of person who loved his own didactic thoughts and speech.

I joined Sid's counseling group, wanting no part of happy, didactic sessions. Walt Disney movies were enough to provide added moral instruction along with rote entertainment. Maybe Sid wouldn't push me to get in touch with my 'inner' feelings. Or compel me to explore a homunculus—a little human—resident in my head. Our first session was scheduled for the next week.

The Group

Sid greeted the gathered bunch of morose men in one of the small windowless session rooms. The room had chairs around three sides, a large whiteboard on one wall, with a door in a corner and a television set in the other corner. Sid asked that we begin introducing ourselves, providing some background of our origin, and the sorry circumstances that brought us into his counseling program.

Levi hailed from the state of Israel. A tall, lanky, dark-haired, olive-complexioned young feller, identifiably Middle Eastern, who seemed somewhat reticent and subdued, and yet talked forcefully. Married into a Middle Eastern family in America, he fought with his wife, fell afoul of the law, and with us in counseling. **Tony** was a short, Hispanic, older man hailing from just south of the border, from Mexico. He was sent to the program for beating his teenage son. **Fred**, a friendly middle-aged Caucasian, was kicked out of his home, with his guns, after his wife closed a garage door on his hand leading to many unflattering words and strong disagreement. I introduced myself briefly as one coming from the other side of the globe, India, and in the program for ungentlemanly behavior with my spouse. There were some more in the group whose names and situations did not register in my mind.

Our group was small, to begin with, though quite diverse, and lacking in enthusiasm. No one expected anything interesting out of our sessions ahead.

Sid began a discussion with his description of what he believed to be an expression of freedom protected in American society. "I am married, but my wife can sleep with anyone she wants to, and I can sleep with anyone I want to."

Smiles of disbelief from all group members.

"What would you do if you came into your house and saw your wife in bed with another man?" asked Sid.

"Kill her," said Levi, with an immediacy that surprised us.

Fred cheerfully agreed, "Yes, you can!"

A good few in the group objected to this blatant disregard for life or the typical norms of civil society.

Levi persisted in his extreme position. "Kill her, I'd say."

Fred laughed. "Yes, you can. But you'd have to be clever about it; claim that you saw a man attacking your wife in bed, got your gun, and shot at him to protect your wife. Shoot multiple times, and tragically, kill them both."

Clearly, Fred had been around guns for long, and perhaps had some experience using them with impunity. The candidate for a vice-presidential post, who shot a lawyer and campaign contributor under the assumption that the lawyer was prey hiding in the bush (which, you may agree, is an assumption well worth forgiving), came to my mind. The conversation swiftly descended into disagreement, with a good few in the group opposing this judge-jury-executioner approach. Yet something about Fred's proposed actions rang a bell, resonated in the mind. I couldn't put my finger on it then. Sid was at a complete loss for words.

Levi clarified further. "See, I am from Israel, of Palestinian origin. It's a democracy there too. But that is what I'd do."

Sid diverted the discussion onto formalities for our sessions, the responsibilities and expectations of participants, etc., and occupied the rest of the session in such matters.

• • •

My own thoughts drifted to that mid-July night in 2007 when I chanced upon my wife's extra-marital affair. It was a hot monsoon night, and a lightning storm was active over a part of the metropolis Dilbut belongs to. I recall that it was about 11 p.m., beyond my usual bed time, and I'd come back down to the kitchen for a drink of cold water. Hearing the fan running in the half-bath downstairs, I headed to turn it off when I noticed the bathroom light on with the door closed. Passing by the door, I overheard my wife talking—something was strange about her voice, and the conversation, and I stood silently by the door listening. I could only hear her voice.

"I'll make some egg curry and bring it over to you."

" . . . "

"Yes! I wasn't sure if I should have sent you that message," my wife giggled.

" . . . "

"Yeah! That was so nice..." she continued giggling.

" . . . "

"Yes! I too really like it in the dark!"

Listening to these late night sweet nothings and declarations from my life partner, I felt a wave of nausea spread in me, overpowering me, enraging me simultaneously. There was no mistaking the tone and substance of her conversation. I knocked hard on the bathroom door and demanded to know who she was talking with.

A quiet, almost whispered, "I'll talk to you later..." emanated from within, followed by a louder—"I'm coming!" in response.

As I waited, I imagined she was deleting suspect messages from her phone. When she came out a few minutes later, I demanded to know who it was she was messaging and talking with, but she would neither reveal that, nor give me her cellphone. As this conversation became more heated by the minute, I knew I needed help—and called our common friends, another local family, and requested their immediate presence.

I had sensed something strange in my wife's behavior in the few months before this incident—but never suspected that a mother of two little children could take such a step outside the family. Or that she could betray any and all promises and her responsibilities toward our children and the marriage. Not after all that we'd been through in the past together…but that remains to be revealed.

When the friends I called—John and Parvathi, also from India— came by, they pressed her to reveal the number called and the circumstances of the call. Maybe she thought there wasn't anything to lose and gave us the number, which I called in the presence of these friends. On the other end was a fellow who was rather nonchalant about his conduct with another man's wife. When questioned, and asked of his intentions, he said he'd enjoyed a level of intima-cy with my wife already, and could make it a long-term relationship after she divorces me. Very glib, very matter of course, and very disturbing.

• • •

Sid's query, about clarifications that members might need regarding the counseling group and sessions, pulled me back to the day's session from trou-bled memories. No, I thought, recalling Sid's *wife-in-bed-with-another* ques-tion, I had not reacted violently to the discovery of my wife's affair and plans. I had instead felt a deep sense of betrayal and overwhelming shock—how could she do such a thing? In our own home? In a home we raise our children in? How could she stoop so low—wait until the children and I fell asleep, to en-gage in her salacious conduct—in our *home*? My home, that sheltered my fami-ly, that gave me refuge and comfort through many family tragedies, was sacred to me. I felt viscerally violated. John and Parvathi could scarcely respond to my emotions; they had no words to alleviate my shock and sense of outrage.

But this was two full years before I landed in the grips of this legal system. Two long years before I became someone who'd engaged in unlawful disorder-ly conduct, falling into a court-mandated re-education program. A program where I'd come to hear that my life-partner may sleep with anyone she chooses to, and that I may do the same regardless of our marriage and its vows.

I was required to follow up with my probationary officer, **Lauren Smith-Green**, after classes began. I was placed on probation—like any other convicted criminal in this system—until my successful completion of the intervention program. Lauren had a second role as an additional counselor. She was a small, short and stocky, white-haired older lady, and was quite pleasant to talk to. She seemed sympathetic toward agonies endured in passing through the process. It was within her authority to recommend that I leave this process and the country altogether. But she did have a condition for such release, that I successfully complete such an intervention program in any country I moved to. And though another had taken this route in the past, it seemed simpler for me to stick with the process here, and with her as my probationary supervisor.

Lauren was taken aback by my description of the first group session. "You are definitely in the wrong group," she said. "Are you sure there isn't a better group to move to?"

I wondered why she thought the *group* was a wrong one to be in. Did the group determine results of counseling? I rather liked the idea of a group that tested the limits of their intervention program. I spoke with Lauren instead about a continuing impasse at home, and about accusations of threats made from my spouse.

"Threats? What threats could *you* have made?" she asked.

"I said to my wife that I'd take her to task in a court of law, given a chance," I clarified. "She knows that I've prosecuted and won civil cases. I am engaged at the moment in a case against a company that stole some of my intellectual property."

Lauren asked if I felt constrained or burdened by not being free. I wasn't sure what she meant, the legal process or my marital nightmare. I replied that I'd always felt free in my heart and mind. I gave her a copy of *My Experiments With Truth*, by Mohandas K. Gandhi, that I brought along to the meeting. You may know of him as an Indian who stood for non-violence, who taught generations before us to be non-violent and yet effective. Freudian thinkers may label such non-violent but provocative methods as being passive-aggressive.

I brought the book along because Lauren seemed genuinely interested in learning about Indian culture in discussions with me. The book could help more; I didn't feel or think much like an *Indian* after a decade and seven years in America. Besides, India is a complex melting-pot, of diverse cultures and races in a smallish geographical area, hemmed in by massive mountain ranges along its northern boundaries and oceans around its peninsular body. There isn't any specific culture that could be called distinctly Indian.

Yet this topic could make for interesting conversations with Lauren. An influx of a large number of new Indian immigrants, into this region of the state, may have aroused her curiosity to learn more about this eastern and ancient cultural tapestry. I knew it to be a complex social fabric that birthed and assimilated multiple religions, and gave rise to much in the way of independent thinking and spiritual pursuits.

Getting Out Before More Trouble

Sid came in with a frown on his face as the group quieted down to begin class the next week. He looked at the papers he brought along and seemed confused—said he'd carried the wrong set of notes and returned to his office to get another. He wanted to talk about violence, and ways to avoid its occurrence, to begin our regular counseling sessions.

"I don't think we have a justice system," Sid declared, back with his notes. "We have a legal system."

Nods of agreement from some in the group, confused looks from others. What do you mean, Sid? Isn't that the same thing, and aren't you just playing with words? Sid said what he meant is that the system isn't necessarily designed to mete out justice as we expect it to do. Because justice is, in most cases, relative: what is just for one may not be so for another. It is simply a system of laws and enforcement, with courts serving to officiate over determinations regarding laws broken and the manner of such infraction. In short, it is like any other government system, prone to manipulation and corruption, though it has been designed to be impartial and fair, more or less, with checks and balances built in.

"Honesty is not always the best policy within the legal system," said Sid.

I could attest to that from personal experience. Consequences of my honesty with law-enforcement included arrest, prosecution, and this re-education program. The police report filed, and conversations with Mindy, my lawyer, helped confirm that for me.

I recall, when questioned by Officer Gormon Grigorevic prior to my arrest, telling him everything that transpired: my wife's absence until late in the night, her lack of response to repeated calls to her cellphone, her return past 10 p.m., and my requests that she and I discuss that disagreement downstairs. She had ignored my repeated requests and those of my son as well. I entered the children's bedroom, pulled on her arm as she lay on the bed, insisting that she come down to discuss the matter. I described the ensuing emotional discussions downstairs, in the course of which she repeatedly called a non-emergency police number, disconnecting the line at each instance. I had no qualms in describing everything that happened to Gormon as comprehensively as could be recalled. It's fair to say I trusted the police then.

It was Mindy who told me that Gormon, who'd expressed surprise in his conversation with my wife, had told my spouse that with what I was telling them, they'd have no problem arresting and prosecuting me. It was as if an adversarial side was chosen by law-enforcement personnel, and honesty by the other side then became helpful ammunition for the system. The other cop, of Hispanic ethnicity—from Feliz, his name—who accompanied Gormon, had looked at me sympathetically as matters unfolded that night. Gormon was in charge, and I'd been deemed the criminal. Judge-jury-executioner mode again.

Execution in this instance was my arrest, and cherry-picking of incident information to facilitate effective conviction. It no doubt added a feather to Gormon's cap and a scalp to his belt. I discovered this only when I had the chance to review a police report Gormon prepared; the one-sided nature of his report shocked me.

What was more interesting was a blatant falsification by Gormon of his administration of Miranda Rights, the right to remain silent and to legal representation, included in that report by him. And Mindy's assertion of the known corrupt nature of Dilbut police—but I digress.

Contemplating Sid's gems of insight and wisdom, I thought only honesty could best serve any relationship, however painful its practice, and avoid delaying the inevitable. Yet what Sid pointed out had more to do with social deception, and, in this case, within a legal system. A skill that could ease one's journey through such social systems and circumstances. The system is an unstoppable machine—if you cannot get out of its way, and land in its grasp, you'd do best to lubricate your path and slip out with careful deception. Nevertheless, isn't such deception only for individual benefit, and not for a greater good?

Perhaps, in systems here, one must focus on whatever benefits oneself. One cannot trust the system, this branch of government, to do right by itself. This society appears to comprise only of individuals and adversarial systems; it is not an integral community. It was all rather confusing. I drifted back to listening to Sid.

Sid was talking about accountability, and—"...putting it behind you," that it was—"...not the end of your life." I thought, instead, "Except for one who, with an arrest record for something as objectionable as violence, may never be hired again in the corporate world." I could not have realized then how accurate this would prove to be. And how this one event would impoverish my little family, and deny me so many opportunities to provide for my children and myself.

Or how a legal system's intervention program that they considered helpful and corrective became a virtual life-sentence for me and my children. But who cares about such individual circumstances? Surely not the adversarial system of laws and law-enforcement; that is quite clear. This system appears to account for people principally in terms of numbers prosecuted and money gained.

We moved on to watching a video on domestic violence, '90s style. According to that video documentary, four women die every day in the United

States due to such violence. The source of violence, claimed the video, is the sense that one is superior. Violence is often used to enforce this superiority. A contrived domestic situation was depicted: cat-hair on an overcoat, and a husband who shoved his wife when she objected to his complaints. An attempt at illustrating moral superiority in one who was wronged, albeit with hair shed on a coat, but resulting in a decidedly immoral act of needless violence. Any connection between superiority and violence seemed tenuous to me.

The narrator declared, "Violence is entering someone's personal space when they do not desire it." He went on to say—"Emotionally rejecting someone is emotional violence." To avoid such violence, he recommended taking a time-out.

I piped up, "What form is the violence done, on children and a husband, when a spouse has an affair?"

Sid admitted that it is indeed abuse of the relationship and the family. "You have to work at your relationship, every day, and whenever possible," he declared.

"That is a very stressful occupation by itself," I retorted.

Widespread laughter in the group; Sid walked around to pat me on the back. Man-to-man empathy, perhaps. I wondered if Sid was engaged in maintaining a relationship himself, as he described that task in class.

I explained my views further. "As a father, my principal concern is the well-being and happiness of my children. I don't think as much about myself—or expect anyone to."

"Happiness has to flow down! You have to work on making yourselves happy, focus on yourself, before making the children happy," declared Sid.

We discussed the oxygen-mask example, in airplanes, where it is recommended that adults put their masks on first before helping with a child's mask. That seemed a bit extreme to me. A contrived situation misapplied to reinforce trickle-down economics and current social practices.

Social situations are not quite the same as a low oxygen crisis in an airplane. I think of an affair by a spouse as a sudden sky-diving departure of a family member from a floating balloon basket. Wheeee! Look at me, I'm out, flying, and happy, says the departee, leaving others in the family scratching their heads in more than a little confusion. And the remaining parent holding the children protectively to prevent them jumping after the happily absconding parent. There is little resemblance in such a social circumstance to the oxygen-mask example.

Perhaps a difference between eastern and western cultures lies in selflessness, a focus on duties and responsibilities in the east, and in self-orientation, a pursuit of individual liberties and benefit, taking precedence over the group, in the west. But aren't instances of familial fracture found everywhere? And aren't such crisis examples over-simplification of complex social situations?

Interested in the exchange between Sid and me, the group asked for a description of events that led to my presence in this intervention program. I spoke of the mid-summer incident in 2007, when I first discovered my wife's split from an integral family, and many intense arguments that led to the presence of police in our home that year. And of similar arguments and discussions that led to the presence of law-enforcement again in 2008, both police visits at my request for assistance. And the events of 2009, when, under the strange circumstances that brought cops to my home, I was arrested and prosecuted. The group members, including Sid, were of one voice, vehement and unambiguous in their recommendation. "You must get out of this! You may soon face greater trouble..."

But getting out wasn't that simple for me. I struggled then with the upheaval in the family, and the lives of my children turned upside down with a caregiver largely missing from the home. An unresolved question circled in my mind. Every sane and responsible adult has the right to do whatever he or she pleases with his or her life. But what right permits a mother to shatter the security and comfort of innocent children in pursuit of better situations for herself? Solutions through the legal system seemed just as uncaring about this question; I wasn't ready to let go until this vexing conundrum could be resolved.

In an all-too-familiar argument around that time, my wife claimed to have harbored thoughts of an extreme nature—death, I imagine—because of me when carrying our first child. She seemed to project her internal unhappiness onto the children as well. Was that meant to convince me that her life, and the lives of our children, would be better with me gone? I tried explaining to her then that there are always two sides to every coin, to any such situation or perception.

I recall also explaining that I required nothing of her, and that she might find release from what she was going through only if she took a measure of responsibility for the difficult problems now faced by the family. The impasse continued unchanged, except for a deafening silence in my home, and confusion and conflict in my mind.

But even more, constraints of the eastern culture, that I grew to adulthood in, did not permit such rapid change in life circumstances. Indian marriage law requires that a couple contemplating divorce go through a period of separation, for introspection and self-evaluation, before reasserting their demand for termination of the marriage. Besides, having passed through a prior marriage breakup, and having seen its effects on a growing child, I couldn't bear to subject two more innocent children to the torment of a broken family. No, getting out of this commitment wouldn't be as simple as a quick and cheap divorce granted in a 'no-fault' state. Not for someone who comes from a culture where such things are looked down upon as a sure lack of character and maturity.

New and Old Stories

The group seemed larger when we next gathered. I'd been waiting outside the facilities, as was common for those who came early, and the crowd outside had also seemed somewhat bigger. Past the holidays, and into the New Year, perhaps more of those required to do so were beginning the program. One new member in the group had a cast on his leg, and came in on crutches.

Sid was in the session room early, chatting with the rest of the group. Sid was short by American standards—five and a half feet in height—but fit, and gave the appearance of being a military man with his close-cropped hair and square features. He preferred sitting to standing when talking with us inside the session room or in his office.

By this time, many among us had settled into specific positions around the session room—a human habit of finding one's place, perhaps. I came in early to choose a chair at the edge of the circle, right next to Sid, away from the door, and some of the regulars sat next to me. With new members in early this day, my usual chair was taken. I found another place in the middle of the circle.

That suited me well, because Sid and some near him were talking about experiences with kidney stones. A group member commented that the stones, when broken and passed on through, caused an awful smell. Another laughed and said it can be ridiculously painful as well, and that you can see some of the stones. Yet another group member asked him if he'd put his stones in a jar. Not exactly a fireside chat about life and love.

With new members in the group, Sid started out with stories from them. The trim young man in a leg-cast was chosen to go first.

Jim was a Caucasian, around thirty years of age, who looked fit enough for extreme sporting activities. He spoke of a wife reacting abnormally to emotional situations, buying new furniture, even new cars, and taking prohibited drugs regularly. As things became more difficult with her, he was forced to petition for a restraining order—a legal order that minimizes contact and interaction to avoid conflict—against her in their separated situation.

On one occasion, with the restraining order in place, he saw her in a public location and waved, and she'd come over to talk to him. Later, he sent a text message to her daughter, his step-daughter, to talk to his separated wife again. The cops then took him in, presumably for violating the restraining order, an enforceable judicial order binding on both parties, that explicitly prohibited contact.

Facing what he thought was a ridiculous charge, he decided to fight the case, and encountered a judge who seemed, in his words, to *hate* him. Jim found, in conversations with lawyers and others in the court, that this judge harbored a deep personal dislike toward men—Jim claimed the judge was gay and identified better with women—and was utterly biased against him. He was ordered by this judge to take drug tests every week, since this was an allegation against his separated wife in the prior court order, and to also attend regular psychological evaluations.

Jim informed the group that he hoped to have the judge assigned to his case removed. In view of his 'undesirable contact' charge, the legal term for which escapes me, he was required to attend the state's intervention program regardless of any developments in his legal predicament. No one had the heart to ask him about his visible external injury after this story. Jim came to us from the town of Dilbut's well-known law and order processes.

Oscar, of Hispanic ethnicity and advanced in years, spoke about having left messages on his ex-wife's telephone answering machine. Oscar's ex-wife cohabited with a new boyfriend who, he soon discovered, had been recently charged by the state—with *murder*, no less! He was concerned about his daughter, living with his ex-wife and this new domestic partner, and called to discuss the matter.

Unable to reach his ex-wife on the phone, he left some angry messages, and continued to call often. Once someone did answer his call, but it was the local Sheriff. They—the cops—were at his ex-wife's residence, questioning her about her new companion relating to the murder charge he faced. What Oscar experienced next was the uncommon hospitality of state holding facilities, and a requirement to complete the state's domestic violence intervention program. Sid welcomed him and thanked him for sharing.

Sid then asked me to detail my own story as well, since I had not discussed it in its entirety or the prior events that led to it. I spoke again about discovering my wife's affair in 2007, and a visit by law-enforcement, at my request, to defuse an emotional disagreement later that year—when they spent more than a couple of hours with my wife, speaking to her about their American family experiences. They made sure to let us know that they had gone above and beyond what they were required to do by law. I recalled being grateful for their intervention efforts and compassion, and having thanked them.

And the visit by police again in 2008 at my request, where they'd separated us by essentially kicking me out of my own home—which I resolved then by calling their supervisory officer the same night. The police sergeant, a female cop, agreed with me that I had every right to be in my home, but cautioned me nevertheless that another call to them that same night could result in someone going to jail.

Explaining the events of 2009, I identified myself as the most guilty among group members, for I did yank my wife's arm. A group member asked if I'd pulled my wife off the bed, which was not the case. I'd seen her rising while on the edge of the bed, and slipping off the edge onto the carpet. I detailed how I calmed my children who'd woken up, sent them to bed, and discussed the disagreement with my wife that fateful night downstairs.

During that discussion, she called the Sheriff's office—not the emergency number—thrice, and disconnected the line without talking to them in each instance. The police then called back, and came over despite assurances from the both of us that they were not needed. I was candid with them, as in the past, about the events of the night. Officer Gormon determined, based on her emotional state, statements, and other evidence they'd gathered—he'd even tried to wake my sleeping son to get him to corroborate the story my wife told him—that I could be convicted, carted me away for paperwork at the local police station, and then off to holding and processing at the infamous 4th Ave. jail in the larger city.

The group heard that all my requests to speak to Dilbut's busy, faceless prosecutors were in vain. Judges I appeared before didn't seem to care to know anything more. The district attorney's office changed prosecutors often as the case proceeded. My lawyer Mindy's detailed letter to them, explaining that I was an entrepreneur in the high technology area, working on creating jobs in the local economy, imploring them to let me get on with that endeavor, went unanswered. I was even stood up in a formal meeting set with the DA's office.

Left with no option, and with a seemingly ineffective lawyer, it became quite clear to me that the system simply wanted me to pay and get on with their well-oiled process and machinery. Hence I did so, a decision triggered, in part, by an intense argument with my wife. I pled guilty to disorderly conduct, and thus joined this counseling group.

The entire group had fallen silent. Someone said prior incidents may have added up...to what could be said to be an overreaction, an overreach. Most expressed surprise that the police would ever think of helping, but no one was surprised that they would take sides where they saw any advantage. I'd felt that the cops arrived that night with a clear agenda. My wife's actions also raised a number of warning flags in my mind. Sid, uncharacteristically, said nothing. There was little else, pertinent to my situation, left to say.

• • •

As I think of the most recent event, of the arrest and vigorous prosecution of Priyavani, I cannot but think that the state and those who represent it use legal processes to inflict immediate punishment, playing judge, jury, and executioner in their domain.

In my situation, I can almost see a need to separate domestic partners engaged in a disagreement that could lead to further harm. But my situation had been only an emotional one; there was no physical altercation. The cops imposed themselves upon the participants due to what may have been calculated, manipulative behavior—my spouse's numerous calls to them and unresponsive disconnection to rouse suspicion.

But in many other instances, of unwanted contact between previously separated domestic partners, arrests seemed quite arbitrary and over the top. Do phone calls and text messages require physical arrest?

So what had Priyavani done to merit an arrest, and, as she claimed in emotional notes to her friends and colleagues, a strip-search? She too was involved in a domestic disagreement with a maid she employed. Having declared that she'd pay wages per US law on the maid's visa application, she paid her significantly less, claiming that the lower amount was fair, because she did provide the maid with room and board—in New York, no less. This domestic employment arrangement soured almost half a year before Priyavani's hospitality at state expense, with the maid going incognito—at which point Priyavani demanded state assistance in locating her absconding maid, accusing her of theft of valuables.

Instead, given rather questionable conduct by Priyavani, with the state and her maid, and noting her minimal regard for laws of the land, the state reacted atypically after a number of interactions with both parties. In this instance, the state chose to work with the maid, for available evidence supported such a stand. US attorney Veer Batata, with the full power of the state vested in him, ordered that Priyavani be arrested and charged. State minions grabbed Priyavani as she dropped her children at school, took her in for fingerprinting, state custody until she posted bail, and the rest of their procedures that they deemed necessary.

An arrest? What were the state's minions arresting here? This wasn't a bank robbery, or a grocery store hold-up, where a perpetrator needed to be stopped, and harmful actions halted, was it? That the state took offense at unconscionable acts by Priyavani was indeed the state's prerogative, and charging her with misdeeds done also their sworn duty. But what justified the public and severe restriction of personal freedom that served no purpose other than intimidation and deep humiliation? Especially when the matter had been ongoing for almost six months, with involvement by the Indian government?

What justified the violation of a strip-search, of invading one's intimate personal space, of an individual charged only with the crimes of falsification of information and breach of an employment agreement, after she'd been taken against her will to a state's facility? Did the state or its minions expect her to be walking around with volumes of evidence, or weapons and contraband, hidden beneath her clothes, as she dropped her children at school? Wasn't a pat-down, and a few passes with metal detectors, sufficient to ensure that she carried nothing on her person of significance?

But wait—arrests serve other purposes, do they not? Put someone in a disorienting, helpless, and sometimes life-threatening situation and they are compelled to talk, often incoherently. They talk either to friends and relatives, through wiretapped telephones, as they reach out for support, or to others in crowded holding cells, providing the state, through recordings of such conversations, with ammunition to continue the process in motion. I learned from Mindy that the state had indeed gathered some such material against me.

Or they become shocked and frightened, and thus easy to dispose of in the future. And bail—the state can then hold a person and deny their freedom until a bail amount set is posted. And when such money is held by a court, they can impose any penalty deemed necessary—all according to their law, of course—in the course of legal proceedings, appropriating amounts that help the state's legal machinery run smoothly. Yes, they did compel Priyavani and her family to post a *quarter of a million dollars* in bail to secure her release. Just as they forced me to arrange for bail, in cash, on a Saturday.

But did you know, Priyavani, that the state that arrested you also arrests other residents and US citizens, guns pointed menacingly, sometimes with choke-holds, quick take-downs, and blows to the head and back? And that they do so with fabricated and exaggerated details of resistance by those being arrested: "Why are you resisting arrest? Why are you reaching for my gun?" Or that police officers may arbitrarily choose to use their batons, tasers, or guns, harmfully and with impunity, to procure the submission they demand?

Or, that in a state down south, you could be arrested if you were a jaywalking girl and pulled your arm away from a policeman who may grab you to detain you for his ticketing purposes? That southern state has the distinction of employing law-enforcement personnel who claim that it should be a relief that while a cop may commit sexual assault on duty elsewhere, as it happened in Detroit, MI, they only touch people on the arm in their locale.

Do you also know that some here, arrested or incarcerated, are subjected to body cavity searches, where they not only have to strip, but squat, naked, in front of others, and cough? All you need to do is watch a recent Hollywood dramatization of true events, *Fruitvale Station*, to see what I describe as common practice in arrests here.

• • •

As I recollect my own arrest, and hospitality at state expense, painful thoughts of helplessness and frustration mix with interesting memories of sadism and empathy seen in people met, on this journey, within the system. But the extreme disorientation and humiliation that I went through is a punishment I wouldn't ever be able to wish on anyone else. Would it diminish your pain, Priyavani, if I recount the ignominious and harrowing details of my arrest and holding before barely making bail?

I wore only my night clothes, a simple t-shirt and shorts, when arrested in my home by Officer Gormon. There really wasn't anything much to search on me. Handcuffed, with my hands behind my back, I was made to stand in my driveway in full view of my neighbors. The cop Gormon was inside, wrapping up his evidence-gathering with my wife. He was reassuring her—I determined much later—that he had more than enough from all that I readily admitted to him to have me arrested, prosecuted, and convicted. Officer Feliz stood near me looking rather sympathetic. He seemed to want to say something, but I did not meet his eyes. I was looking instead to see if any of my neighbors saw me in my predicament. I couldn't really tell—it was about 11 pm.

I wasn't allowed to see my little children—I didn't think to ask and neither did the cops—before being carted away by Gormon to the Dilbut central station for paperwork. The drive was uneventful except for the discomfort of having to sit on a hard squad-car back seat with my hands cuffed behind. At the station, Gormon cuffed me to a bench within, and completed his arrest data entry with information from me. With his documentation at Dilbut done, he explained that I needed processing through the 4th Ave. jail in the larger city, and escorted me back to his car. Before getting into the back seat again, I asked that Gormon cuff my hands out in front—and was grateful that he complied, though I now understand that this is against regulations.

As I stepped into the squad-car, he stopped me, saying he had not administered my Miranda rights as required upon arrest, and proceeded to do so. I paid no attention until he asked for my agreement. More than a couple of hours after arrest, and after my discussions with him, the disclosure of any such rights seemed quite redundant to me.

It is hard for me to recall, now, details of that night. The years and pain have faded and suppressed these memories. But I do remember arriving at the back of the 4th Ave. facility, and being herded, along with others brought in, into a line going through a security procedure. Two cops in official blue uniforms were standing off to the side of this line. As we shuffled past, I asked one, "Excuse me, Officer, since it's late, and since we may be held through the next day, will we get a toothbrush, or soap?" He sneered at me, and turned to his companion. "What does he think this is—the Hilton?" I did not press him any further, and passed through a metal detector and a rough pat-down.

A number of us were then led into a hallway for the first of many procedures—our booking photos, and surrender of personal items carried in to surly attendants behind counters. We waited in turn to be asked to stand in front of the height scale, facing front and facing sideways. As we waited, I noticed Gormon waiting along with us to ensure that I and another 'collar' he'd brought in with me were both successfully pulled into the system. The reality of my present situation began to register consciously, and tears flowed from my eyes. I buried my head in my cuffed hands and turned away so that Gormon, who was watching, wouldn't see.

Once entered into the system, we were herded, cuffs removed, into one of many holding cells, and I found myself in a roughly five by twenty foot cell with as many as ten others. At about the middle of this cell, against a long wall, was an open toilet seat, with two waist-high half-walls jutting out halfway into the room on either side. All along the longer walls was a concrete bench interrupted every couple of feet by long metal handle bars that stood an inch or two above the surface, separating sitting spaces. The bars served presumably to handcuff inmates to, but also to prevent anyone from sleeping on the concrete bench.

This was a sitting and standing room only holding pen, with an open toilet, crowded with a number of inmates. Steel doors opened into the cell from either short wall, with a small square window that opened from the outside in each door at about shoulder height. The cell felt rather cold. I learned later that the temperature was set to less than 65°F in the cells to minimize germ and bacterial growth within.

There was a sturdy wall-mounted telephone in the cell that looked like a payphone, but didn't need any coins. One could make only local calls from the phone. It would inform you, upon attempting a call, that all conversations made through the phone will be recorded. What I did not know, until I made some calls from the phone, was that the phone also identified itself to the call recipients as one situated within the central jail, which information recipients must acknowledge and accept before any conversation could ensue.

I sat in a corner away from the door, feeling rather cold, and occupied myself with studying inmates in the cell. A good number were Hispanic, some Black, and a good few Caucasian as well. I held the dubious honor of being the only one of East Indian origin, but nevertheless did not seem to be getting much attention from anyone.

Some were very young, no more than teenagers, tattooed all over their arms and chest, wherever skin was visible, and seemed quite comfortable with their situation as if it were a regular walk in the park. Others were quiet, clothed in full-sleeved jackets with hoods, and seemed appropriately dressed for such confinement. Most appeared, at least to me, to be younger than myself. One Caucasian—forgive my use of ethnicity for identification, none of us introduced ourselves—was also tattooed on his arms, and looked weather-beaten and rough.

The younger members conversed merrily in colorful street-speak that I do not care to reproduce in a book. The older ones remained quiet and tried not to look each other in the eye. Some members appeared to be attempting sleep, crunching their bodies in unnatural positions over and around the metal bars embedded in the concrete benches.

Two cops came by, opened the steel door at my end of the cell, and pushed in two more into the already crowded cell. Now there was barely enough sitting space for everyone inside. Those attempting sleep were deprived of their additional space allowance. One of the younger occupants took this change in circumstances to occupy the toilet seat and relieve himself, flushing the toilet every half-minute so as to minimize any odor from his unavoidable call of nature offending everyone else. As the night wore on, a few took to lying on the dirty floor and catching a few winks. From sheer exhaustion, I followed suit and lay among them.

One of the newly-delivered occupants appeared completely out of his senses, perhaps drugged out of his mind. Short, a little on the portly side, with fair skin that had a slight yellow tinge, he had on a full-sleeved shirt tucked awkwardly into his pants. He was barefoot as well. He seemed to have little consideration for anyone's personal space, falling on us as we sat together on the concrete bench—this in part drove me to descend to the floor. The drugged individual followed me down as well, and lay between myself and the rough, tattooed, older cellmate.

Drifting in and out of sleep, I noticed the drugged fellow moving closer and trying to press himself against me. After avoiding his unwelcome advances a number of times, I retreated onto the concrete bench and leaned against the wall instead. Being hit on by an over-medicated, possibly amorous inmate was a jail experience I could do without—but is now etched in my mind.

With me now unavailable for his attentions, the chubby fellow turned to the tattooed older man, also on the floor, as I watched this situation drowsily. It was perhaps after two of his attempts at getting cozy with this new potential victim that the victim turned ferocious aggressor. Before anyone could even register the event, the tattooed Caucasian launched a few powerful punches in quick succession into the drugged fellow's face. Though his body shook from the attack, the punches did not seem to faze the amorous addict in the least.

I was now wide awake and alert, shaken to the core by violence at such close quarters, ready for any further expansion of the situation to include others in the cell. But it fizzled out as quickly as it began. The drugged cellmate staggered from the blows, but simply moved away from his violent antagonist and did not bother anyone else. No one seemed concerned about the incident either.

I turned to the camera mounted in a ceiling corner, and fully expected a team of cops to rush in…but nothing. Not even a casual visit by cops to check on the beaten man's now visible and growing bruises. Callousness? Negligence? Apathy? Standard operating procedure? It was clear to me then that in the holding cell, as it may also be in long-term incarceration facilities, we were all on our own. Rules and civil behavior no longer applied; survival may well be determined only by cunning and brute force.

Hours dragged on interminably as we persevered to get whatever sleep was possible. With no windows in the cell, or clocks, we had no sense of time. It was only our bodily sleep cycle, the circadian rhythm, that let us know it was still night. Some hours later, I called my friends John and Parvathi, and they promised to work on getting me whatever legal help could be obtained in short order. This turned out to be one of their acquaintances, who, they assured me, would follow up with the police on my progress through the system.

After what seemed to be a few more hours, a steel door opened, and bags of prepackaged food were handed into the cell. A breakfast bun, peanut butter in a cup, an orange, and a drink of some kind, all packed in a plastic bag. Most of my cellmates set to devouring this feast rapidly. One advised me to eat quickly, for the trash disposal team was expected shortly thereafter. A few minutes later, a trash collector appeared, and we emptied into a sealed corridor through the steel door at the other end.

Once trash in the cell was collected, a clean-up crew sanitized the floor and sitting surfaces with chemicals. Spread of germs and disease through the holding cells, and close human contact within, was a known feature of the incarceration facilities.

More hours later, I was called out of the cell by cops to be taken through a formal process of appearance before a judge, who would read out the charges against me, and determine release conditions. This time around, my conveyance was the 'dog wagon,' a small truck with its insides subdivided into compartments, one on each side of the vehicle with small diamond grille windows, and one in the middle with no windows. I was pushed into a side compartment of this wagon, handcuffed, and soon realized why the vehicle was called the dog wagon. There was barely enough space to move forward or backward. One could sit only by turning sideways, and had to watch out for one's head hitting the slanted top edges of the vehicle as it moved. No, the state is not concerned about seat-belts or on-road safety for criminals under its responsibility, never mind any right of presumption of innocence. It does not take much imagination to realize that not even animals would be transported in such discomfort.

The wagon rolled out of 4th Ave., and I was grateful to see some sunlight through the tiny window. We stopped at a holding facility in another part of the metropolis, where a young, stocky fellow, no more than a year or two above twenty, with a large black patch of what seemed like dead skin on the underside of one of his forearms, joined me in my side of the dog wagon.

He seemed chatty, and given my brief exposure to sunlight, I conversed with him enough to learn that he'd gained his permanent black skin patch through MRSA gathered from unclothed contact with surfaces inside many jail cells he'd been in. MRSA is a bacterial strain highly resistant to treatment. It is quite common in the holding cells and incarceration facilities of the state. He was hospitalized by the state due to the severity of his bacterial infection. They'd managed to stop it, but not before the starkly visible damage. He seemed dismissive of it, but I wasn't so sure that I would, at my age that was twice his, survive such bacterial infection.

As we were led into the civic center in Dilbut that housed the courts, through back doors into a holding area, I saw the same cop who'd mocked my request for toiletries at the 4th Ave. intake line. This Hispanic member of law-enforcement—from his name, Carillo—seemed to enjoy playing sadistically with the emotions of those in the state's unrelenting grip, presumed innocent or not. His face had all the refinement of a Halloween mask. It was a face not even a mother could love.

He was engaged in loud conversations with those awaiting a court appearance, declaring that judges may not come in during the weekend. And then we'd all be carted away to one of Sheriff Waspoia's infamous tent camps for the weekend, roasting in the summer sun, with violent bullies and predators for company.

In time, an officer came in to inform us that a female judge had put in an appearance, and the sadistic cop changed his slant to discussing how she'd been making bail release determinations. It's rather redundant to indicate that he worked at raising our hopes, with claims that the judge had, just the past week, let many in arraignment leave without bail, right from the courtroom, on their own recognizance. It is also not hard to now see why those arrested and subjugated by law-enforcement refer to them as *pigs*, which I hardly think stands for 'people in government service,' though you may be forgiven for such an assumption.

A short walk, and a climb up a spiral staircase, led us directly and surprisingly into a courtroom. There, we were all gathered in the jury section, some gloriously attired in overalls of white with wide black stripes, and all with handcuffs on. There was only the judge and two cops present in the room. She went through each person's situation, setting bail at significant amounts for each and every one of us. Some she would not release at all, and had to resign themselves to going back to the holding facilities or to Waspoia's tent camps.

When my young dog-wagon mate's turn came, I was surprised to see him quite composed and vocal. He addressed the honorable judge not as y*our honor*, but simply as *judge*. He was evidently conversant with the system and its processes, and spoke quite lucidly and firmly, but was not successful in obtaining any concessions from Her Honor.

Then came my turn, and I didn't have a chance to say anything much at all. My hastily arranged legal assistance was nowhere to be seen, nor was my wife in attendance, though she'd assured me over the jail telephone that she'd objected to the police taking me away. With no one to speak for me, the judge put in a protective order that prevented me from going back to my home and children. She set my bail at a thousand dollars in cash, and sent me on my way back to holding to await payment of said money to secure my freedom.

The sadistic cop, with the Halloween-mask face, grinned with evil satisfaction as we humbled criminals filed out in dead silence.

We were shunted back in the dog wagon to 4th Ave., where I was hustled into another cell with just a few occupants this time around. Until now, I'd suppressed my need to relieve myself; using a sitting toilet in full view of others within the same room wasn't something I'd ever had to do before. Apologizing to my new cellmates, who only looked bemused, I did use the open toilet, standing, and flushing often, to relieve my full bladder. Anything else would have needed a bath, and I just couldn't.

The next round of sustenance came by, and I ate very little of it to ensure my intestines could hold out. There was no water in any of the cells. I saved my cup of water, from the meal, to ward off thirst over the next many hours. Come to think of it, we inmates were not given any fluids outside of our meals, which, in dry Wariduna, could only be another health hazard.

In the meantime, when the cop on the beat in my cell corridor passed by, I inquired with him about my paperwork process. While he did take my information down and check, he had no encouraging news to offer. Discussing this situation with my new cellmates, I gathered that it was a common thing for the 4th Ave. jail to "lose the papers" of someone in custody, forcing them to stay in holding for a number of days before release. One of them even claimed he had already been in holding for more days than he cared to remember.

I'd previously called my friends, who assured me that they'd obtained the necessary money and deposited it at the Dilbut central station as advised by authorities there. But there appeared to be no communication between the Dilbut and 4th Ave. locations affirming completion of bail posting. Instead, upon inquiring again with the cop walking by, I was told that payment had to be made in the location I was being held in, or they wouldn't release me. I called my friends again, and asked that they withdraw the payment made at Dilbut, and bring it to the 4th Ave. location. They in turn assured me that the lawyer helping out was calling the 4th Ave. location hourly to inquire as to my progress and release.

Eventually, I was taken for fingerprinting, and moved to another crowded cell. My now regular requests to the cop taking people out and bringing new ones in clearly annoyed him. I'd lost all track of time, and harbored no small fear that my paperwork might be lost, the end result being a transfer over to a tent camp around the metropolis.

I called John once again. "John, I won't last another day here, and could be bundled off to their tent camps which I do not think I'll survive." Desperation was beginning to set in. John assured me that the lawyer was doing all she could to help, but that did precious little to calm my fears.

Another officer passed by my cell, a fit, young man, and I enlisted his help. He made a diligent effort to address my concern, taking my name and all other necessary details. Shortly thereafter, he returned with detailed information about my status, assuring me that I had been entered into the system, and that bail hadn't yet been posted at the 4ᵗʰ Ave. location. I thanked him for his kindness, noting that he had a European look about him.

Soon, the European-looking officer came by of his own accord, and told me that bail had been posted for me in their system, and that he was waiting for release paperwork to be ready. I asked him for his ethnicity—I wonder why I was so interested in that aspect—and determined that he originated from Poland. The land of hard-working people, famous for its jokes, where people do not take themselves too seriously. This Polish officer seemed to be genuinely concerned about the welfare of another in trouble.

In time, he came by to escort me to a half-way hall, where further paperwork was handed to me, and where I was allowed to rest with some comfort. He chatted with me briefly, while a number of other inmates, waiting in this hallway, were moved to another room that had inmates awaiting release. Names were called; inmates cheered those whose turns had come at regaining their freedom. My turn came soon enough. I was handed back my belongings I'd surrendered the previous day. As I walked out, I saw the Polish officer standing by, and thanked him again for his kindness before getting out.

It was late in the night as I stood on the street corner, awaiting John and Parvathi, who came by soon thereafter to give me a ride home. I apologized for my disheveled, smelly state, and sat away from them in the back of their car. Parvathi pointedly informed me that my wife had arranged for the bail money they posted, but these details mattered little to me. The protective order in place prevented me from going home to see my children.

My wife declared that it would be perfectly alright with her if I did come home to the children. But something deep within my mind cautioned me not to do so. What I had gone through, in the past day and a half, seemed to me only the beginning of a struggle for survival with known and unknown enemies facing me. I asked John and Parvathi to drive me to a second home bought toward the end of 2007 as a gift for my wife and for the family. A house bought as a change we could all move forward with, leaving unpleasant memories behind in our first home. One that could now become a change that tears my home and family apart.

As my friends left, promising to return with food, they handed me the disinfectant, antibacterial soaps, and other toiletries I'd asked them to bring along. For the first and only such time in my life, I coated my entire body, head to toe, with disinfectant, and antibacterial soap, and washed it off in a hot shower, repeating this process once again. Funny how frightened we can be of the smallest of creatures on earth. I scrubbed as I'd never scrubbed before in life. But nothing could wash away the humiliation and a growing sense of disillusionment I came to feel at everything I'd gone through.

Needs and the Clueless

The group was in roll-call and class fee payments collection when I joined in the next week. Some in the group paid Sid in each class attended, having to pay from what they earned every week. Sid kept a running score of their payments. Twenty dollars per class. Twenty dollars for an hour-long discussion, with a barely qualified counselor, and others in similar predicaments. When you think of it—compared to psychiatrists and their \$150/hr. and up rates—this was eminently affordable, with a flexible payment plan to boot. Given the number of program attendees in each class, Sid and the state collected as much as three hundred dollars for an hour. Yet, for a bare minimum wage-earner, twenty dollars was more than a couple of days' nutrient allowance. Some didn't have money that week, and were allowed to pay the next. A couple of new participants including a medical doctor had joined the group.

Parting with his twenty for the week, Jim asked, "Does the money collected go to the state?"

Sid turned to him with an inscrutable look. "No, it goes to the company contracted by the state to hold these classes. This is not a non-profit organization."

Sid skipped me as he continued polling; I had paid in full before beginning classes.

I couldn't hold back my question. "But doesn't money collected in fines, or for classes in traffic violations, go to the police and the courts?" I knew that it does, for an instructor in a traffic class had given me a full account, but was keen to know how many organizations profited from this stream of captive participants in DV classes.

Sid agreed. "Yes, a part of a traffic violation payment does." He did not elaborate any more about the money he collected.

"What did you do, Sid, to get to hold these classes?" asked Jim instead.

"I earned a Bachelor's degree in Behavioral Psychology. It actually took me almost twenty-two years to get my degrees—my family plans and misadventures got in the way. I did my Master's in a couple of years, though."

"Behavior has statistical variance," continued Sid. "It is rarely deterministic—so we also study statistics in behavioral psychology. I was an engineering major, for a while, in my long path to getting my degrees."

That bit about statistics confused me. "Isn't statistics used mainly for studying large groups of individuals, and not individual psychology alone?"

"Yes, that's true," said Sid.

I didn't press him any further. This was, after all, a diverse group.

"I had an enlightening thing happen to me," continued Sid. "My life circumstances caved in, and I went through extensive counseling."

So our counselor had lived through some sort—or the same sort—of turmoil we'd all gone through.

"Engineering and science seemed rigid to me. Life is flexible," he ventured.

Science, rigid? Science is nothing but the exploration of nature, in our attempts to understand it, and life, Sid. It changes as we make new discoveries; it is constantly renewed. I kept thoughts that didn't go along with Sid's slant on things to myself.

A group member asked him about his ethnicity. "My last name is McIntyre. I'm Irish," said Sid.

"Back in the day," he continued, "everybody was screwing everybody anyway, and you really did not know who you were…"

From a counselor, a truly comforting observation!

Sid carried this thought further. "A recent blind test for paternity found fully one-third of children born in a hospital not related to their fathers."

Oscar spoke up, "I know of a father who did the test, and found out that one of his daughters was not his."

"What happened then?" asked Sid.

"Nothing," replied Oscar. "They probably split."

This brought back memories—of similar suspicions on my part—but I suppressed them. Except that my wife had been attempting to use my suspicions as an explanation, and justification, for her own betrayal of the family. I'd have to face this again someday—but not alone. 'Everybody was screwing everybody anyway,' and, 'You really did not know who you were'—is this a guide to the development of social norms and laws here? Absence, and irrelevance, of identity? And a grand, perennial spring break party for promiscuous adults? Clearly, repression will not work with a freedom-loving population, but isn't being entirely permissive the other extreme? What do people in such strange circumstances do with their natural suspicions?

Sid continued, "Women commit domestic violence more than men. Women are also more inclined to be physically violent. The problem is, if men get violent, there is usually a visit to the medical emergency center."

He was right, of course. Even in my circumstance of mid '09, in the days after my arrest, my wife visited a medical treatment facility in the hospital, where she worked, to check on pain she felt. No, it wasn't her arm I'd pulled, or her shoulder, but her *hips*, because she'd fallen down onto the soft carpet in the bedroom—as she sat up from the box-spring and mattress bed that lay flush on the floor, without any bed-frame, to suit our small children. A slip of about a foot and a half, because she was at the edge, with the children in the middle of the bed, from the bed to the soft carpet, landing on her cushioned rear end. I saw this, and she'd waved off my offer to help.

The interesting thing was that X-rays, and a full check-up at the hospital, did not determine any cause for concern. The attending doctor speculated that she might have incurred a *slight* pelvic separation and corresponding discomfort. She limped enough to put Quasimodo to shame in the days following. I could imagine other ways by which that presumed pelvic separation could have come about. More interesting was how she sought medical opinion: she did not go through her normal insurance coverage for this checkup, X-rays, and medical diagnosis, for they would most likely have refused her such a claim.

And she conveyed, through our friends John and Parvathi, to gullible old me, that she had not approached her insurance company because the state, prosecuting me, could then have obtained records of her alleged injury. Sure, I believed them, that the cops did not ask her to do this, that the state would not ask for and obtain records from the hospital she worked in. That they'd all conspire merrily together, to withhold such information, to help me in this decidedly adversarial legal system.

And that she did not go to her workplace hospital just to be sure to get a check-up and radiography done, with something usable against me. No—her workplace, because that is where her affair in '07 began, was definitely on her side of the matter. That was evident when I communicated with them then to resolve the matter of her affair. I remember my lawyer Mindy asking me to take a good few photographs of this alleged fall, which, when discovered in my preparations for trial, seemed to infuriate my spouse—"Oh, you took pictures, did you?"

But I did not discuss this in the group. It probably wouldn't be all that interesting to them anyway, the stories from the new additions might be.

Sid finished talking about himself. "I am in a classic rock band now. In the past, I got tired of all the circumstances, fell asleep in my pants, let my life collapse around me."

He was no doubt in better circumstances now, with a couple of psychology degrees, lecturing a motley group of no-good bums, and jamming with scrappy pals occasionally.

"If something's got your goat, let it be known," declared Sid as he summed up his life-lessons.

I will, Sid. That is why I take down notes in these classes, to lend clear detail to my memories when it is time to let everything out. The state's definitely got my goat—no, my ram—by the horns! I don't think Sid was quite comfortable with my note-taking in his class. But he did not oppose it—how could he, when he provided notes himself?

We moved on to stories from newcomers into the group. Two new fish.

"Fresh fish! Fresh fish!" cried some. We did *so* look forward to their fascinating tales of woe. The power of commiseration in promoting healing. Better than Sid's monologues, and old videos, or his Freudian behavioral psychology notes. It must have encouraged our new additions to find such a friendly and receptive audience.

Paul was a man of many years, a widower, who sought to change his lonely life by finding a new partner. He was tall—near six feet—and rather heavy-set. Fair, with blond gray hair, and pleasant looking, he gave the impression of being a school teacher or a sports coach. Paul met his prospective partner at a crowded online dating place, a *find-your-suitable-mate.com* web site.

The woman he met on the site seemed nice at first, and Paul had worked on spoiling her. He sent her a dozen roses, three separate times, on a single day. He took her out bowling, and to other activities they both enjoyed. She had three children from a previous marriage. Paul readily accepted them and included them in these activities. He was quite eager to develop this relationship further; his need did not go unnoticed. His new-found girlfriend began to talk of marriage, and Paul asked her and her three children to move into his rather empty house. All this in just a few weeks after meeting her on the online dating site.

By his own admission, Paul was desperate for companionship. He advanced this romantic relationship rapidly, and even considered proposing to his new girlfriend on the Cardinals board—a local baseball team's stadium scoreboard. But when the new girlfriend and her children moved into his house, Paul found out in short order that his lonely heart had misled him. The children simply refused to listen to him. They would leave all the house lights on, despite his repeated requests that they turn the lights off when not needed. The new girlfriend slept in his bed for a few nights and then moved downstairs to a room alone. She did not seem to care about his requests regarding her children and their obedience, their compliance with his wishes in his home, or the complete lack of that aspect. Paul soon felt that things weren't really working out.

After a week of getting to know each other, he had seen enough, and asked this girlfriend to move back out with her children. "*I am not going to,* **bitch**, *what are you going to do about it?*" was the woman's exact response, per Paul. The argument escalated as they moved downstairs. She was on the third or fourth step, of a second set of stairs leading downstairs, with Paul following her a few steps behind, when she suddenly sat down and began rolling down the stairs, calling to her children and telling them, "*Look how he is hurting me! Call 911!*" Her twelve-year-old daughter did, right away. He moved to get the telephone to call a friend, but his girlfriend hit herself on the face with the handset, holding on to his hand at the same time. Paul pulled away from her and left his house.

The police arrived soon, and took him into custody without much discussion. He was barred by the court from returning to his house. Paul approached a lawyer, and served an eviction notice upon the woman. She left a few days after, and when she did, took everything she could carry with her, including toiletries. Paul then attempted to prosecute her for felony theft. But he had to face the state and its due-process pending against him first.

At his trial, he faced a number of witnesses against him. The woman and her children were brought in by the state; Paul hoped to counterbalance that with twelve character witnesses. Despite all who spoke highly of and for him, the judge declared his complete lack of belief in his version of the domestic incident. The woman's story changed every time she provided it, in the police report, when she took the stand as a prosecution witness, and during defense cross-examination. Her versions did not match her daughter's recollection. Her twelve-year-old daughter testified to seeing Paul standing over her mother who lay on the floor. The police provided video and other photographic evidence against him. They did not provide any of the information he'd given them. It was, as may be expected, an entirely one-sided stance by the police at his trial.

The judge found him guilty. **Guilty**—*convicted*—hence sentenced to a token few days in jail, and the twenty-six-week DV counseling program. Paul was distraught, and in tears, as he recalled his painful experiences. He asked for a paper tissue and had to leave the session room.

At one point, during Paul's long but gripping description of his experiences, he said that this—his painful saga—might have been a blessing in disguise. When he returned to the session room, Sid asked of him what he thought contributed to the court finding him guilty. Paul believed that the twelve character witnesses he'd brought in had no impact in determining how the court viewed the facts of his case as presented by the state. It wouldn't have mattered if twelve apostles had been brought in before the judge. The facts were damning indeed. Goodwill could simply not overcome the apparent truth of evidence gathered.

The police indicated that the woman victim of Paul's crimes appeared to have marks resembling injuries on her face. The twelve-year-old saw and described an intimidating situation. She claimed to have been harmed by the event as well. The woman spun a tearful, impressionable tale of violence and helplessness. Paul was the only witness, biased as may be assumed, to his version of the event. He stood no chance in the adversarial processes of the legal system.

I wondered why Paul thought of his experience as a blessing in disguise. Was it his only way of consoling himself, of being rid of the pain? He was clearly not intending to continue his new relationship—asking a woman and her children to move out after having them move in but a week before surely couldn't mean anything else. In making that decision, he brought upon himself a terrible injustice, assuming his version of events to be true, with great humiliation and suffering that wouldn't be forgotten easily. Had the experience made him wiser and perhaps less prone to such traps?

The sentence, upon Paul's conviction, of a token few days in jail, didn't make much sense to anyone either. He did say that when he was taken in, his paperwork had indeed been lost, and he remained in holding for a good number of days. Was this—the sentence of a few days—the system's way of covering up its own incompetence, or willful cruelty, that led to his extended suffering? With the excess days he spent in holding before making bail, Paul did not have to spend any more time incarcerated after his conviction.

I recalled that the judge accepting my plea agreement also said that she'd give me credit for a day spent incarcerated before making bail. *Credit*—for incalculable suffering! She seemed to think only in numbers, in terms common in finance, having set aside some of my bail money posted for the state's fees and fines.

I thought then, "Go ahead, compound my agony, having forced me to spend a day jailed despite a 'presumption of innocence.' You reinforce painful memories, of treatment as a criminal and as an animal. You harden my heart against all that you stand for." But I did not say anything to the judge. An elderly lawyer, who stood in for Mindy at my plea hearing, had a few choice words that he addressed to the judge instead. His tone and scorn for the judge and the state's processes astounded me, but were inconsequential in the formality that the hearing was. I didn't thank Her kind Honor for credit she magnanimously granted me, or for any learning from the torment suffered.

The group had fallen silent, listening intently to Paul's tale of horror. We moved on to the next new story, of a repeat offender, **Lopez**, one who'd been through this program before. He was not very forthcoming with his act—he said he'd blocked the path of a girlfriend who was in a closet, and that she rushed out, and called the police. He omitted mentioning how she came to be in the closet in the first place, frightened enough to want to rush out. A judge sentenced him to the maximum duration of probation and counseling—fifty-two weeks, a full year—so he was sure to be in this class for a long time. There was something rather different about Lopez, which we'd learn later.

Responsibility and Accountability

In the next class, after the usual roll-call and payments, Sid said he wanted to talk about responsibility. He took an example, that of a Baron and Baroness, with the Baroness involved in a clandestine love-affair, the old Drawbridge Exercise you can find in a quick search online.

Briefly, when the busy Baron was away on his duties, the lonely Baroness ignored his dire warning to her to not leave the castle while he was away. She left to spend time with her clandestine lover in the village, instructing her servants to leave a drawbridge to the castle—which stood on an island in a wide river—lowered until she returned. After many pleasurable hours with her lover, she returned to find the drawbridge blocked by an armed gatekeeper. He implored her to not cross the drawbridge because the Baron had ordered him to kill her if she did so.

To enter the castle without crossing the drawbridge, the Baroness asked her lover for help. But the lover, claiming they shared only a romantic relationship, denied her the needed assistance in her time of peril. She then begged a boatman for help, who demanded money for his services, and a friend, who took a moral stance, against her, since she had disobeyed the Baron. Everyone she approached thus proved unhelpful.

She eventually returned to the drawbridge and crossed it on her own. Despite her fervent pleas to the gatekeeper to spare her life, he killed her as the Baron had ordered him to.

The exercise involved listing, by decreasing culpability, those responsible for the Baroness's death. Sid simplified the task, for those among us who did not want to evaluate shades of responsibility, and asked us only to identify who we thought most responsible. It felt strange that in a counseling session, for domestic violence, the instructional exercise used was one of extreme violence and assignment of blame.

Nevertheless, the group got to it and we tallied votes. The Baron got nine votes in all as the most responsible, while the gatekeeper got four votes. Jim, our leg-in-a-cast member, gave the Baroness his vote. What registered in my mind then was only that there were fourteen group members in all, not counting Sid. But some are more easily remembered, while some just shrink into their places, barely touching the group's collective consciousness. The general trend of votes was as expected, that the Baron, for planning and ordering that the deed be done was considered most responsible, and the gatekeeper was also held responsible as the perpetrator.

Only one in the group, Jim, held the Baroness responsible, which was interesting. Despite her infidelity, and lack of respect for her husband's wishes, it appeared that the majority empathized with her. I could only think that must have been due to the tragic nature of what had befallen her, and not really a rational analysis of what led to the tragedy. Sympathy overrules cold reason readily. The test seemed more about judging one's human responses. Opportunists would perhaps align with Jim, and push blame onto one to whom it wouldn't matter any more, so everyone wins. Why fret over what is past?

"The one who seems none the worse here is the Baroness's lover," said I, as we discussed the exercise. "He enjoyed what he chose to, and took no additional responsibility. Though his actions lacked what we may call conscience, he is the least affected, so long as he is not discovered."

Laughter all around, and general agreement.

Paul spoke up, "Being the lover is the easiest thing to do, maybe the best in today's culture. Take what you can, and run—or cut your losses, and run."

Sid tried to redirect the discussion toward taking responsibility. "There are consequences… The lover may not be in any committed relationship…"

No one paid heed to what Sid said. You could say that the exercise did not produce a specific result he was hoping for.

It reminded me of my own circumstance, and the apparently conscience-less individual involved romantically with my wife, Bert Burgess. Yes, I did track him down with all the calls and messages my wayward spouse exchanged with him at all hours of the day and night. These days, one can obtain almost any information about another from a mobile phone number.

His statement to me, when asked if he'd had physical intimacy with my wife, and about his intentions, was that he had indeed done so, and was looking to make it long-term. That sounded about right—his first reaction elicited on being caught red-handed—this was all that he cared about, for that was his nature. There could be no empathy expected from him, nor any compassion, in conversation with a troubled and wronged husband and father.

Yet, there were indeed serious consequences. I approached the workplace that had allowed such close, uninhibited contact between married individuals—I'd learned that their affair began with hugs during a workplace incident—and asked for a full investigation, which the folks there were compelled by law to undertake.

And Sid was also right in that such a lover may not be in any committed relationship. I determined from additional conversations, with my wife, that this Bert Burgess was previously married, and his wife had left him, and their marriage, because she'd realized her own lesbian nature. He apparently was neck-deep in debt at that time as well, having lived a life of relative excess. As a consequence of their divorce, he was forced to sell an expensive home that he'd bought and place his personal belongings in a storage facility. His casual relationship with my wife, and statement to me when caught, made a lot more sense when I discovered these details.

I wondered what exactly was the thought experiment intended with the drawbridge exercise. Compiled in 1978, it perhaps held little relevance three decades, a generation, later. Nevertheless, the State of Wariduna, in its wisdom, appeared to be employing deeply patriarchal and violent examples to convey its messages.

Levi engaged me in a side conversation meanwhile. "You know I am an Israeli Arab, from Palestine originally. Did you know how much suffering Arabs went through under the English? You Indians benefited from them. I have an Indian relative, a sister-in-law."

I begged to disagree, since I had, by then, sworn allegiance to America. And also because the known history of mismanagement of resources by colonial forces in India included gravely under-reported holocausts documented in a new book, *Late Victorian Holocausts*, by Mike Davis. I recommended the book to Levi for his edification. I was introduced to it by my son's history teacher, Ms. Sheila, who also hailed from Poland, coincidentally.

Not having made any progress with the drawbridge exercise, Sid asked if anyone had seen *Lion King*, a Disney animated cartoon movie. He asked if we remembered the baboon whacking the lion on his head, and the conversation following, with the lion asking, "What did you do *that* for?" and the baboon, in his sing-song Jamaican accent—Disney often adds fun sub-themes—replying, "Doesn't matter! It-is-in-the-past!"

Jim piped up, "So what are we learning? That violence is allowed, and we get on with our lives?"

"That is just not the point," replied Sid. "If you come across an injustice, it helps to move beyond it."

Huh? Not sure Disney intended that part to mean that an injustice may be left unaddressed, Sid. The lion did explain later in the movie that he saw that incident as some sense being knocked into his head—it was a boon to him, not an injustice.

The group discussed injustices in general. Lopez began talking about his religious inspiration, *Jesus*—the Hebrew name *Yehoshua* translated through Greek and English—and how every injustice is a test. We learned only then that Lopez had enjoyed long-term hospitality from the state prior to his current predicament—a decade or so. He underwent many of the state's correctional programs while incarcerated, and had "found Jesus." So much for the separation of church and state. The state does not hesitate to employ any church where convenient.

Everyone fell silent while Lopez downloaded his version of theology. Sid queried him about the origin of his understanding of injustices being tests, to which he answered, "From above." There really wasn't much to say to Lopez's proclamations; no one could discern if he meant what he said, or said what he thought would win him some favors or attention.

Paul changed the conversational direction with a picture of a pet lion on his cellphone. He had a friend who owned such animals, including tigers and bears, and lent them to movie studios. He passed his cellphone around, and sure enough, there was his friend standing beside a so-called king of the jungle in the picture. Having initiated a discussion on *Lion King*, Sid was glad to go along with the diversion.

Paul continued, relating an incident that happened to him the week before class. He was in a Starbucks drive-through, and saw his ex-girlfriend, who'd had him convicted, immediately ahead. She backed her car and blocked him, and did not allow him to pass. He had to climb his car on a curb to get around her. When he managed to get out of the drive-through, he found her in the parking lot attempting to block him again. He went home. Some time later, there was a knock on his door—cops had come along to ask him why he was harassing her. He described the events to them. Later, he found her following him again, coming as far as his house, and called the police to report that event. They informed him that they did not have officers to spare to go to her place and question her.

A good few in the group shared their ideas. "You should have called 911 right when you found her blocking your way, Paul, rather than trying to find a way around," said Jim. "Catching her in the act, they may have been able to do something."

Paul let the group know that prosecutors had not yet approved of his complaint of felony theft against his ex-girlfriend who carted away all that she could when she was evicted from his house.

Sid recalled another story, of roommates, a guy and a girl, where the girl owed the guy a large sum of money. They had fallen into an argument; the guy had taken a knife and destroyed her couch that was worth around the same amount of money. She called the cops, and they arrested the guy for domestic violence and criminal damage. Though this seemed like a situation that did re-quire police presence and subsequent action, some in the group disagreed. Sid pointed out that any act that appears or is violent, in a domestic situation, could raise suspicion in the cops' minds.

I recalled an incident where my wife alleged that I harmed her. She was getting out of her car, and had a bag in her hand, with groceries, slung over a shoulder. I'd waited to take the bag, but she did not hand it to me. I took the bag away from her grasp—she did not let go easily. Instead, she turned, stared at me, and said that I'd rotated her shoulder. She's an occupational therapist, a nurse who deals with such injuries. I apologized, saying I was simply taking the bag. It wasn't hard to see that she may have been thinking of additional ways to get me in trouble with the state, for this was after my arrest, and during my prosecution. Or playing a power card, when she had the state, prosecuting me, on her side.

Sid popped a surprising query. "Who in the group schedules sex like I do? Put it on your calendars! Avoid the resentment of missing it." Did we really need to know that in this class, Sid?

Levi spoke up, "One-night stands are the very best. I've done it all—but one-night stands are the best."

The group laughed, and Levi continued, "Don't take her to your home. Go to a hotel or motel. No responsibilities, no commitment, just a fun night. Don't go with trashy women, though."

"It's a crap shoot," said Sid. "Even children of counselors and religious advisers could be crack addicts, criminals." He was coming up with strange thoughts this class.

Levi, quite vocal this day, declared—"It's just the culture. So many from other cultures come into this country and are destroyed. I had a friend who brought a girl, a Russian woman, a good person. But in a month's time, she was completely changed, worse than any American woman, partying, drinking. He brought her from Russia, but she did not display their values."

I wasn't so sure—I'd been reliably informed that it was far easier to get laid in Russia than here. It seemed more likely to me that the absence of close family members in a new location here in America may have led to the Russian girl finding traditional constraints lifted.

Sid opposed that blanket condemnation vigorously. "Why would it be negative for her to find her freedom here?"

"Is that what freedom is all about?" asked Jim. "Doing anything and everything one feels like? My ex will surely agree with you. She'd probably want to make pot and drugs freely available too."

The session descended into veritable chaos. Everyone talked over one another. Perhaps the discussion touched a rather sensitive spot in the collective mind. I could hardly hear what was being said, much less think any more about responsibility. It was the end of the session anyway, and the session room emptied, while I stayed back to have a word with Sid—who sat in sullen silence as the group dispersed. He looked troubled, and rather unhappy with the session, but agreed with me when I pointed out that we tend to overemphasize freedom instead of discipline in the present day.

Excessive Force

Lauren, my probationary officer, had set another meeting with me about a month into my participation in the court-mandated program. She asked how my learning progressed in the classes, and of how things were at home.

I spoke about my wife's difficult, uncontrolled interactions with our children. "You are a messed-up kid," and, "You need to take pills or go to counseling," were among her declarations to my son, who sought clarifications from me. I explained to Lauren that it wasn't easy to see a parent taking out her frustrations upon children in this manner.

There was, of course, precious little communication between the adults in my home. No intimacy or activities together of any sort—we were no more than housemates now, caring for two little children. I was far more cautious than I'd ever been in life. But that wasn't really a dramatic change. After two children and numerous other life and business events that I'd gone through, including an ongoing lawsuit that severely impacted my new start-up efforts, I truly had withdrawn from what I assumed were matters that did not need as much attention. It is fair to say that I did not persevere at maintaining the relationship, taking it for granted given kids in the family.

"What are you looking for? What would be the best thing under these circumstances?" asked Lauren.

"Bringing back affection into the relationship could really help the whole family. Nothing dramatic, no jumping into bed, or any intimacy. Just affection. So the children pick up on good vibes."

She asked what I was doing to bring this about, and I mentioned my request to both my children as an example. *Do one thing every day for mom that will make her happy.* I clearly didn't think it required my personal attention or involvement.

She said nothing. I'd informed her, comprehensively, of my efforts in '07, with guidance from my friends John and Parvathi, to bring back happiness into the marriage, and into her heart and mind. Surprise flowers, chocolates, lunches, dinners at restaurants, vacation trips to various places, and deeper engagement with her family were some such. At Pravathi's recommendation and urging, I'd purchased another house—that the family did not need—in my wife's name that year. Despite all those efforts, there had been no change whatsoever in my spouse; her attention seemed elsewhere entirely. Lauren knew that I'd abandoned such efforts by the end of that year.

．   ．   ．

As I waited in a corridor of the intervention program offices with others, for the earlier session to finish up, Paul approached me and started a conversation. He said that his judge refused to believe him, denied his request for a restraining order against his ex-girlfriend, and told her instead that she could call the police if she saw him anywhere near her, which would lead to Paul, the plaintiff in this proceeding, going to jail for six months. I advised Paul that he should seriously consider leaving this place if at all possible to avoid further danger, particularly if his ex-girlfriend was indeed baiting him as he informed us all.

Conversation in the session this day began with a tragic instance of gun violence. A Dilbut cop, a sixteen-year veteran Lieutenant of the force, a detective, had been shot and killed recently. He had pulled over a car with an obstructed license plate. Something he probably need not have done, said a group member.

"It's a dangerous job…" said Sid.

"There were fifty cops chasing these perps," Lopez objected.

A typically quiet group member piped up and said that while he felt bad for the cop's family, the attention given to this incident seemed overboard.

"Look at the fire engine there and all those glossy pictures. I bet, if it was some Joe Schmo, there won't be a fraction of that level of attention or care as they show for a cop," he asserted.

Another spoke up, agreeing with him. "What about the Peoria situation, a sixty-seven-year-old man, tasered twice, and shot to death for DV? And what about the homeowner, fighting an armed intruder, shot six times by a responding cop? Six shots with a police weapon—do they shoot to kill, to leave no witnesses?"

That homeowner, who'd wrestled an armed intruder down and was taking his weapon, survived, but was confined to a wheelchair, permanently, due to his wounds. It was clear that cops focused on how not to get killed, or sued, in performing their law-enforcement duties. Reminded me of Fred's suggested method—in resolving a *wife-in-bed-with-another* situation—employing extreme prejudice.

I related a personal incident in which I woke up at night, in my house, in my bed, with three guns pointed at me by three Dilbut cops. This was some years prior to '07, resulting from a door not properly closed by my wife that had swung open in the night. The home alarm system activated while everyone slept upstairs. My wife slept with our children in the kids' bedroom. No one heard the loud alarm downstairs. The cops came by a while later to find the door open. They'd come in, climbed upstairs, and found me sleeping in the bed alone.

Sid disagreed with my implication. "How would you expect the police to respond? Maybe you were in bed with a knife at someone's throat."

I didn't provide any further details; it seemed pointless for us to debate police methods. It is easy to realize that the gun-happy cops could, quite readily, have shot me multiple times, without any further thought, had I reacted in a nervous manner that they could have interpreted as a threat. And, with three guns pointed at a target less than a body length away, I wouldn't have had any chance at survival.

As it happened, I'd woken up, very much aware of the guns pointed at me, with my hands raised, and asked them if I could check on my family before anything else. They allowed me passage to the kids' bedroom, where I found the door locked, and upon inquiring if everything was fine, I heard a muffled response from my wife, while the door did not open. By this time, their guns lowered and holstered, the cops explained that the alarm system signal they saw brought them over to check on the house. I asked them to help me search the house to ensure that nothing was amiss, which they did. They left afterward with sheepish looks on their faces, or so I remember.

I did recall that two of the cops who came by appeared to be young, and were probably in training. But three guns? All pointed at someone obviously sleeping, and alone, in the big bed in the big bedroom of the house? What were they thinking? Memory fails me now, but I think they offered an explanation that they thought I might have been a perpetrator who'd decided to take a nap after a crime. Did they get that from the Dilbut training manual for cops?

Sid had, meanwhile, provided handouts for the group to look through and discuss. Topics du-jour were violent behavior and performance, virulence, brutalization, and belligerence. Big words for us simple folks. We read through silently as he completed his roll-call and payments collection.

As Sid continued to discuss characteristics of violent behavior in the handout, I wondered what violence really meant to me, and about my experiences of that aspect. In two decades of life and work in the country, as an adult first generation immigrant, I had never once been accused of being violent by anyone. Yes, I'd been known to be angry, and yell, even in professional workplaces, but there it always ended, often with apologies from me for my behavior, whatever the circumstances.

It's also true that I'd been subjected to quite some physical punishment as a child—spanking—by my late father, but he had rules—smacks below the waist, and only with justification. Except that he did break his own rules on some occasions. But I had been a willful child who had little or no respect for any adult authority. I am sure I tested my parents' patience on a number of occasions.

And yes, I too had gone through high school with my share of experiences of being bullied. By the time I graduated from college, I'd grown big enough,

and well aware of my own physical capabilities, knowing that I could recipro-
cate any violence that came my way. Violence would usually not come my way.

Yet here I was, accused of domestic violence, and in an intervention program intended to satisfy the state that all they could do to change my violent
nature was being done. What was it that convinced them that I was the violent
participant in the disagreement? Was it because I was quite tall, and at 6' 3", a
foot and an inch taller than my wife? Why did Gormon decide that fateful
night that I would be the one to go through prosecution? Was it because I'd
told him about my wife's affair, and our continuing disagreements, a common
factor in many male-inflicted domestic violence injuries in the country? Or was
it something personal with him?

My thoughts drifted to contemplating the story of Andy Dufresne in
Shawshank Redemption, a moving narrative, in which he was convicted
wrongly, of dual acts of extreme violence, and tormented in the custody of
the state. I smiled internally at my own over-dramatization of the present
predicament.

Talk had moved on to relationships. A group member spoke about emotional pearl-harboring. While he made preparations to leave, his ex-wife asked
him, "Do you think we'll ever get back together?" He did not want to be cruel,
but this left him more than a little confused as he moved out.

Sid jumped in. "Whose box of problems is that? Statements like that—
there you go, running away—isn't that a problem clearly in her mind? She has a
difficulty, and simply threw that into your box. Say to her: *This is about you,
dear, not me.*" Sid *must* be Irish. He didn't say 'honey.'

It was graduation day for the emotionally pearl-harbored member in the
group; he'd completed his twenty-six weeks. We wrote him notes on his graduation certificate. I wrote that I hoped he would give it every effort and chance
to mend his broken relationship. More pearl-harboring for him to think about.

●   ●   ●

I missed the next class because of illness all week in the family. We were
allowed to miss three classes with prior notice, which extended the program
duration by as many weeks as classes missed. I was grateful for assistance from
my wife's sister Binita, who stayed with us at the time as she prepared for a job
and residence in the country. I took her out often for car-driving practice, and
she helped out with the children.

That week, there had also been another altercation. My wife was helping
my son with his homework, and in a disagreement with her, he said—"You are
mean! Stupid!" My wife ran to her sister Binita and cried her heart out, pro-
claiming that my son's behavior was caused by his father who showed her no
respect. Confronting this accusation, I demanded an explanation for what I felt

was wrong and unfair—what parent would teach their children to disrespect the other half raising them?

My wife claimed that my son had seen me being aggressive with her from a tender age. So now I had, by my very nature, and interaction with my wife, caused my son to be disrespectful toward her. I had, by what she called being aggressive, nurtured my son to be the same way. Sid, the intervention program counselor, will surely find a description, without much difficulty, for this male malady in his advanced psychology notes on violence.

What next, I wondered, an accusation for being too firm in family decisions? I was grateful to have Binita present at this time, for she witnessed how I managed my daughter's willful behavior that afternoon. And she saw how I reasoned with and convinced my son to go to his piano class—that he didn't want to, but his mother insisted upon—ensuring that he went by her wishes earlier that evening. Yet, my alleged aggressiveness had been influencing my children to be disrespectful to their mother, or so claimed my wife. This was, much as Sid put it, about her, not about me.

Batterers

Next week's session began with a worksheet titled *Obstacles to Partnership*, asking to identify unrealistic expectations of a partner, presumably a male partner in our group. Staying silent under any and all conditions popped into my mind right away. Living through the accidental death of my little sister in '03, watching my father slowly deteriorate and die from this heartbreaking tragedy three years later, and having my pet dog Rusty die later the same year—these were life events I'd faced. Managing a lawsuit threatening the survival of my start-up efforts, bringing up little children, and having to deal with a wife chasing after an affair, betraying all her promises and responsibilities toward a family—this was my lot at home with my partner. And yet being forced to listen, over and over again, to all of her *pain* that she wanted to express in justification of her actions—something just did not seem quite balanced in the situation.

Levi, from the Middle East, recounted his challenges. His wife and her brother had delved into his things in storage and taken away his gun that he loved. They'd apparently lied to him about his keys having slipped out of a bag, and about not having touched any of his items. Levi objected strongly to his gun being *stolen* as he termed it. He spoke of wanting to sue those who misappropriated it, but said he did not because it was his spouse and her brother. The group asked if he was married when this occurred. Levi confirmed that he was.

Sid provided a legal view. "It cannot be theft, because property belongs equally to the spouse as well, and given her concerns with your violent ways, she could be deemed to be justified in taking the weapon away from you."

Levi added that his wife and her brother had informed him that they'd handed the gun over to the local police. He'd checked with the cops, and determined they did not have the gun in their possession. He felt that her uncles, particularly one who was ex-FBI, were plotting to 'F' him. Not the failing grade sort of 'F' either. Levi spoke of a curious desire to help him get over these concerns and problems. He wanted to slap his wife four times. No more than that, just four slaps exactly. The group set to teasing him about his desire to slap someone silly, but exactly four times.

The doctor who had joined the group spoke up, asking Sid if he could change to an earlier class to fit his schedule. The group wanted him to enlighten everyone with his story before he left. He gave an interesting summary that seemed eerily familiar.

In view of his difficulties with his wife, friends had determined that he would benefit from a personal and unsolicited intervention, and had, in his words, broken into his home. As the intervention went awry, he'd touched a man on the chest, and the police had been called because of the alleged break-in. The police tried to subdue him in his agitated state, tasered him *thrice* while he struggled on the ground, and charged him with assault and disorderly conduct. Standard operating procedure, voiced the group—an arrest is a foregone conclusion in such incidents with intervention by cops.

Sid said there should be slots in the previous class and asked the doctor to get in touch with Dave who ran that class.

Another group member raised his situation of being set up with thirty-six classes though the court had required only twenty-six. Sid advised him to call the intervention program office, and put it in their court for resolution, cautioning him that if it was a therapeutic determination, that he needed thirty-six classes, he'll have no luck getting around that.

• • •

As Sid continued with roll-call and payment formalities, my thoughts drifted to an incident in the morning. At breakfast with my son and daughter, we'd fallen into an unnecessary argument about what was set out for breakfast and what they should eat—and that had become a confrontation. Right then, their mother called, and my son continued complaining about me with her on the phone. Out of frustration, I compared his behavior with his mother's—which led to an offensive outburst—"Shut your mouth!"—from her, while my young daughter was on the line with us. I replied only that our daughter could be learning these habits from her.

Later that morning, I called my wife, who was on a trip to another state, to explain a challenge I saw with our son, and the need to inculcate implicit respect in children for their parents. She insisted that our children needed religion; I responded that I'd not agree to exposing children to brainwashing that is common in religious instruction. We nevertheless agreed that just as religion can be a one-way conversation about conduct, we needed to build implicit respect in our children for discipline and guidance from parents. She said some face-saving thing and disconnected the call.

Religion has always been a touchy topic in my relationship with my wife. When she first knew me, she had been quite happy about my open-minded approach regarding religious beliefs. This came in part from my family's origins. We were a tribal clan associated with Hindu temples for a thousand years or more, employed as soldiers and keepers of temple premises and property. We were thus entrusted with the task of protecting and serving Hinduism, and many family members were devout Hindus. And this way of life, guided by its ancient texts, has always been an inclusive philosophy accepting of all forms of belief, including that of non-belief in divine entities.

My wife's path to religion, on the other hand, had more recent origins. Her grandfather had converted to Christianity. This was compelled in part by penury, and also by social oppression, in prior Indian society, that looked down upon lower social classes. He'd led his family into this alternative choice that came along with the activities of missionaries in India. In an argument with my wife, I'd called this conversion a lack of faith and of consistency, an easy way out, and not one that is disciplined and enlightened. It is fair to say that I considered such conversion to be a convenient option for the weak-minded. She'd been vehement in her denial then that such was the case. She resented my feelings about her opportunistic religiosity—she hadn't spoken about or practiced her religion in the first decade and a half that I'd known her.

I called her again, later that day, to apologize for yelling, which started her off, once again, into her descriptions of life with me, and of her shutting the door metaphorically. She asked what I called for, and listened to my clarification that it was only to apologize. She again said something inconsequential and disconnected the call.

I wasn't about to agree with her on her thought that our children needed religion. They needed critical thinking, and the ability to comprehend anything that they came across with rational and scientific thought, far more than religion. I'd grown to adulthood questioning the tenets of Hinduism, which is a philosophical path rather than the religion it's often misconstrued to be. But I did prefer its acceptance, of all ways of life, to the patriarchal and differentiating approaches of Judaism, Christianity, and Islam, Abrahamic religions in general. But there wasn't any way to bridge such differences with my wife, who sought religion only at times of great stress.

Reflecting upon these interactions with her, I began to realize that all my efforts at unity in the family weren't really getting us anywhere. Civil discourse may permit one to agree to disagree, but may not bridge deep, fundamental differences that I'd been blind to, or naively assumed to be inconsequential.

• • •

The group meanwhile had moved on to discussing *pit bulls* and *cobras*, as illustrative examples of battery. Sid declared that men are classified as batterers of women, for statistics showed that two to four million wives are severely assaulted each year by their husbands in the United States. And that *half* of all women murdered were victims of their husbands, ex-husbands, boyfriends, or ex-boyfriends. The comparable statistic for murdered men was a fraction, *one-sixteenth*.

Sid did not clarify why cobras were employed to symbolize acts of extreme violence by men. A common reptile in India, the cobra is worshiped by simple folks in the land I come from, as are many other living things for qualities admirable to humans. A book written after the O. J. Simpson[1] double-murder case and its aftermath, by two psychologists, *When Men Batter Women*, reviewed in the New York Times in 1998[2], may have a lot to do with this rather unfair characterization. In that arguably opportunistic book, psychologists portrayed male behavior in dark extremes, employing these animals, and our revulsion to some of their behaviors, for dramatic effect.

So that makes all men batterers, Sid? If they are aggressive, clamp down hard, and won't let go, they are then pit bulls, and if they are unemotional, and strike with great speed, cobras in the grass? You mean us men in your counseling class, surely, for we'd been duly deemed, one and all, violent or prone to violence with our domestic partners by the state. Yet the statistical fact of half of all murdered women harmed by their partners was indeed frightening.

Sid spoke of his ex—it wasn't clear if that was a wife or a girlfriend—who hit him, which went on for about two years. He said he'd felt like hitting back at one point. Had he threatened to do so, or caused any fear of physical harm in his ex-'s mind, the legal definition of assault would have fallen on him like a bag of loose hammers. But Sid only said that hitting is just not acceptable. We wondered when we'd hear more about our counselor's own misadventures.

Another group member, Duane, who'd inquired about being asked to attend thirty-six classes instead of the typical twenty-six, began talking about his past problems with his ex-partner. A group member piped up, interrupting him. "Duane, I don't mean to be offensive or anything, but when you first came in, I thought you'd need thousands of classes! I was scared of you. But now you seem close to normal." The repeat-offender group member Lopez laughed his guts out rather too loudly for comfort. The entire class dissolved into jibes at Duane, who seemed to brighten up at the sudden and pleasant attention that descended upon him.

Surprisingly, Sid talked about three participants he'd come to know in his four years of counseling who were innocent in his mind. One was accused of grabbing his wife by her throat. He'd denied it, and Sid said that he knew that was the truth from his ready response to the next question—"Did you ever touch you wife [roughly]?"—with the answer, "Yes, many times. Just not this time." In another similar instance, a man and wife were involved in a disagreement when cops arrived, called by neighbors—the wife was a cop, and the man knew that she'd lose her job—whence he took the blame upon himself. Sid said that couple continued to remain married.

Yet another case was a man prosecuted for spanking—the man wanted to

1   http://en.wikipedia.org/wiki/O._J._Simpson_murder_case
2   http://www.nytimes.com/1998/03/17/science/battered-women-face-pit-bulls-and-cobras.html

stop, but his kids had run at him, and were quite unafraid of him. Absent any cooperation with his requests and instructions, he'd resorted to the only thing he could, which, though permitted by law in the State of Wariduna, was nevertheless prosecutable if deemed excessive.

Innocence. Was I innocent? An anguished query to my wife had elicited an interesting reply—she'd said to consider the prosecution I'd been going through as just retribution for all that she had to suffer with me. And what had I done to cause her such unforgivable suffering? Given her my life in marriage, two beautiful children, a beautiful home to live in, and another home with a backyard pool as a gift, friendship, companionship, and love in no small measure? Along with the quirks of any ordinary man, anger, discipline, impatience, risky business ventures, and consequent financial stresses?

Not once had I strayed toward any other woman after we married, though a common failing in many men. Evidently, no good deed ever goes unpunished. I would have considered myself guilty had I jeopardized the family's integrity. But insisting upon a conversation with her to sort out her extra-marital interactions and her questionable behavior at a difficult time for the family—a controlled exercise of a modicum of manliness—was not something I could feel guilty about, despite her emotional distress or the state's ready conclusion about my conduct.

A Widening Gulf

Jim, with his leg still in a cast that he explained was from a skiing accident, suggested the group ought to be let off ten minutes early since we'd stayed that much longer for a previous class. Some agreed, while Sid conducted roll-call and payments collection.

In the general banter ongoing, Lopez, the repeat offender required to go through fifty-two weeks of classes, piped up, "I had to take matters into my own hands this weekend."

Someone asked, "You weren't alone, were you?"

Jim and others listening burst out laughing. Lopez wasn't sure if he understood what was implied, or feigned incomprehension, and did not respond.

I drifted away into thinking about a difficult time with my son as I drove my children back home from school that day. He wanted music in the car, the radio turned on, with songs of the wilder variety that I just couldn't listen to. I refused to turn on the radio, and that upset him a good bit. He called me *mean* a number of times; perhaps it relieved his frustration. I'd employed silence—no response—which only got him more worked up. At home, he continued with his complaints. I gave him a hug and told him it was alright, though it really wasn't.

The kids' mother had returned from her out-of-state trip, and had been giving me her typical passive-aggressive treatment again. She had now begun to sit in the back of our van when I'd drive, avoiding the front passenger seat next to me. She cooked food at home for herself and the children and stored it away in the refrigerator, leaving me to fend for myself. I'd begun to wonder how I could manage to live with such interaction, that I did feel to be insulting, and had been thinking of moving on, moving ahead, and closing this miserable life-chapter. Yet thoughts of my children held me back.

My kids' mother, and her good friend Parvathi, ridiculed that as well. Parvathi, a bit of a mother hen, knew and befriended my wife before I met with her and John. They—the women—now called my concern for my children "hanging onto their coat tails." I appreciated Parvathi's kind intervention in my troubles with my wife, but could not understand this rebuke that came from her.

While it is true that women carry, give birth to, and nurture the young, is it not the father's role to protect, mentor, and build their character and identities as they grow? Doesn't a son look to a father as his first example to emulate, and a daughter look to him as the first loving, caring, and nurturing man in her life? Do they not carry the father's clan name traditionally, thus affirming their kinship?

Parvathi had previously cautioned both my wife and me that the stresses a family goes through in a split could require many visits to child psychologists to counsel children of the family as they grew. Why then did she so demean my focus upon the well-being of my children, as they coped with difficulties the family fell into? Her ridicule of my devotion to children and family hurt deeply. It also reflected more than a little immaturity in her that distanced me from any further assistance she could offer to resolve our predicament.

Sid completed his administrative tasks, and fielded a question from a group member, a BYU (Brigham Young University) graduate. The young graduate asked if the group could go on a field trip. Group members laughed, but field trips are typical in any program, so the query, however inane, stood.

"Okay, a field trip. Where could we go?" asked Sid.

"I don't know, the zoo, maybe?" said the BYU grad sheepishly.

Sid dug deeper. "What can we learn, from animals, about DV?"

Knowing Sid was heading to dismiss the young graduate's ideas, I spoke up. "Perhaps you haven't come across this, Sid, but researchers have recorded a Chimpanzee actively mediating, resolving conflict between two others."

"Really?"

"There is much to learn from animals," I continued. "Ants, for example, form a highly successful species, having lasted for a hundred million years and more without any change. They display extreme discipline, a possible factor toward their success."

Sid disagreed. "I wouldn't call that discipline; it's not something taught and communicated among them. Ants are rigid, maybe, and organized and precise, but not disciplined."

Sure, Sid. Science is rigid, and so are ants now. I didn't venture the biological fact that worker ants that fall out of line are dealt with immediately by soldier ants in some species, with such matters often decided with extreme prejudice. Soldier ants are much larger than the workers, and a crunch with their mandibles neatly severs out-of-line workers' heads from their bodies. It is hard to conceive of ant actions as being rigid or programmed. On what basis would such decisions be made by these intelligent beings? Two steps away from the food or construction line to follow gets the head chop?

But they are evidently organized, as Sid pointed out, with well-defined roles in their social structure. Sid clearly wanted to be the knowledgeable teacher, the counselor, and that was just as it should be. I was happy to have turned his focus away from the young, naive graduate.

A new member, **Manuel**, had joined in; it was story time for us. Manuel had been overly vocal in his disagreement with his ex-wife, and had 'cussed' her out. There had also been two previous incidents of altercation between them with police involvement. Manuel's ex-wife testified in court about being afraid of his evil eye. She hailed from Mexico, where such concerns are common among members of the general population. Needless to say, things did not go too well for Manuel. The judge bought into Manuel's wife's fears of his evil eye and its violent intimidation. Rightly so; legally, any form of threat of harm, perceived by presumed victims, is viewed by diligent keepers and enforcers of the law as conforming with the definition of assault. Manuel spoke of the system demanding money from him, of its insistence that he pay the state in one form or another.

Manuel's distinct impression of the system's wanting to profit from someone in its grasp hit on my sensitive nerve. I launched into how there had been no 911 (emergency) call, my wife's explanation to the prosecutor that she called the Sheriff's office because she felt I was *mocking* her, about how the state and its prosecutors did not care to listen to me at all. And how they ignored corrective actions taken, in attending parental anger management classes at my own initiative, giving it no consideration.

My passion prompted the group to ask me to continue with what I'd gone through, though it seemed rather repetitious. I pointed out that I readily admitted to being aggressive and pulling my wife's arm, but also asserted that there had been no intention toward or perpetration of violence, in typical form, on my part. I detailed how my wife too had rushed at me, and how I had to hold her hands firmly, away from my face, to stall her aggressive behavior. She had been so forceful in coming at me, that my fingers gripping her arms had left impressions that the cops had photographed as visible evidence of my alleged violent conduct. And, employing my honest admissions, the state branded all of my actions criminal. I now carried that label on my record.

I characterized the state's actions as vigilante in nature, of how they'd called in, came in unsolicited into my home, and how they deemed me, on the spot, the criminal to be prosecuted. It was fair to say that Manuel's story stoked my own smoldering fire against presumed guilt, and injustice, by the state.

Sid attempted to explain the state's behavior. "There is zero tolerance; *the State throws ninety-seven people under the bus to get two or three really bad ones.*" He spoke about the perception of violence, about how almost any action, even including one's very presence, could be perceived to be intimidating and interpreted by the state as DV. As the group listened with some disbelief, Sid tried to backpedal, indicating that the state does this so the *ninety-seven* thrown under the bus can see how bad it can get. We get it, Sid, thank you. The state's the bus, and you, a modern **Arnaud Amalric**. We are the ninety-seven crushed under it, the doomed *Cathars of Béziers*.

The group voiced that the label *sucks*, and that the damage can be perma-

nent to one so labeled. The actions by the state, I continued, could compel me
to leave Wariduna and the country to be able to find gainful employment. Or
impoverish me and compel me to explore new, alternate occupations. Though
I didn't reveal this in the group, thoughts of a life of white-collar crime had
also crept into my mind.

Sid strove to justify the state's approach. "It used to be different in the
past, but the pendulum has now swung the other way." He said that certain
high-profile cases, that my lawyer Mindy also alluded to, the O. J. Simpson case
in particular, had prompted a number of states to act. The states provided new
guidelines, to their law-enforcement cadre, to err on the side of caution. This
produced large numbers of instances of unjust prosecution of men under the
DV umbrella.

A *pendulum*? Is that what the justice—no—legal system is, here? Something that swings to an extreme, and then back the other way, passing for a
fleeting moment through the middle? It may have been just an illustrative
model Sid employed, but his pendulum sure had swung hard against me,
knocking out any expectations of fairness and equal treatment. This pendulum
was not only an unstable system, it was, in the hands of a ruthless and single-
minded collection of authorities, a hammer of social injustice and repression.

That reminded me of our many unilateral actions, arrogantly undertaken,
including invasions. Action that resulted in unimaginable suffering for innocents, as in recent wars waged to liberate countries, to teach their ancient people how to govern themselves with our laws and law-enforcement. And of
rough statements—"Boot on BP's throat"—from none other than the head of
the country's administration, bringing to mind an image of violence far removed from the diplomacy that might be hoped for. I recall emailing Lauren
about this—after my matter had concluded—with not a word back in response
from her.

What was most troubling was the same righteousness, with which our
ways, of convenience and rampant materialism, invaded other ways of life
readily, overcoming and ruining them. Is this integration and inclusion, wise
and considerate cultural assimilation, or is this an extreme approach that could
give rise to and foster fundamentalism?

Sid did let us out early; no one seemed to be in a mood for further education by the state.

I had a long chat with my wife late into that night, as I recall. Conversations with her had become even less rational and constructive than in the past.
I explained to her, in as many ways as I could, that my only desire was to find
happiness for our children and herself. And that I had no other agenda whatsoever. But nothing seemed to get through to her. She seemed to want her
"life" back, repeating vehemently—"Not with you." I suggested that she act
upon that desire, and leave, but that brought—"But I have two children

here!"—from her. She seemed to want to experiment with the two houses idea, with the children shared. I asked her how it would be fair, to the children, to have their lives so disrupted solely to fulfill her wants; there was, predictably, no reply.

It occurred to me then that I struggled with a wayward mother, in a free-for-all society, to maintain a reasonably stable home for my children. Neither of my two children, young as they were, had any desire for a breakup in the family. Perhaps they'd seen too many such instances in their school, a private organization selected by their mother, where I found, to my surprise, that more than one-half of the children enrolled were from single-parent homes. In any case, they were set against any formal separation in the family. But all signs pointed then to a split of some kind. I thought that I might even be forced to leave the country, given my arrest record that would be revealed in any background check for a corporate job, which could precipitate the split.

The discussion with my wife ended badly that night. I was forced to admit to her that given her mental state, I knew that my efforts would be futile, and friendship in my heart for her was dying. Yet, the next morning, I talked—no, listened—to her again, apologizing for having kept her awake quite late the previous night. She launched into descriptions of her *pain*, over and over again, which I could only listen and agree to.

I had to explain, again, my intentions in bringing her back to this country after she left it for good. This was an event way back in our past, when my relationship with another girl that developed after a breakup with my wife, who was my girlfriend then, had caused her much anguish. She left the country after I declined to heed her pleas to me to marry her. It had been a constant refrain from her that I had not really loved her. But would my agreeing to marry her, just because she asked, have proved that I loved her?

Was that really true? Did I not love the mother of my two little children? It is true that due to difficulties over a long period together, I'd left Wariduna, and a house we shared here, with nothing but my clothes and my old car. I left to another state in the northwest of the country, thus breaking up with her. This was more than a decade before events with the state changed us, parents of two small children, into adversaries in a legal proceeding. It is true that I left—the state and relationship, but not my friendship with her. When her stay in the country on a work visa came to an end, shortly after I left Wariduna, I helped her in every way possible. This was the second time she left the country for good. The first time that I helped her leave was when I'd fallen deeply in love with her, and, against my pleas, she'd decided that her life lay elsewhere—but that is a story yet to be told.

Having moved away, it is also true that I came to know another girl, whose brother literally pushed her onto me to begin a new relationship. She became aware of that to the extent of interfering in this relationship, penning and leaving an emotional letter to my then girlfriend at her doorstep, days before leaving the country. After the turmoil that followed, I brought her back and married her, as she had desired, for she stood by me at a time of great difficulty. I did so against the advice of good friends then.

Could I have done all that without love? Is there no love in caring for the needs of another, regardless of one's own? Perhaps this was a relationship doomed from the beginning, for it began no differently from how her relationship outside the family began in '07. It also began as an affair more than a decade and a half ago—one she pursued relentlessly, that I joined in with little resolve—which I succumbed to eventually, against the advice from my then apartment mates and friends.

But turn the question on its head—did this woman really love *me*, or did she love the security and convenience of having me as a companion by her side? Did she only desire *the idea of me*, a romance, a dalliance, an escape from her troubled past? Was it a distraction from boredom or the plainness of her prior life, when she pursued me with such determination, to the extent of unexpectedly relocating near my university? In today's terms, that is akin to stalking. She had even offered to help me pay tuition as I worked to obtain my graduate degree without the funds to do so. An offer that I declined immediately.

And, when this rocky relationship eventually transformed into mundane domestic existence, with its typical challenges, and lack of attention and romance, did she simply fall back into her pattern of loose conduct, her natural tendencies? Or was this, as writer Margaret Atwood said, a crass human realization, "Longed for him. Got him. Shit."

More Stories

The next week, Paul, the widower, said he met with Lauren too, and that she conveyed a *hi* to Sid. He had good news, and seemed excited and full of good cheer. His ex-girlfriend had been subpoenaed, summoned by prosecutors to appear in court, to explain the theft she was accused of committing when she vacated Paul's place.

Paul was bursting with his desire to share this news. "I was really excited," he said. "This was the fifth time I'd been to the prosecutor's office to ask about the status of my complaint. In all my prior visits, they told me only that it was under review. I was really happy to hear she has been summoned!"

"You feel vindicated she has to own up to what she did," said Sid. "This doesn't absolve you, but she played her part in what happened."

Paul didn't respond. He didn't need any absolution, I thought, smiling at Sid's obvious attempt to play both sides of the matter. There wasn't much guilt that Paul needed release from, or forgiveness for, other than decisions made in haste, and a distinct lack of caution, perhaps. I admired his persistence in seeking a measure of justice, and congratulated him on the result.

Ken was a new addition to the group, hailing from Mexico, the populous Hispanic country south of Wariduna. Ken married into a Caucasian American family. He said that his wife's family members discriminated against him at every opportunity. These relatives were enthusiastic supporters of Sheriff Waspoia's crusade to rid Wariduna of undocumented immigrants, particularly those from south of the border. Coming from that part of the American continent, Ken stood at a distinct disadvantage with his American in-laws.

On the day Ken fell afoul of the law in Wariduna, in Dilbut to be precise, his wife asked him not to go to a social event because her family was planning on attending that event. He couldn't take that in silence. The conversation turned into an altercation; they yelled back and forth. He threw a glass cup from the balcony, shattering it. As his wife left the home, he locked her out, with their child with him in the home. She panicked and called the police, and a Dilbut cop arrived soon thereafter.

When the cop came by, Ken was busy cleaning broken pieces of glass, and did not pay much attention to the man of the law. Under the charge of DV, Ken was arrested and processed through the 4th Ave. facility. He spoke of being transferred in cage-like vehicles between the jail and court. A protective order prevented him from going back home for two months. As court proceedings continued, Ken took a plea offer to avoid further difficulties.

Ken described how the Dilbut cop wrote up every charge he could think of, most of which were dropped by prosecutors. In particular, he described how his action of leaving the cop's presence, to bring a broom to finish his cleaning work, was characterized by the cop as a threatening act. The cop claimed that Ken had armed himself with a weapon. Clearly, a thorough officer and gentleman of the law. Asked why he fell at the receiving end of a two-month protective order, for an incident that seemed relatively minor, he indicated that it could have been due to the police report, and the number of charges filed against him.

The group had a good laugh over Ken's experiences and the form of Dilbut law-enforcement. It was the only thing that the ninety seven thrown under the state bus, as Sid described such events, could do. Besides, it was common knowledge that law-enforcement lacked their needed additional heads, had experienced pay cuts over many years, and in general had become a disgruntled group, prone to taking their frustrations out on those they had authority over.

Ken also spoke of his wife's apologies to him for what he had gone through, and indicated that they remained together.

"You mentioned your wife apologizing. Did you apologize to her?" asked Sid.

"Of course—many times," said Ken, without any hesitation. "I know what I did, and she accepts what she did too. We've also done some counseling together, though that doesn't satisfy the state."

"Does the discrimination by your in-laws not trouble you?" I asked, wondering how he survived his oppressive social situation.

"I've dealt with it all my life," he replied. "I lived in an all-white neighborhood as a child growing up. I am used to it. But it can be tiresome."

Coincidentally, Sid showed the group a video on domestic abuse, in an interracial family, with a black husband and a white wife. The family had three children, who witnessed daily abuse of the mother by the father. This carried on for a long period of time; the children videotaped some of the abuse, and that became evidence in the case against the man. He was sentenced to thirty-six years in prison for his violence and abuse against his wife and the mother of his children.

While the group discussed this situation, a loud member claimed that the thirty-six year sentence was handed down because it was a black man abusing a white woman. Had it been a white man abusing a black woman, there would not be this level of outrage, he asserted. Sid stayed silent. The class dispersed after the video.

I left class encouraged by Ken's situation. Despite his humiliating interaction with his in-laws, and flare-up in a domestic altercation to a painful phase for him and his wife, they seemed to be happy together, which promised a happy future for their child. His wife clearly did empathize with him, see things from his point of view, and cared enough about him, and their marriage, to be able to subjugate her own ego. He seemed quite mild-mannered as well, which must also help.

· · ·

The next day, my spouse informed me that she had travel plans, for the end of April, to visit her sister Binita, who'd moved to the northeast for her new assignment. As I had previously planned travel to France, to present a tutorial at a workshop, I couldn't agree with her new plans. She then insisted on taking the children along with her. I denied approval for the expense, and for taking the children along, just to satisfy her whim, in complete disregard of my requests.

The discussion flared into an altercation, with her calling me a *bastard* that my son heard quite clearly. On a prior occasion, his mother had asked him to spell 'H Y P O C R I T E' to my face, telling him that was his father. I explained to my son that such actions and behaviors by adults are not typical, and are entirely unacceptable. Nevertheless, this wasn't the only instance where both my children observed such interactions between the adults in their lives. In the years since their mother's affair, my words and speech occasionally did descend to unacceptable depths. All I could do then was remind my spouse that our children do register, and may well emulate, these behaviors, which would do them little good as they grew to adulthood.

I was beginning to see that little would change in the mother of my small children. Browsing through the family's phone bill earlier that month, I'd discovered multiple text messages from her to an acquaintance, Ganesh Mathai, in India—all on Valentine's Day, the 14th of February. This was an unsavory fellow who caused much sorrow to my parents in India. My little sister had fallen prey to his manipulation, which my mother revealed to me long after I was introduced to him. His frequent and recent interactions with my spouse did not escape my notice—one too many messages, telephone calls, emails—and I'd asked of my spouse that she stay at a distance from this individual, and avoid communicating with him further. She evidently did not heed my request.

After my little sister's tragic demise in a traffic accident in '03, and interactions with Ganesh confirming his sleazy and opportunistic nature, I had disconnected from him, but he had been attempting to continue contact through my spouse. Upon finding this, I'd called and talked with Ganesh's spouse in India, voicing my concerns about his undesirable contact with my wife at a vulnerable time for my family. Yet, her continuing behavior, particularly after the adversarial legal event I had to face, was deeply disheartening. My spouse not only disregarded advice and requests from me, she continued to communicate, uninhibitedly, with those outside the family who may not have had good intentions toward us. Perhaps I failed to see that *she* may not have had any desire to help me in my efforts to save this family.

I did feel then that there was little worth saving in my partnership with the mother of my children. Yet, I was resolved that the happiness of our two little children would remain uppermost in my mind. The sins of the parents must not become punishment for their children.

My wife called later that morning, and apologized for calling me a bastard, asking me at the same time to not put her down in front of our children. I wondered aloud how I could do that, and tried to make her see that neither my intentions, nor my actions, were so directed. It was nice, nevertheless, that she showed a measure of empathy, and did acknowledge hurt caused. I thanked her for her call and apology.

But the recurrence of altercations, with disrespect and disregard so openly displayed, could only do more harm. Wasn't that also grave abuse of children experiencing it? Wasn't that domestic violence too? I'd begun to lose respect for the kids' mother. I felt a significant change in my perception of this human being. Though connected by shared parenthood, I saw her now more as a selfish person, causing harm to others, uncaring as to consequences. I should have listened to advice from friends and steered clear of her—but that's in the past, as Sid put it, and it can only help to move beyond it in this circumstance.

Dressing to get to the next weekly re-education, I was upstairs in my bedroom when I heard my children fighting and screaming. The keyboard instrument downstairs was being played at the same time. When I heard screaming from my daughter a second time, I came to the stairs to look. Finding their mother playing on the keyboard, I assumed she'd take care of this clash. As I finished dressing, there was more screaming, mixed now with yelling from their mother, who appeared to be insisting that both children go to 'time-out,' probably because their fighting interrupted her playing.

My daughter ran up the stairs, asking something or the other from me, which I agreed to so as to pacify her, while her brother resisted going to time-out because it really hadn't been his fault. His little sister insists on playing video games with him, that she cannot do well in, and frustrates him. And she tends to be rather aggressive with him physically—hitting him with her fists often—it is typically not his fault in these clashes.

As his mother turned the television off, my son tried to prevent her from doing that, and I watched her shove him roughly, something no adult should ever do with young children. His mother showed the very same aggression seen in my daughter, that comes from a small physical frame and a strong will. She employed such aggression to discipline a child of nine years, unable to convince him with reason. I could do little to prevent the incident.

Recalling my own childhood, I remembered my vocal objections to a punishment regime that distanced me from my parents. I'd said to my mother, up-set at a spanking, "Punishment for something I'd done, I can accept, but a beating, just because you are angry, is not okay."

As I drove to class, my son called, and tearfully requested to be allowed to continue playing the video game he was engaged in before his mother inter-vened. I asked him to think about possible effects of that action, and to play a little while later. It twisted my heart that I had to ask a small child to think about his adult parent's frame of mind and behave accordingly.

I couldn't help but think that we were failing as parents in ensuring a hap-py home for our children. These incidents, in our home, and family, were far too common. We weren't just failing—we *had failed* miserably in being family.

• • •

At class, the group engaged in casual banter while Sid worked on roll-call and payments. A new member appeared quite knowledgeable about soccer, or football as it is known in the rest of the world. He shared his opinions about Beckham, who apparently had a great free kick, and Donovan, who, in his con-sidered opinion, was a better mid-fielder and unselfish as well. Sid asked this new member for the usual description of events that brought him to our group.

Jerome was a talkative young father, of two little girls, who came home one evening to find his wife online and his daughters trashing their walls with marker pens. He fell into an argument with his wife, and threw the marker pens at her. She left home after this fight. A few days later, he was charged with disorderly conduct. He pled guilty, and had been assessed a stiff penalty and a half-year of DV class. The penalty in his case was $1700/-. Now di-vorced, he worked with his ex-wife on looking after the children. He continued to spend time with his divorced spouse, trying to mend the relationship. Jerome claimed he was part Sicilian, and a good soccer player, playing profes-sionally where he could. Sid welcomed him to the group.

This day, the group discussed negotiation, discussion, and decision owner-ship. The topics were simple enough and did not include any new or interest-ing insights. My thoughts drifted to other matters.

A group member, who I felt was a level-headed individual, piped up, "What I've learned from all this is that she's just not worth it! Just walk away. The best revenge is to do it calmly." He seemed to be in no mood to negotiate anything with the individual who caused his presence among us. The psycholo-gists, who published a study on men as batterers of women, would have la-beled him a cobra batterer for taking revenge by leaving his troubled marriage unemotionally.

As classes proceeded, I wondered what all this would lead to. Not that I expected any novel understanding, or a miraculous change in my view of life and relationships. But all that I heard seemed only to confirm my own suspicions. A biased view of events by the state and law-enforcement personnel. Widespread over-reaction due to a highly publicized double-murder case, with incompetent prosecution failing to convict a known abuser—in this instance, black—for a brutal act of ending two arguably innocent lives, both white. Corrupt officials in government who worked the system to their benefit. And numerous instances of domestic discord, with undeniable similarity in circumstances despite cultural differences.

The state's intervention did little to benefit any participant in its mandated counseling program, much less help resolve difficulties and unite families. Was I learning anything at all? Anything worth learning? It did not seem likely that I could do what I'd sincerely exhorted the emotionally pearl-harbored class graduate to do—try to get back together with a difficult spouse.

Expectations and Demands

As I think back now to the year of my re-education, by the State of Wariduna, I wonder what I'd expected from the state. And what was expected from me as I journeyed through the process the state put me through. It's safe to say that I was no more than a *perp* to the state—a number, a feather in the Dilbut police's and DA's hats of a case successfully identified and prosecuted by them. And fines as well as fees paid, for a re-education program, put into play by some authority of the state that could be shown to be profitable and useful from the numbers passing through.

It has been almost five long years since domestic discord and state intervention started me out on this journey. With the stamp of a criminal arrest on my record, I have found no corporate employment in this duration. Not that I shirked trying; every such attempt resulted in a typical but inexplicable termination of contact, by interviewing entities, near the end of the selection process. That's just about where the human resources department, in a company interviewing someone, conducts a background check. No one says a thing, of course—it's illegal to discriminate—but who in their right minds would hire one prosecuted by a state for violence, domestic violence particularly, for positions where he would need to manage, motivate, and inspire many others?

Who in the corporate world would think that a lack of self-control, a propensity toward violent reactions, can be accepted in a team? I cannot teach in any educational institution, or so I was told, since a clearance by the state cannot be granted to one arrested for criminal matters. An assignment to teach in my own children's school fell through upon my disclosure to them of this fact. No, the state had condemned me to impoverishing circumstances, with my corporate record and reputation beheaded by their indelible stamp on my character and life.

But I knew this the moment it occurred, and used this period of virtual destitution to compile two engineering text books in my area of expertise. And to prepare to write this complex story. Little good could come from what I, these circumstances, and the state, had driven my family into. The state's processes only reminded me of a management refrain, common in the industry, "The beatings will continue until morale improves." Or, as Sid, my good intervention program counselor characterized it, "We'll throw you 97 under the bus, and run you over and over again, until you learn to get up by yourselves." I prepared myself, knowing this outcome, to explore new pathways in life.

• • •

That brings me to you, Priyavani. You *must* have felt even greater outrage and disbelief at what the United States of America, where one out of four humans jailed in the world live[3], subjected you to. A deputy consul-general, a civil servant of another country, a person of prominence both at home and abroad, treated with such disrespect—how was your arrest and holding even conceivable? Me, I understand, I am an ordinary man, subject to all the practices of the state and of society here, but you, an honorable deputy consul general? How could you have expected this affront to your freedom, to your modesty, and to your respectable position in world society? There is a good bit amiss here—something clearly does not make sense. How did Veer Batata, presumably an honorable man of the law here, decide that you should be subjected to the state's treatment reserved for all it deems to be criminals? How did matters come to such a pass with a diplomat, a government official of another country, one with whom diplomacy surely is the first path taken?

I know you may not like to recall the unspeakable humiliation you went through. And you certainly will not speak with me, an ordinary American, one who relinquished his citizenship of the land we both originate from. To comprehend the state's actions against you, I must build your story from the bits and pieces available in the media.

The truth does matter, does it not? We both hail from India, where *Satyameva Jayate*—from the Mundakopanishad, an ancient Indian text, *it is only truth that wins*—is inscribed on the national flag, and ingrained in us. In constructing your story, from its key events listed, forgive me if I am not as near the truth as I should be. Take comfort, if you will, in what we believe with all our hearts, that it is truly only truth that wins, not untruth.

In the last week of June '13, you returned home from a trip to find your maid, Seeta Jacob, to whom you had entrusted your two little children, missing. You informed the Office of Foreign Missions and the New York police of this event. Seeta was your domestic help, brought over from India, who stayed with you at your residence. Why did she leave, and what did you convey to the state authorities, other than that she was missing? She had complained to you that you were paying her less than what had been promised, less than what would be fair. You made an agreement with her to pay her less than $600 per month, while asking her to be available all day, every day. She hoped instead to be paid according to the hours and effort demanded of her. You did give her a place to live in, and food as well, but $600 per month? Was that because she hailed from India? Why did Seeta feel compelled to leave the security of your residence, and seek shelter from others in the Indian community in New York?

3   Chris Jordan, TED talk "Turning powerful stats into art," Feb. 2008

Seeta sought help from a lawyer, and a non-profit agency with an anti-traf-
ficking program, to try and resolve this disagreement. You characterized their
interactions with you as *aggravated harassment* and filed complaints with the
state. Though officials in India and the Indian Embassy here involved themselves in the matter, you tried to resolve your differences, accompanied by Indian consular officials, in a civil meeting with Seeta. But neither you, nor the
consular officials who attended this July '13 meeting, were willing to consider
Seeta's requests or her grievances.

In the meantime, one in your family, your father, with a controversial past
including involvement in a fraudulent housing scam, is reported to have contacted Seeta's family in India, warning them of dire consequences if she continued with her complaint. Seeta's husband, in turn, filed a complaint in a court
in India about her treatment in New York, alleging that she had been kept in
conditions of slavery and bondage. He also informed the court of the threat
conveyed by your father to them, but this complaint filed was inexplicably
withdrawn in a few days.

You, and other involved Indian officials, had Seeta's diplomatic passport
canceled with effect from the day she is thought to have left your home. On
what obscure legal basis was this done? Put yourself in Seeta's situation—in a
strange country with little to no means of survival, having her own country declare her to be an illegal entrant into the country she had been brought to
legally by you. What was it that you expected her to do—come to you and
plead for help? Or was this your attempt to force the start of legal proceedings
against Seeta by immigration authorities in America?

In September, the US Department of State contacted Indian officials to
determine the truth of Seeta's conditions and grievances. At that point, you
and Indian officials contacted accused the aggrieved and hapless domestic help
of attempting to subvert both Indian and US laws. You had a court in India issue a non-bailable arrest warrant for Seeta. Again, what was the legal basis for
such an order by a state? What crime had Seeta committed, in the jurisdiction
of the Indian court you filed your complaint in, that she needed to be arrested
and held without bail? I can only imagine that you made allegations of theft
against Seeta and perhaps of breach of contract on her part. But how does
that dispute merit a non-bailable arrest warrant, from a court with no jurisdiction over where these alleged acts took place?

In early December, the US Department of State brought Seeta's husband
and her two children to America to give witness to the allegation that Seeta was
treated as a trafficked human being. You were then charged, arrested, and processed, as is done here for anyone the state wishes to act against and has sufficient evidence to prosecute. Can you deny that the violations alleged by the
state occurred?

None can deny the horror of the arrest and strip search you experienced.

It was very difficult for me to watch it online as well. But perhaps you do see, from my own and many other situations I've written about, that this is what the state commonly does here. You, and I, and countless others, have gone through indignities of public and repeated handcuffing, searching, and being held with drug addicts and other accused criminals. Could you have expected anything else, given the deep revulsion that the American public and state feel at anything that resembles human trafficking?

Do you see that the demands of Indian state officials, prompted by your umbrage and the efforts of your father who'd also served in the Indian government, and their one-sided use of their legal system against a helpless victim, jarred unacceptably on shared, universal principles of fairness and justice?

I hope you do read this someday, Priyavani. Perhaps you'll come to see how so many ordinary people face trying circumstances, fall afoul of laws and norms of the land, and suffer consequences, while continuing to figure out how to be strong for those who need them to be so. I hope you can see beyond illusions of class and status, beyond your hurt and humiliation, and identify with the anguish and struggle of ordinary people everywhere. Isn't that just what your chosen role in society is, that of a civil servant?

· · ·

Back to the year of my re-education, by the State of Wariduna, we had an additional ten-minute wait before class started the next week. As the group filed in from outside, and the corridor, I chatted with Sid casually, complimenting his recent haircut. Sid said that he'd asked for all of it cut. Jerome piped up, and spoke about a place close to our intervention program center—named Knock-Out—where they'd cut your hair, and do so in lingerie. Girls, of course.

Levi snorted. "120 bucks, man!"

"Would anyone pay that?" queried Sid. I wondered as much.

Jerome smirked. "Yeah, for that kind of money, you could go to the Asian Rose and get a hand job…"

"We don't need that [sort of conversation]," said Sid.

Jerome continued, but Sid interrupted him firmly. "We *don't* need your explanation of what results are at Asian Rose."

Roll-call and payments proceeded, while someone well behind on the number of classes he needed to attend asked if Sid wanted to hear his excuse.

Sid turned that into a teaching point. "I don't want an excuse. Do you have a reason?" A discussion about excuses and reasons began.

Sid posed the question to the group. "Can anyone help him out? What's the difference between an excuse and a reason?"

Group members spoke about taking responsibility, about not trying to get away with something.

Ken piped up, "Perhaps he has a reasonable excuse?"

Chuckles all around.

Sid began to talk about humans only wanting to seek pleasure, and avoid pain, prompted perhaps by the Asian Rose exchange. This seemed such a simplistic characterization that I objected, pointing out that a basic feature of human nature is altruism, which could be seen as seeking pain to achieve benefit for others. The group wasn't following the discussion well. We got into definitions of altruism and examples in everyday lives.

I cited examples from animals including Bonobo monkeys who share their food with strangers, and Octopuses, where a mother octopus starves for months or years, tending to her eggs, and dies in this act. Sid claimed that for animals, such behavior is purely instinctive, that there is no conscious thought involved. I countered with social mediation and fairness evaluation behavior of monkeys to support conscious thought in such actions. Even more astonishing are examples of animals such as cats, dogs, and pigs that put themselves in harm's way, to save others, often not their progeny. I had the good fortune to observe and learn from the actions of a mother hen who protected her brood against a cobra. No, animals do accept pain for possible greater good—and we humans are animals too, Sid. Freudian psychological theories are just that, theories, with limited validation or application in comprehending nature.

Sid spoke about his love for languages, and I asked him how many he was fluent in. He said he was fluent only in one. I pointed out people from other cultures being fluent in many—myself in at least four, having had schooling in all four of these languages. Levi pitched in, for he too knew at least three, coming from the Middle East, where he interacted with multiple ethnic groups.

Others in the group diverted the conversation with tangential comments. But I persisted with this train of thought, linking it to the main discussion, bringing it to the point that the use of good words, phrases, and sentences, conveyed far less violence, contrasting it with the language of civil dispute resolution—lawyer-speak—which hides much threat of violence. Sid did not dispute that.

Moving on, we talked about books and of vicarious learning from the stories within. The group didn't really want to talk about books much. This wasn't exactly a language prose and poetry gathering. I mentioned that I was nearly done with writing and editing my first engineering text book. I recommended *Siddhartha* by Herman Hesse to Sid; he said he'd read it. The group dispersed, and Sid shook my hand as I left class this day. A little out of the ordinary.

• • •

Later that week came another altercation at home. My son came to complain to me upstairs, disturbed and crying, because his mother refused to agree to a Hawaii vacation the kids and I were planning. I intervened and asserted that we were indeed going to Hawaii. My wife asked if the children could go along with her to visit with their maternal grandparents at her sister's new location. Given these and other travel plans, I disagreed, and asked that the grandparents come down and visit with them here—particularly since the children had traveled all the way to India, the previous year, to see them upon their mother's assertion that her father was dying.

Back upstairs, with the kids out of earshot, she continued this discussion, calling me *pure evil* as I endeavored to explain further. In her mind, everything I said or did was with ulterior motive, and with harmful intentions toward her. Having listened to many unflattering characterizations by her, during our arguments, including *hypocritical preacher* and *venomous cobra*, I'd developed a layer of thick skin to deflect these. But 'pure evil' seemed a bit much and I demanded that she explain this.

Her explanation was that I was preventing the grandparents—who, incidentally, had swallowed her story-line and declined to help me—from seeing their grandchildren. I asked my son, who'd come upstairs to hear his mother calling me evil, if I was preventing them from seeing their grandparents. He did not think so at all, because I did agree to have them come and visit the grandchildren if they wished to. He had come to confirm that his mother did agree to going to Hawaii as was being planned, and not to mediate in an adult disagreement. He ran back downstairs.

Was this in any way appropriate, a child resolving accusations made by his mother against his father? How much more would the family have to suffer? But what other pathway could I take? Silence might work better, perhaps.

It was at this point in time that the kids' mother began demanding a split in the family, a divorce, a house, the children, and $50,000/- she said was owed to her. She threatened to take my statements over to prosecutors of the state, claiming she perceived them as threats, and harassing and badgering. I assured her that I'd welcome any such escalation, and that I was prepared for anything that came along. She said she'd go to court, and obtain what she wanted. I welcomed that as well.

This brought memories of a curious incident in the months when I was prosecuted by the state, with her as a witness against me. While discussing the case across the kitchen table, she had asked me, with a smirk, "What will you give me, if I get the state off your back?" My outraged response, accompanied by a thump on the table, had been instantaneous. "Nothing! I'll fight to bring out the truth in court on my own. I'll give you nothing." When questioned about this behavior by Parvathi, who heard about it from me, she claimed she was only being sarcastic, that she hadn't meant it.

My lawyer Mindy had talked with her before trial, and instructed her not to appear as a witness in court, to avoid giving the state any more ammunition than what they had already gathered. Though she agreed to do as advocated by Mindy, I'd always kept this incident, of her demand for material self-benefit from the situation, in mind, and after the state's prosecutors stood me up at a meeting set, I caved in to the state's conditions. *I did not trust her any more.* And, with the State of Wariduna out of the way, I was now prepared for battle, any battle that I might have to face.

The only nagging concern in my mind, educated now by DV classes of the state, was the very real possibility of her fabricating another situation that could land me in trouble again. I thought it prudent to relieve her frustrations by giving in to some of her many demands.

Fool me once, shame on you; fool me twice, shame on me, so said someone wise. My instincts and fears about my so-called spouse had largely become reality. Any decisions regarding marriage or family, and its unity, now needed to be approached pragmatically. But could I trust her parental instincts that could keep the needs of our children uppermost in her mind? Or would that belief be foolish as well?

Growing Frustration

The next week brought another altercation with my children's mother, and a curious new demand for a mediator. When asked how a mediator could help, she said she wished to discuss her pain, and ways to manage children and parenting under the circumstances. Pointing out that everyone involved in the matter had experienced much pain, I told her I'd like to address the humiliation and anguish caused to the entire family by her affair. And her continued disrespect for the marriage and for me. She'd suggested, in '07, when caught in her unfaithful act that she, I, and her "friend" sit down, and talk, as adults. She'd claimed then that the other male involved could even apologize for interfering in this family. I proposed that as a good first step to address challenges in our present predicament. Disagreeing with that, she continued to demand a mediator.

She called later that day to reiterate her demand for a mediator. She threatened to meet with Lauren, my probationary officer and counselor, on her own, and make her demand, which I happily agreed to. I had no doubt at all that Lauren could handle her demands better than I could. She then said she'd ask for a session with Lauren for the both of us. I pointed out to her that relationship problems of a decade and a half, and more, may not be addressed in a single session. And that marital and familial discord may require six or more months of sessions in discussion with a skilled, professional counselor. Clearly something the state's processes taught me, which I was only too glad to pass on to her.

But given that this could be an expensive and an emotionally burdensome process, I asked for her expectations, which she declined to elucidate. What came across to me was simply that she had certain wants—money, the house, kids, and freedom from me—that she thought might be achieved through a mediator. I made it amply clear that if it was her expectation that she'd be able to satisfy these *wants* of hers that my family did not *need*, the thousands of dollars that might be spent in such counseling could well go to waste.

I called Binita instead for help. I'd copied her on a couple of text messages exchanged with the children's mother, discussing these demands for a mediator, so she'd know what was being communicated to her sister. Binita called, and obtained my descriptions of petty behavior by the kids' mother—such as complaining about a pork and vegetables dish left in the refrigerator that I'd consumed, despite being more or less vegetarian, since it remained uneaten for a few days, because it was "hers," and not mine—and promised to speak with her sister, and perhaps calm her down. I explained to Binita then, as I'd done when she'd stayed with us for a few months that her sister was free to do anything she wished to, as long as it did not harm the children or the family beyond tolerance.

I had also made this as clear to my errant spouse as could be done. She was free to go. Free to take any of her earnings and money along with her as she may wish to. Free to live in the second home on the next street, as long as she did not deny the children its use, and me the ability to play with them there if they so wished. She was free to leave, but *not* to drag innocent children along with her on a path that could break this family apart.

I was resolute on that point, that I'd do anything and everything possible to prevent her splitting the children away from me. That I would not hesitate to reveal every action of hers, that could be shown to be fraudulent or illegal, perpetrated when she married me, such as her deceitful assurance to me—"All divorce papers had been signed"—in connection with her first marriage, claiming she was legally free to marry me at that time. I had seen no such signed papers. And, it took a US government investigation, in connection with my citizenship application, to uncover details of her prior marriage.

She asserted that she hadn't been previously married, that it wasn't recognized formally, and included that into my citizenship application. It was embarrassing beyond measure for me, in '08, when the interviewing officer of the US government had me telephone my wife, and correct information relating to her first marriage. She supplied false marital data for my citizenship application—for what obscure reason, I cannot know until it's fully investigated—and I promised to not hold back, in my search for ammunition, were she to try to harm the children and me again. A promise she knew I'd keep, come what may.

She'd assumed false bravado, knowing she and her family could fabricate documents from India with relative ease, perhaps even persuade her ex-husband to back-date such documents. But she knew this would be a fight for the truth, which I was certain to undertake with great vigor. And the possibility existed that she'd lose not only the civil dispute, but also her legal status in the country.

Yet that I could not desire, for it would hurt my children. Her fear, of these severe consequences, may be the only thing that prevented her from proceeding with a battle to secure her wants, regardless of anguish to the family. She had done everything else she wanted to, in life, hurting so many others along the way.

I promised myself that I'd never speak to the children's mother about these matters, or the past, again. The truth about her mind and heart was unmistakable, my disappointment most extreme, and no good could come out of revisiting past suffering. I wished no further debate on the situation, and only to look forward. I had begun to contemplate bringing the split to reality in natural ways, without any middle party or mediator participating. Fifty thousand dollars? Sure, it's a large sum of money, but a worthy investment for peace. The second home? Perhaps a sacrifice that could be made. Lack of a partner in looking after the children—a hardship, but necessary in our circumstance.

The next morning involved another altercation no less than a crazy circus act. As voices rose, my little children witnessed their mother ranting and raving in frustration. I tried to calm both children, and relieve their concerns about these loud discussions. Ultimately, to end the needless and hostile argument, I too raised my voice, while explaining the need for it to them simultaneously.

Out of desperation, almost, and yet in all sincerity, I asked to give their mother a hug to calm her down. I was conscious, all along, that my raised voice or touch could be construed negatively in another unsolicited intervention by the state. My spouse reacted with her typical, exaggerated disgust. I persisted, assuring her that I did indeed love her, telling the children too that I loved their mom. But she responded with anger, rejecting my assurances. Did I love their mom? I loved my children with all my heart—that extended to what they loved too. And their happiness now depended upon my self-control in this agonizing circumstance the family had fallen into.

She pulled out one of my class papers, that compared behaviors considered violent with those that complemented them in non-violent ways, and alleged that I'd subjected her to each and every violent act described in the paper. What could I have done then, but stay silent? It was time for my weekly re-education by the State of Wariduna. I was only too glad to leave for class.

• • •

Sid was holding a sheaf of papers as he conducted roll-call and payments collection—copies of the same document, with descriptions of violent behaviors my spouse accused me of earlier that afternoon. There was general chatter about meat, red meat in particular, and about how it wasn't conducive to a gentle nature. An awakening of an understanding of vegetarianism, and its social and cultural benefits, I thought. Sid said he stayed off red meat, and stuck to chicken and chicken burgers.

The group began discussing examples of people advocating and teaching non-violence in our lives. For some, mother figures and grandparents came to mind. I dug deeper to find clear role models.

My mother of course advocates avoiding violence to the extent possible, but does assert that men require a measure of manliness or *Purushottvam* as it is called in my mother tongue. Perhaps this has to do with traditions and practices of the clan and community we hail from. I recalled that men in my extended family either served in the nation's military, or ventured out to far away lands to provide for the rest back home.

A bit of digging into my family's past revealed that I belong to a martial culture in India, known for its traditional martial arts and natural healing practices. There has even been a military brigade formed under my clan name. Loyalty and obedience to family and to our way of life is innate in us. Violence, in defense of family and community, isn't unknown to me; it is part of my tradition and learning. Such training isn't off-limits to girls either, some of whom learn our martial arts until coming of age.

But I did recall a good friend, and roommate, when at university in India—Ramnarayan—a most humble and considerate person. He was, always, a voice of moderation, a person called upon to settle conflicts. And Krishnan Iyer—a manager at a company I worked in right after my first degree—a kind, gentle man. He advised me to not be so approachable and attached to line personnel I supervised. He was compelled to convey this to me by his superior, who felt such interaction on my part made me "dangerous."

And then there was Bala Natarajan—another humble, helpful mentor, whom I reported to in a large corporation I worked in, for many years, here in America. He embodied non-violence, and helpfulness, in all his interactions. But privately, his frustration with backstabbing peers and colleagues, and management that gave him no support, would pour out often to me. He would also tell me that I reminded him of himself. And my children of course—thoughts of them reminded me to be non-violent, to set an example they could admire and learn from. Tragically, Krishnan Iyer and Bala Natarajan passed away much too young; good men who took upon themselves far too many burdens of others, I thought.

Lopez, having enjoyed state hospitality and its correctional programs, and having *found Jesus*, opened up, revealing that he had been jailed for almost a dozen years. He said he dealt with a large number of diverse personalities in an enclosed space. And that he'd caught a harmful virus that required employing safe sex techniques. He also said that he felt he'd used his wife, by getting into a marriage, because he thought he would not be able to have sex otherwise. The group including Sid remained silent when Lopez spoke...what could anyone say to him? He invoked fear, more than empathy or sympathy, in the few who listened to his monologues.

Sid guided the group discussion on to what he called *Wheels of violence*, intending, perhaps, to talk about violence perpetuating itself. He talked about a need to *judge the situation, not the person*. On the topic of physical intimacy, in a marriage, provoked in part by Lopez's monologue, Sid asserted—"You have to earn it!" He pointed out that a participant in a previous class said, "I am married, and I expect a certain amount of sex," in a forceful, demanding manner. That evoked much laughter. Nevertheless, I delved further into this topic with him, asserting that in many other countries and communities, being denied such benefits of marriage can be grounds for divorce.

He accepted that. "Maybe so, but not in this country. Here, we call it *rape* if you insist upon your sexual needs while your wife does not agree to it."

"Sure, Sid, but physical intimacy is certainly one of the benefits of marriage," said I. "How does one get there?"

"You have to earn it," he replied tersely.

I pointed out to him, laughing, that this, exactly, was my response to my spouse, that such intimacy is not to be taken for granted. I'd said to her that—"One must deserve it."

My spouse used that as one of her complaints, and justification for her extramarital conduct, that when she approached me, I had denied her physical intimacy. That I hadn't adored, admired, and desired her, but made her work for love. How low can one's self-esteem be that it must be replenished by others? I told Sid that my wife would not be happy with his recommendations.

• • •

Back home that evening, I described this class discussion to the children's mother. She reacted as had become common then, with a threat of calling Lauren, for a discussion with her, that my counseling was not going per her expectations. I assured her that my counseling was not meant, in any conceivable way, to address her demands. Her assumption, that court-mandated counseling was intended to assist her, served only to prop up her ego, her low self-esteem. I assured her also that I'd conveyed these threats of hers to Sid, the counselor. And that she could meet with him, if she desired to 'have it out' on this topic.

My friend John called, in the evening, to address my request for an interview with a local pastor for my wife and myself. I thought this could be a safe path to pursue in any mediation she desired. A pastor would be unlikely to recommend splitting a family, and my wife appeared to have found religion again in the years the family passed through turmoil. She'd *found Jesus* too, much like our buddy Lopez in my group. What I did not know then was that her regular visits to a savior was for bliss of the emotional and physical kind, for her rendezvous with her new-found boyfriend.

In the discussion with John, she demanded to meet with the pastor on her own, insisting that she'd like to convey *her* story, and then determine if he'd counsel the family. I pointed out, to her and John, that this was exactly why it was important to know her intentions and expectations, before beginning any sort of mediation—because her efforts aimed to vilify our relationship and defeat my attempts to bring happiness into the family. She seemed only to want *her* way, to see things only from her perspective. How poor is one's vision, and how limited the mind, if one has but a single perspective? To what purpose is mediation with one unwilling to see another point of view? John excused himself from the conversation.

The discussion continued into an argument, with her asserting—"I have no choice, but to talk to Lauren." The argument escalated, and she recorded a statement from me—"If you do anything more to harm me or this family, I will ensure that you learn the biggest lesson of your life." She recorded this on her phone to convey to her friends at the Dilbut prosecutor's office. I asked that she delete the recording, for it could bring no good, and could be used out of context harmfully as is often done by the state, but she refused to do so.

Pointing to her many actions of abuse, of myself and the children, I reminded her that her threats and statements such as—"The prosecutor told me that one call to them is all I need to make to have you back in jail"—could lead to prosecutorial misconduct, as continued intimidation and provocation. I do recall asking her to identify this *one-call* Dilbut prosecutor she began to refer to, someone she claimed could "put me away." I truly looked forward to meeting her and this prosecutor on a level playing field.

Later that night, given our irremediable conflict, I asked my spouse if she'd be happy with my departure from the country to restart life elsewhere. A heartfelt, sincere question, but a difficult step for me. I had, in years past, been forced to leave a young son in the care of his mother in India when I left that country, and he had suffered the absence of a father as he grew. Yet, circumstances appeared to force me to repeat that mistake of my past.

"I have three more months of class attendance to fulfill the State of Wariduna's requirements," I continued. "When done, I can, quite simply, just leave. The houses and capital invested will provide some security and happiness for the children. And I will be entirely out of all your lives. Should I do that?"

"No, hang around here for the children," said she.

But how long could this go on? She did little to make our lives better. She sabotaged all that I did—arranging for a pastor to mediate, for instance—in a relentless drive to cast me as the devil. She strove to obtain agreement, from everyone, with her individual path that would split our family. I pleaded with her to not jeopardize the little remaining happiness of innocent children. Yet, as motherly wisdom informed me a while ago, my heart was inadequate to the task of melting the resolve of one so selfish and self-willed.

I also felt it wasn't just between us—the adults—that she worked to create divisions. On a few occasions, she drove my daughter to school, while my son refused to go with her because he liked driving to school and back with me every day. It was a wasteful practice to take two cars to school—I'd ask that she take my son too, but given his objections, she took only my daughter with her. She seemed less comfortable with my son, who had a penchant for asking questions, and of not aligning with her religious affiliation. Not being able to bond as comfortably with my son, she appeared to be cultivating a bond with my daughter, one that diminished my daughter's communication with me and with her brother. I asked her to not do this, to not create divisions in how our children identified with both parents.

Parental alienation at a tender age, and its resultant harm, could be irreparable. But inquiries with the kids' teachers then did not reveal signs of emotional distress or isolation in them. They did well at their school, but I knew that the environment at home could hardly help them develop emotional and social strengths. Yet, what could I do? Giving in to their mother's demands would break us all apart, and destroy any sense of security the children had. Besides, how could I be there for them, every day, when they needed me, with a family split in two?

I was determined not to succumb to circumstances, despite my troubled query to the kids' mother. But keeping my self-control and sanity intact, under constant conflict with no feasible resolution, was proving a challenge beyond any I'd faced before.

Letting Go

In the next class, Sid invited everyone to attend a concert, by his rock band, playing at a drive-in amphitheater of another residential city in the metropolitan area. He indicated it was a free public event. Family members could come as well. One of Sid's band members had been through these classes for assault. He'd engaged in a scuffle with the bartender at the place they were originally supposed to play at. I was tempted to ask if Sid's band member friend was Irish as well. Sid seemed to like hanging out with many of us violent criminals.

Bantering about violence and movies, someone in the group mentioned *Law Abiding Citizen* as an interesting example Gerard Butler starred in. Another pointed to *300*, also starring Butler.

Sid shared a memory of violence from his youth. He described his father taking an unloaded shotgun, aiming it at his brothers' heads, and clicking the trigger, asking, "You ready to do it my way now?" The group listened in pregnant, hushed silence. He continued, "My brothers are fine, but my father feels like shit." No one asked him why. I couldn't help wondering if it was just remorse that made him feel *like shit*, or his present circumstances, that may have come about from his conduct. Sid's twenty-two year wait before completing his degree was beginning to make more sense.

Continuing with the topic of disciplining kids, Sid discussed spanking, pointing out that more effective than such physical punishment is positive reinforcement. The group disagreed and pointed to such rewards fostering a sense of entitlement in children, and worse, dissatisfaction with small rewards. I had to agree with the group, pointing out that my son often asked for money to complete any chore around the house. Discipline had become a dirty word in my household, almost synonymous with punishment, rather than with building character as it should be. A clear impression of expectations not met often worked better in my experience.

Sid countered, "You've got to let them know their responsibilities around the house. Explain that they belong to a family."

"I have a hard time explaining that to adults, much less children!" said I. "I reason with my son, but to little effect. His typical response is 'What will you give me?'"

Group members with children agreed with this description of challenges in raising kids in today's American families. Sid described results, with positive reinforcement, with his present girlfriend's pet cat—that would urinate in his bedroom—trained successfully to do its business outside through inducements with food. Someone said if his kids were to see that, they'd figure out how to train you to give them goodies by doing things you will not appreciate, and will invent new and improved training methods as they grow. Kids are smarter than one may think.

I wondered if Sid had any kids or had been around kids much. He had mentioned hitting rock bottom in his life in class—was it a life event that disrupted a normal family situation for him? He'd also mentioned that he'd been arrested, charged by a state, and had to go through counseling and similar re-education prior to his Master's in Psychology. And that he separated from his ex-partner and started life anew. Perhaps he'd gone through an interrupted family life. The class ended with this discussion.

• • •

Before class the next week was another altercation, with a now common refrain from my spouse, "I want my freedom." And—"Give me my money. I've earned more than $500,000/- over the past ten years. Where has all that money gone?" This came up because she'd received her annual statement listing her earnings and contributions to the social security fund over the years. My own statement for the same period, minus a few years I spent at school, showed more than one and a sixth of a million dollars earned, twice her earnings, which I did relay to her. I attempted reassuring her that I was investing in an individual retirement account in her name.

"I want my own account. You control everything. I'll start my own retirement account," she insisted.

"Okay, as you wish."

I did indeed take care of many of these financial matters for the family. She tried her hand at investing in the equities market and had been frightened by how easy it was to burn money in such activities. This was left to me, someone more comfortable with such risk-taking. Yet now I was to blame for *controlling* everything.

At the counseling group, Sid began talking about masculine and feminine characteristics. I could have listed a bunch of contrasting aspects, but remembered one in particular—that my mother had told me of—called *Chanchalamanasthithi* in my native tongue. This is a distinctly feminine behavior of flitting from one thing or idea to another. It could be a valuable trait, a multitasking capability, if applied well. In contrast, men are known to be sequential or single-minded at any point in time.

Though one could call it sexist, feminine and masculine neurology determine these traits, observed and labeled correctly by traditional wisdom. These aspects can also be noticed at a high level in gender-based roles adopted in traditional hunter-gatherer society. The hunter is single-minded in his pursuit, while the gatherer takes stock of a number of things at the same time. I remained silent nevertheless as Sid continued with his ideas about gender determined traits.

He then showed us a video documentary, narrated by Jackson Katz, who described himself as an educator, author, filmmaker, and social theorist, long recognized as one of America's leading anti-sexist activists. The movie illustrated how American society reacted to the growing acceptance of equal roles and status for women. In it, Katz cited, as examples, how the size and ferocity of sport wrestlers increased over time, to being far more muscular and violent in aspect, and the gradual change in the manly depiction of action figures and comic book characters.

My mind wandered to the invitation Bert Burgess had sent to my spouse's cellphone in '08—to watch Ultimate Fight Championship bouts on television at his place—that I caught because she seemed furtive about the mobile phone. That, coming after the '07 dalliance between them, had flared into another altercation.

Getting back to the anti-sexist video, fighting in cages with bare hands, and excessive violence, did seem all too common. That Bert would watch displays of gratuitous violence, in his pursuit of entertainment, seemed right in character for him—unable to put himself in the shoes of those who suffered from such acts of violence, he probably lacked any and all empathy. That he would continue contact with my spouse after many explicit requests, conveyed through his friends and workplace, not to do so, also seemed quite in character. Noting my own digression, I drifted back to pay attention to Sid's video.

Katz described a dramatic increase in the size of guns used in movies, with small pistols changing to Clint Eastwood's .45, and then to Rambo's typically stand-mounted weapons held in his bare hands. There seemed to be some commentary on Rambo—I'm not sure if it was in the movie or in the group—of Rambo the man executing a country's military goals while the country itself vacillated, and popular movements within the country opposed the war direction that was pursued. That thought reminded me again of my simplistic view of masculine and feminine traits. Perhaps democracy is inherently feminine. And it avoids guns, and overt displays of the capability for violence. But the trend in the American democracy seemed just the opposite, with vigorous political activism to maintain one's rights to all sorts of guns.

Talk of Rambo also brought back memories of the first and only fundraiser I organized—back in my engineering undergraduate in '85 or '86—to raise money for a college music club. We'd screened *First Blood*—the first in the series of Rambo movies—and it was a great success, along with another teenage fantasy movie that had a scene with girls dancing around a camp fire, pulling their t-shirts up and exposing their breasts to hoots of approval from boys. During the screening, I'd paused the movie right then—at the raunchiest scene—and my audience of young undergraduates had hooted much like the boys in the movie did. There were girls in my screening audience too, who didn't seem to mind the fun. My thoughts were indeed drifting.

Sid's point, or his opinion after the video, was that masculine and feminine characteristics lay in the mind, that women could exhibit these aspects just as much as men. I thought equating sexes in this manner seemed much like the idea of creation of the heavens and the earth in six undefined days, a sweeping simplification and approximation of nature in other words. But I remained silent. Sid was the counselor, and he knew what he was doing.

The group dispersed, rather confused that day. A multicultural group of men learning American social theories about men and women. And to avoid violence while learning that popular entertainment showed only an increase in violence over time—in a seemingly desperate desire to assert differences between the sexes. But hey—Jackson Katz was the social theorist—he must be right.

All explicit inculcation in society appeared to highlight differences between the sexes, and romanticize vice as excitement, while people individually were being held responsible, and punished, for falling into the very same vices. Society took no collective responsibility for any of the symptoms of its own enculturation. A case of *do as I say, not as I do*—not a precept easily resolved in the group's simple individual minds.

· · ·

Later that week came more abuse from my spouse toward us all. This was her exhibiting some masculine traits, perhaps, recalling my learning from class earlier in the week. She snapped at me when I asked who'd be taking my son to his soccer game—"Don't I always take him?" I'd asked because I was planning to take my daughter over to a school 'open house' event, and did not know if my spouse wanted me to drop my son for his soccer practice on the way.

I took some *upma*—a simple south Indian snack I'd learned to prepare—to her, upstairs, which was curtly declined. That was me exhibiting feminine characteristics of conciliation with an offering of food I prepared—or was that just me, or just a natural response to the situation? More of her bad temper fell upon the children and me. It was a relief to be out of the place with my daughter. Feminine approaches did not appear to work with a spouse in a masculine mood.

Her demands for mediation became more urgent as days passed. She claimed to want her freedom, but wasn't willing to leave us—me and the children—to our devices and lives while she enjoyed her freedom. She became quite insistent about her $50,000/-, the house, children, and freedom from me. Contemplating all this, and that she'd passed her fourth decade of life, which makes one concerned about retirement and associated financial challenges, her demands seemed typical to me, but rather lacking in consideration for the happiness of our children. These incessant confrontations began to chip away at my resolve to keep the family unit integral.

I wondered if my own thoughts about leaving, perhaps even leaving the country, could be on the right track. But the thought of leaving little children in the hands of one I could neither trust nor admire, and of having them suffer the same loss of a father, that their stepbrother had endured, troubled me greatly. I didn't think her 'mediation,' which in all likelihood meant a quickie divorce permitting her to proceed with her own plans, could produce results any better than my departure.

I met with Lauren that week—and talked about positive developments in my situation. My first engineering textbook was on its way to being published in a month. The corporate lawsuit I faced in another state, a state one didn't *mess* with, had been settled with a small amount paid to me that could help me survive one more year without employment. Though the contingency fee agreement with my lawyers specified that 70% of any settlement would go to them, they took only 50%, which was something I was grateful for. Not the additional money, but the simple act of splitting the fruits of our labors equally. There is much to be said for this core American idea of equality. I also mentioned my spouse's endless demands for mediation, and it occurred to me that Lauren could help mediate. She seemed agreeable to it; I filed it away in my mind as something to explore.

The lawsuit that ended in a small settlement won in '10 began in late '06, prior to my family situation spiraling downward. It began with a customer for my first start-up company, the only large customer I worked with at that point, breaking their agreement with me. They took the intellectual property I developed for them for their own use without licensing it from me as agreed.

My wife was the financial controller of my start-up company then, reflecting an Indian tradition of the wife holding keys to the treasury of the home. I sought her counsel on settling the matter with this rogue customer, but she offered no decisive input, and left it to me to determine the next steps in the conflict involved.

A large sum of money was offered as settlement for the breach of contract between this customer and me. Nevertheless, on a matter of principle, because they flatly refused to license my intellectual property, I'd been forced to investigate a lawsuit to resolve the disagreement.

In that process, we found that my company had been sued without any intimation to me. The legal system in that state permitted such action, a hidden weapon prepared and aimed for firing if ordinary negotiations fail. It is akin to a concealed weapon in one hand, with the other extended in a seemingly friendly interaction. Learning of this lawsuit filed, I had no option but to join the battle.

This extended battle exhausted my energy and finances entirely. My spouse provided no assistance whatsoever. Instead, she greatly added to the burden with her dalliance begun in '07. Facing financial, physical, and emotional ruin, I had repeatedly attempted to let go of this corporate legal battle as being inconsequential compared with the difficulties my family went through. But the skilled senior lawyer who assisted me in the matter was both wise and compassionate. He helped to continue prosecution, despite my wholly depleted financial reserves, by entering into a contingency representation agreement with me.

With his assistance, we brought the matter, after more than three and a half years of long and exhausting battle, to a successful end. To say this was a burden lifted from my mind and life is a gross understatement—it was no less than what Atlas, bent over as he carried the earth, may have felt when relieved of his burden.

But I reached another conclusion from this legal battle—and this wasn't the first one faced where our strength as a team was tested—that my life partner lacked the wisdom, the mental and moral courage, to stand with me in meeting these challenges. She provided neither useful counsel, nor the strength needed to face extended, debilitating conflict. I struggled entirely on my own. She, for her part, will no doubt say, it has always been my habit to get into such conflicts, it was my fault this happened, and that she therefore didn't want any part of it. I'd heard that a number of times in the past, and did not solicit it in this instance. She merely added to the enormity of the burden I faced then in her grave deviation from family unity. Any remaining regard, in my mind for her, did not seem worth holding on to anymore.

Some Useful Sessions

Sid was absent for the next class; his colleague Dave stood in for him. We continued viewing the remaining portion of the Jackson Katz video about masculine and feminine aspects, and violence.

My thoughts drifted to a conversation I had with a senior school teacher at my children's school. She was an old-timer at the school, a grandmother, and had very kindly attempted to mediate in the early stages of the mishap that befell my family in '07. She had good reason to, for as she explained it, such events typically have a life-altering effect on children, and are best avoided. I recall that she advised my spouse—controversially—that men like Bert Burgess may only be interested in exploiting women for company and sexual gratification, or for their entertainment, and that she should ignore the sweet nothings such men whispered in her eager ears, and focus instead on what is best for her family, not for herself. That characterization seemed to me an accurate capture of the behavior of such men to me. In later conversations with me, she'd gone so far as to assert—"You do not know girls...men can be aggressive, but girls can be vicious! Be very careful." I knew she spoke from extensive life experience, and respected her words.

The principal of the school, a wise lady with a doctorate in child psychology, also cautioned me, "Do not buy another house for your wife, even as a gift for the family—that will be her pathway **out** of the family." These words remained in my mind, as wisdom arising from many years of life and living, wisdom proven right in my own life as well, and I paid little attention to the video by the social theorist.

After class, which was occupied by the movie and uneventful, Paul grabbed me in the corridor and blurted—"You've got to listen to this!" He seemed quite animated, and I paid due attention. Paul had met with another man at a bowling alley, arranged by his church for single folks, who, it turned out in their conversation, had dated the same woman who had put Paul into his current predicament. That man Paul met experienced very similar things: the woman called the cops on him as well, and had stolen things from him too. Paul was bucked by this finding that confirmed his own experiences. The other man also met her at the same online matchmaking site.

Sid was back for the next class. Paul caught him before class and narrated his not-so-surprising new finding. Perhaps Paul sought some empathy and understanding from Sid, that he really did not deserve the classes or the nightmare that had descended upon him. I thought instead that the other man Paul met could gain from the classes we were attending, from the commiseration and discussions we engaged in together. That line of thought surprised me. Did I now come to see these classes as being helpful?

There were a couple of newbies in our group—**Jamil**, and **Bill**. Jamil, who was Jerome's friend, talked about vigorous disagreements with his ex-wife, but continued to see her and their children. He was a friendly young African-American man, who seemed composed and clear about his priorities, which contrasted starkly with his friend in the group. Jerome seemed agitated, disturbed, and emotional in class this day. He said it was due to button-pushing by his ex-wife Natasha.

Asked about his story, Jamil said he'd engaged in a loud disagreement with his wife, and their neighbors had called the cops. When they came over and talked to Jamil, he happened to mention that the scratches on his hand came from crashing his fist through a door. The cop asked to come in, talked with his wife, and determined that this event occurred in the course of the argument with his wife. That sealed Jamil's fate. He was duly arrested, processed, and sent to our group. This then led to his divorce, but he continued to be intimate with his ex-wife, taking care of their two little children together.

The discussion moved on to Jerome, who spoke about having been threatened with a restraining order by his ex-wife that morning. Jerome also sees his ex-wife on occasion, while being antagonistic about his broken relationship with her. He described his previous day's get together with her as amazing. She'd come over with their children, and had stayed the night. He spoke—as was his style—without inhibition about having had a great orgasm, about that being a great relief. And that his ex-wife had enjoyed herself too. In the same breath as he recounted these experiences, he said he *hated* her, which the group found hilarious.

Jerome said his ex-wife talked about him all the time to the caregiver who looked after his children when they worked. And that she did so quite negatively, leading to what he said was treatment like a doormat by the caregiver whenever he'd go to see his children there. He spoke of recently having offered to pick up his children from daycare, which his ex-wife curtly refused. Despite this, she called him later to ask him to collect the children, which he did. No one seemed to treat him with any respect, in his words.

Jerome was evidently troubled by interactions with his divorced spouse Natasha. The group cautioned him to be careful in his conduct with her. Jerome queried the group about what he ought to do if his ex-wife asked to be intimate. The group asked him to not indulge in that activity. He asked why not, and I spoke up, saying it would be the mature thing to do, to not give in to what could be manipulation on her part. The group agreed strongly, with Sid tagging along.

Bill, the other new participant, had a troubling story to relate. Married to a Vietnamese girl, he fathered three kids, and had been getting into arguments with her occasionally. On one occasion, he shoved her roughly. She fell and lost consciousness. He called the cops, and eventually joined us here. Bill was quite callous about his teenage son who seemed to lack respect for him. On one occasion, the thirteen year old challenged him, asking him about what he might do, physically, and Bill lifted him by his throat with one hand. On the flip side, the boy wouldn't listen to him at all, refused to learn, did poorly at school, and did not respect him. I wondered aloud who could really be held responsible for the child acting out, and not doing well at school, but Bill did not respond.

Sid thanked me as we dispersed at the end of class. Perhaps I'd spoken once too many times in the group this day.

• • •

In the next class, Sid asked Jerome if things had changed for him in any way. Jerome said his ex-wife wished to participate in our sessions, be a 'fly on the wall,' because she thought he was making her out to be a monster in his group discussions. He said she seemed to think—over Chinese food, this time—that he was taking the classes seriously. I wondered if Sid noticed that Jerome did not give his own opinions, but simply conveyed those of his ex-wife's, even about himself. Or that it was she who detected change in Jerome. Self-awareness is not an easy thing for Jerome, perhaps.

I wondered if the State of Wariduna and its many minions such as Gormon and Sheriff Waspoia could ever be self-aware. Perhaps they were, in their own way—they always knew what to do to maximize benefit for themselves within the system they functioned in. They had a clear focus on self-benefit, on learning how to work their system to that end. A system of laws and enforcement, which comprised of coarse, rigid tools and methods ill-suited to guiding a complex and dynamic society's change, or its refinement and growing consciousness.

Sid asked if anyone remembered his crock pot example—of his disagreement with his girlfriend, and how he'd helped his girlfriend overcome her fear of leaving the cooking pot turned on without any attention paid to it. And of how he'd accomplished this by leaving it on, a couple of times overnight, presumably unintentionally. The group reminded him that he'd discussed it a couple of times previously, and he desisted. It didn't seem related to Jerome's situation, or any other that group members struggled with.

Sid then showed us a movie starring Julia Roberts, *Sleeping with the Enemy,* where her character was married to an abusive husband who valued her as a trophy, and abused her at home and in bed. He showed an explicit intimate sequence where the husband was shown apologizing to her, attempting to compensate for prior bad behavior. But he subsequently engaged in gratifying himself sexually with her, ignoring aspects of intimacy in such a manner as to almost constitute rape. Her anguish, at the way in which her character was used by the husband, was evident. I couldn't bear to watch the scene, and looked around to see Sid watching us as we watched the movie clip.

That movie reminded me of another such where I wasn't able to watch any more. It was a movie show my girlfriend, who became my wife, took me to, a decade and a half ago, titled *Indecent Proposal*, starring Robert Redford and Demi Moore. The idea, of a husband and wife taking a rich man's offer, of a million dollars for a night the millionaire wished to spend with the wife, was too much to bear. I had vacated my seat in the theater as Demi Moore left to spend the night with the rich and handsome millionaire in the movie. My spouse seemed quite at ease with the situation depicted, and was surprised by my discomfort.

Empathy isn't very common in a society chasing after entertainment—I wondered if that was what Sid was looking for.

A Turn of Events

There was talk about speed traps, roadway cameras recording vehicles traveling above speed limits, while Sid conducted roll-call and payments collection in the next class. A group member leading that discussion said the State of Wariduna removed these systems from freeways because they weren't making as much money as expected.

Another group member, with his hair in a ponytail, said the smart thing to do is to ignore any citation received in the mail because there is no way to prove receipt without signature confirmation. Yet another said the state expected to collect as much as $90 million, but had only gained $9 million or so—and hence the vanishing act by the freeway cameras. A smart business decision by the state to pull out of a public safety measure that generated low returns.

Sid started this class with a discussion about the variety of people coming into our DV class—such as cops, rock stars, and others.

"Shouldn't a cop be let go after a DV incident?" asked the ponytail hairdo member.

Sid disagreed. "No. It was actually a useful class for the cop. He'd been influenced by the class to let others go. He realized the human side of situations."

I couldn't resist—"Shouldn't every cop go through such a class? Before being allowed to make DV arrests?"

Laughter in the group, while Sid looked thoughtful.

Paul had news, a positive turn in his situation, and was eager to share. The previous day was his ex-girlfriend's birthday. Paul had her served with civil litigation papers. Chuckles all around in the group. Paul said his ex had an arrest warrant pending because she had not appeared in court to respond to criminal theft charges. Asked for his recommendation, as the victim of her alleged theft, for any deal the state makes with his ex, Paul suggested a fine, three days in jail—because he'd put in four for a misdemeanor charge with no need to have done so—and payment for damages. I wondered about Paul's ex's three children in all this turmoil.

Ponytail, one of the quieter group members, in a talkative mood this day, pointed out a couple of people with injuries—me with a hurt foot in a crepe bandage, and a new member with a hand in a cast. I explained that my right foot had folded inward under me, bearing all my falling weight, after a volleyball spike on uneven ground, and the ankle joint had become dislocated. I'd put it back in place myself, but needed a firm bandage to keep the joint immobile. The new member had broken his arm by boxing hard.

The new participant—**Romero**—had fallen into an argument with his girlfriend, which escalated. He tried to get out of it, but couldn't, and pulled her by the arm out of the apartment, locking the door. He went to sleep, and woke to find cops at his door. Arrested, he was jailed and put into DV class with us, because his girlfriend called the cops, and because there was some alcohol involved. All he desired was to get her away from him in his inebriated state, so their argument could be done with. He had instead been charged with assault, disorderly conduct, the whole nine yards as we say here in America. This was in Dilbut again, the city that Mindy—my *lump-sum* lawyer—assured me was the most corrupt she and others knew of in the state.

Another new member, whose name I do not recall, argued with his girlfriend in a parking lot, and broke a car window with his fist. It was the driver's side window, and she was in the car, in the driver's seat. She called the cops. He had been charged with causing criminal damage and with disorderly conduct. This was his second offense; he was in for a full year of weekly classes.

Yet another was a young kid, barely nineteen, who fought with his mother, punched a hole in a dry wall—the sort that dents easily when a doorknob bumps it—and went to sleep. His mother called the cops, who came by and arrested him on typical charges. He did not live with his mother any more after his arrest and prosecution. Spending some days in state detention, he enrolled in our class. This young kid remained quiet for the entire session after giving us his story.

The group dispersed, depressed by this steady stream of entrants into the program. It was clear that the default reaction by the state to any disagreement, involving the other sex, was to imprison and process the participant deemed to have been violent, which, in most cases, led to jailing the male participant. Is this what '*Protect and Serve*' means? Or did it fulfill other agendas of the state? I couldn't help but remember the words of Daniel 'Big Dan' Teague, the loquacious, one-eyed Bible salesman, in *O Brother Where Art Thou*, "It's all about the money, boys! The gol—darned—money!" as he whacked away at his two picnic companions with a log. You cannot blame the state for making hay while the pendulum swings, I suppose. They have to compensate for financial losses in their other public programs, don't they?

•   •   •

Before class the next week, there came another volleyball injury, with a buddy of mine dislocating his foot like me, but his foot had come away from his shin bone entirely, and had no way of going back into place easily. He'd been taken to an emergency treatment center nearby, and I paid him a visit. His greatest concern was that he wouldn't be allowed to travel with his family on a trip planned many months previously. Doctors had to sedate him thrice before they could pull his dislocated foot out and back into position over his shin bone. Surprisingly, he had almost no swelling on his dislocated foot, while my foot had swollen to near twice its normal size. Perhaps it was because he had been pumped with drugs. No middle-aged volleyball for me anymore. Without employment, and associated medical insurance, severe injuries can easily bankrupt a family in the American system. Fortunately for my buddy, his wife's insurance covered him.

At class, I gave Sid a DVD of the movie *One Flew Over The Cuckoo's Nest* starring Jack Nicholson, since he'd said he hadn't seen it when asked. He was pleased. Will he be pleased after watching it, I wondered. He seemed to have missed my meaning.

Lopez, who'd been jailed for more than a dozen years, dominated conversation this session. He'd now acquired a new roommate, a girl 300+ lbs in weight, who, according to him, disrespected him. By not being at a work-out place she said she would be at. Sid and the rest of us were surprised enough to let him continue, though we typically ignored his comments.

Lopez said a friend had asked if he could take this girl in as a roommate. She was known to him, having spent some months with him in the past.

He said she made breakfast for him even though he'd told her he didn't want any.

Paul cut in. "Doesn't she need to eat?"

"Yes," said Lopez, "but she left bacon, sausages, eggs, and stuff out for me. She's tempting me to eat and be unhealthy. She's disrespecting me."

Sid got into the discussion. "So she disrespects you because she makes breakfast for you? Because she said she'd be at the workout place, and wasn't?"

"She told me she'd be there in thirty minutes," replied Lopez. "I went there, and couldn't find her. She's not accountable."

"Why should she be accountable to you?" asked Sid.

"Because I couldn't account for her."

"How old is she?"

"Thirty one or thirty two... She has a kid."

"So are you responsible for her?" asked Paul, this time.

"She disrespects me," replied Lopez.

Paul came around to the food question again. "Because she was considerate enough to make you breakfast?"

Lopez rambled on. "You know the joke about a redhead, brunette, and a blonde? God was talking to the three, and would give them what they wished for, but would dismiss them if they fibbed, or said something unbelievable. So the redhead says, 'My life's so hard. My boyfriend, who likes to have sex often, [did something unbelievable and unmentionable]'—and poof, God makes her vanish. The brunette says—'I live with my mother and husband, and I think my husband cares more for my mother than me'—and poof, she vanishes as well. Then the blonde says, 'I think…' and poof, she too is gone."

Crickets chirped in the session room.

Sid was stupefied by this digression, and attempted, without success, to employ his *belief-rule-action-results-change* or BRARC cycle to Lopez's problems. While the group prepared to bury Lopez, I tried to combine his various story fragments into a sensible picture as Sid and others listened, and wasn't successful either. Yet I knew what Lopez tried to convey was only that in his personal experience, women said things that just weren't believable, and he found it disrespectful. Sid continued to employ his behavioral cycle to determine the root cause of Lopez's sense of lack of respect he perceived from his new roommate. This group member's future prospects didn't seem very bright.

Paul described a situation where he felt disrespected. He had allowed his twenty-three-year-old son, who couldn't afford a place of his own, back into his house. One day, after an evening out, his son returned late at night with a male friend and a girl, and passed out on the sofa downstairs. His companions took this opportunity to visit his bedroom and use it—for loud, prolonged sex—until Paul's other housemate was forced to knock on that bedroom door at *3 a.m.* Paul felt this behavior by his son showed only disrespect. He tried to speak to him to express his strong disapproval. But his son just didn't want to, insisting that he discussed it with the other housemate who'd been disturbed that night. Paul wanted instead to talk to his son, in the housemate's presence, which did transpire.

Dispersing after class, I made sure to convey to Paul that having allowed his grown son into his home again, and despite the kind of behavior he believed he could expect from him, he might need to resign himself to challenges that came along.

· · ·

Did you also feel disrespected, Priyavani, by your maid Seeta, whom you brought into the country, and into your house? Few know that as a deputy consul general, on assignment here in New York, you earned about $50,000/- a year. And that if you were to pay your maid at the hourly wage indicated in her visa application, $9.75/hr., with her working for you at forty hours a week for fifty weeks in a year, you'd be obliged to pay her $19,500/-. This, along with other expenses, could amount to 40% of your salary. Despite perks granted by your government for a senior official in Foreign Service, such as a free apartment and transportation, you could have found yourself unable to meet a high standard of life, expected of a person of such social standing, if a large chunk of your earnings were to go to your house help.

So you had her sign a second agreement with you that negated your prior employment contract with her, which then invalidated your statements to the US government on your maid's visa application. And in this second agreement, one dated after her visa application was submitted, you added terms that specified payment of less than $600 per month to Seeta. These terms superseded previous payment arrangements, giving your actions an apparent cover of legality, and required that you pay her about 12% of your annual salary.

A win-win arrangement, certainly, given that a typical Indian housemaid can earn only about one-half that amount, working in four or more homes in India, and could not have gained the comforts of a New York apartment, with good food, and needed healthcare. Private room and board in New York surely costs more than a thousand dollars a month, which benefited Seeta and you as well in her constant availability. The numbers do work out. I can see why Seeta agreed to your clever scheme, and hence to being bound by it. Is this why Seeta's actions enraged you, because you felt that she disrespected you?

This isn't the first such instance of complaints by house help, in homes of foreign officials, in America. Haven't other such domestic employees raised objections to difficult working conditions in the past? Didn't two other Indian government officials in New York face civil litigation to resolve grievances of domestic employees brought into the country in recent years?

One cannot know what transpired between you and Seeta, but her complaint seems no different from that of others who objected to conditions resembling bonded labor and slavery. Twelve hour days, with no days off from continuous work, and no activities outside of the confines of one's working environment—how different is this from being a beast of burden? And salaries that in no way compensate them for the efforts they put in. Would you, Priyavani, agree to such conditions of existence?

But I have lived in similar conditions, twice, in days long past. Discriminated against by those who employed me, given my land of origin, I have labored, both in the Middle East and in America, under the suffocating yoke of unfairness and oppression, and have yearned and struggled to be free. And yet I did find empathy and respect, in these disparate environments, as I freed myself from the situations I'd voluntarily entered into. Is this where things might have turned sour for you? Because you could not put yourself into Seeta's situation, and see it from her point of view?

You felt Seeta was engaging in extortion, and you and your father employed your enormous influence, within the Indian government, to intimidate Seeta and her family in a manner incomprehensible to folks here. You had her national identity—her passport—canceled by your government. How does anyone accomplish that? How can any government negate its recognition of a citizen because of a civil dispute between its citizens? Can you imagine the astonishment you caused here, whatever be the influence you and your father may wield in India?

Can you see it for what it is, the arbitrariness of those with authority, a form of corruption most vile? As for the reactions of the Indian government to your arrest and arraignment, to charges two more of its officials faced in civil litigation in America in recent years, I think they reflect immaturity in diplomacy unseen elsewhere. The removal of concrete security barricades around the US embassy, cancellation of import goods privileges for US diplomats, threats of arrests of same-sex partners of US officials, and reissue of diplomatic identity cards with warnings of possible arrest on serious infractions—these and other actions by the Indian government exhibited only a desire to retaliate. Threats of harm made against Seeta's family, allegedly by your father, required a relocation of her family here for their safety and your prosecution. Can you not see that while you might perceive Seeta as an extortioner, your actions and those of your helpers reflect oppression and unreasoning violence?

You have succeeded thus far in what you and your helpers set out to do, Priyavani. You were granted a diplomatic post with full immunity, and since your country denied waiver of this protection, you were asked, under diplomatic conventions, to leave the country. You have also succeeded in having your indictment, made by a court after you gained full diplomatic immunity, dismissed.

Nevertheless, given that your objectionable actions occurred prior to being granted such freedom, you remained prosecutable under American law upon that protection being negated by your government or by circumstances. And, having left your diplomatic post in America, which gave you shelter against prosecution, you have been indicted again, within days of the dismissal of your prior indictment. Did you not declare, "The rule of law has prevailed!" when the first indictment was dismissed? How do you perceive your re-indictment just a few days later? Do you see it, perhaps, as a relentless pursuit of law-enforcement?

Curiously, your predicament is, in some ways, similar to mine. Your husband and children, said to be citizens of America, are here, and may not wish to return to India. Your father asserts the family will relocate to India. It is hard to see things working out that way—your husband, an academic here, isn't an individual readily dictated to by you and your father. He and your children may well enjoy greater opportunities here in America. Yet, in any culture, eastern or western, Indian or American, the need for a mother to be with her children is greatly respected. Judges in America often favor mothers in divorce and custody arrangements. It is important for the children that both you and your husband are with them—how will you accomplish this?

As with Lopez, of my classes several years ago, and my children's mother,

I am afraid for you, Priyavani. The media reports that you attempted to have Seeta sign a document including an admission from her that she took items you reported stolen. And that she had her lawyer read the document and explain it to her, after which she obviously did not sign anything.

It is also reported that you told an American colleague, as you left this country, "You've lost a good friend. It is unfortunate. In return, you've gained a maid and a drunken driver. They are in, and we are out." If so, do you know that a poem by Emma Lazarus, engraved into the foundation of the Statue of Liberty at Ellis Island, not far from where you came in and exited the country, says, "... *Give me your tired, your poor, your huddled masses yearning to breathe free...*" near the end? Yes, we prefer the poor and the downtrodden to the high and mighty here in America, though I am not quite sure why it was so then. Emma's sentiment shared by the people may not have been the only reason that founders of a national symbol had the poem engraved beneath it. Nevertheless, bravado and disrespect ill suits a representative of a nation founded on the principles of truth and nonviolence. Nor does it suit a mother who must guide her children well.

• • •

Was I outraged when I discovered my wife's affair? I think yes, briefly perhaps, as I think back to the events of mid '07. I remember having sensed something strange in her a week or so before the night of my fateful discovery. All my attention then was on the lawsuit I faced—and an absence of any business activity in my start-up—and I was not paying any attention to my wife. Standing across the kitchen island in our home one day, a week before discovering her dalliance, I said to her that I thought she might be engaged in something disruptive to the family, and pleaded with her to not do such things that I did not and could not know. Events proved my intuition accurate. Upon discovery of her conduct, my first instinct was to seek help from John and Parvathi. Outrage was replaced, in my mind, by a greater need to mitigate damage, to minimize harm to everyone.

I spent the rest of that year rebuilding my relationship with my wife, with Parvathi's input and many interventions by her and her husband John. I took part in conversations with Parvathi, John, and my wife, taking strong criticism from Parvathi, hoping to calm the heart and mind of my children's mother. Disrespect wasn't what I thought about. There were clearly deeper emotions and aspects to comprehend and resolve in that situation.

Outrage rose with vehemence in me when I read the report the cop Gormon Grigorievic filed the night of my arrest. He'd twisted my statements into a confession: "*He said he grabbed her by the arm and pulled her out of bed which cause [sic] her to fall onto the floor.*" Grammatical mistakes included, his cunning characterization of facts fit Gormon's agenda very well. He added, "*She had red marks on her left wrist. These marks would be consistent with someone grabbing her by the wrist and pulling.*" No, Gormon, the reddish marks arose because I had to hold her arms away from my face, and do so with some force. Besides, the marks were not on her wrists, but in the mid-forearm. But Gormon's intentions were glaringly evident.

He added, "*I placed him under arrest...at 2254 hours. I placed handcuffs on him and performed a search of his person. I placed him in the back of my Police car. I read him Miranda at 2300 hours.*" No, Gormon, that—your notation of administering Miranda immediately upon arrest—is a blatant lie to cover your omission, an intentional one that undermines your credibility. He wrote further, "*I attempted to talk to their nine year old son who witnessed the fight. He would not wake to talk to us.*" Would you have had a child bear witness against his father, twisting his words too, to suit your agenda, Gormon? Did you obtain his parents' explicit permission to wake and conduct your interrogation of a minor child in the family home? You, Gormon, are guilty of violation of a child's civil rights, and an intention to abuse a child and his family, in your eager endeavor to disturb a sleeping child without due permission from his father.

Curiously, he also added, "*He had a $100 bill in his posession [sic], these are not allowed at the 4th ave. jail so I impounded it into property at 75 E. Civic Center Dr. for safe keeping.*" That did not make much sense—I was in my house wear; why would I have any money in my pockets, much less an uncommon $100 bill? And why were these bills not allowed in the 4th Ave. jail—could it be that fake $100 bills were a matter of controversy here in Wariduna? Had I been foresighted enough to anticipate needing just one hundred dollars when the domestic situation worsened to involve the police?

I first read Gormon's report at Mindy's office, and couldn't contain my emotions. She assured me this was Dilbut's standard operating procedure—they'd do anything, without reservation, to achieve their ends. She said this continued because no one held them to account.

Along with Gormon's report, I also read my concerned spouse's victim impact statement. Needless to say, her statements confirmed my instinctive feelings about her that I'd resisted accepting for long.

She'd spun a moving story of alleged long-term abuse by me: "*Since 2003, I have been verbally/emotionally abused by this defendant. On and off, he has been physically abusive (shoving, pushing, pulling me by my hair, squeezing me forcefully) when I attempt to stand up to his abuse. Since the recent incident my physical symptoms (increased heart rate -120bpm, difficulty breathing) have exacerbated. I am very fearful of mine [sic] and my kids psychological make-up. My children are very confused about what's going on.*"

As for a section that asked for financial loss resulting from the alleged criminal offense, she'd filled it out with—"*Emotional trauma and constant psy-cho-somatic symptoms—(1) Increased heart rate—up to 120bpm, (2) Irritable Bowel Syndrome (3) Sudden weight loss up to 20lbs (4) Hair loss (5) Difficulty breathing (6) Low self-esteem (7) Crying and depressed (8) Difficulty focusing on day to day activities (@ work and @ home) (9) Financial burden when I have to take days off 2 to* [sic] *the above.*" You left out world hunger, poverty, and every other human condition and affliction, you lying, two-faced hyena. It took you until the ninth itemized sentence for a proper response to the question asked.

Do you realize how incredible it is for you to blame all of your illnesses upon the incident, upon me, whom you refer to respectfully as a defendant? Mindy, watching me as I read through these documents, offered to speak with this so-called life-partner of mine. My inflamed emotions would clearly not help in conversation with one whose manipulation and deception had been laid bare.

This allegation—abuse—appeared to come readily to my spouse's mind. Its roots could have been experiences in her childhood that she recounted to me. She had spoken, crying inconsolably, about her own mother having brought another man home while her father was away, and of finding this stranger lying next to her, of being sexually abused by him. When asked how her family stayed together after such conduct by her mother, she said her parents talked the matter over, and her father continued to look after the family for the children's sake. She has harbored a phobia against men ever since.

This came up first when she befriended me two decades ago, in her vehement assertions of abuse by her then husband, a Christian preacher, who remained in India. She accused him of extreme emotional manipulation, and of physical violence against his own father. But this phobia evidently did not prevent her from pursuing the very same pathway, that her mother chose, when she could do so with impunity.

I suppose nature isn't easily denied. It is fatuous to hope that learning, through examples in families and society, may help overcome such innate urges.

The pattern of her conflicted interactions with men through life to this point showed that she'd internalized learning of a different sort, one that she could readily employ to her own selfish benefit. Her claim of abuse by men was an effective means for her to accomplish her desired objectives where she could easily apply them. Sociopathy is an apt description for her manipulative self-serving behaviors, her lying and deception, a need to aggrandize herself, a distinct lack of remorse or any sense of shame, irresponsibility, and promiscuity—but this would not occur to her at all. I realized with much sadness that one so colored by troubling experiences may view others only as painted in the same color. But her accusations of abuse by me, her second husband, asserted for the most part verbal and emotional ill treatment, pointing to physical actions incidentally.

· · ·

Self-awareness is a difficult crown to bear, for with it comes self-doubt, and self-sacrifice. Ego is a far easier mental construct. It is easy for one to be proud of one's accomplishments, wealth, and any station in life achieved, and to express this in any number of outward ways. But when one looks inward, and evaluates one's thought and conduct in relation to hopes and aspirations for intellectual and spiritual growth, self-doubt inevitably rises within.

After the initial outrage felt, my heart and mind filled with overwhelming sadness at reading what my so-called partner wrote about me. I could see that the kindnesses shown, sacrifices made, my implicit respect and love for this person I'd chosen and dignified as my partner in life, mattered little to her. I was nothing but an abuser—to her individual mind and heart that did not function as an integral part of the family that I was building with her. When a stronger entity, the state, intervened in our lives, she saw the possibility of self-benefit and familial bonds turned into adversarial accusations from her. I quelled my sadness, for convenience dictated that she view me in this fashion so as to readily dismiss all other aspects that would raise self-doubt in her—this was her way out, mentally, and the second house and distance from us all a similar way out, physically.

She could not be expected to view the situation outside of herself. She had clearly been caught with her pants down, and saw this condemnation as the only way to elevate her own actions in her warped mind. She would not be able to sacrifice her ego, her wants and demands, her self, for strength and greater happiness in the family. Shame and remorse would not enter her mind. I realized that I had foolishly hoped for love and commitment from one incapable of anything but shallow self-serving emotions.

The Last Few Classes

The next class was dominated by Jerome's problems with his ex-wife and kids. He seemed quite disturbed and depressed. His ex-wife, Natasha, had backed her pickup truck into a corner of his car and crushed it a good deal. She didn't have money to pay for damages—and they both had kids to look after as well. Jerome flew into a bad state, and didn't talk to her for twenty-six hours—yes, *twenty-six hours*, said Jerome, just over a day, which sufficed to cause her much concern.

She called the police requesting that they check on him. When they came, Jerome, quite understandably, did not open the door, and they prepared to break in through the garage door. Facing the potential of further damage to him by the state, he did open the door, more disturbed than ever. After brief explanations, the cops apologized to him and left. He then fell into an argument with Natasha, which led to her threat of not allowing him to see his kids again. Hence his blues.

All of us in the group reassured him that she could not keep him from seeing his children, given the existence of a visitation agreement that is enforceable by law. It would be well within his rights to call the cops if she did not let him see his kids when he went by to do so. He'd just have to get over his aversion of the police. And get out from under Natasha's dominating control.

The group welcomed a new member, and Sid asked for his story. He was an ex-felon, who, in a discussion with a counselor during his probation, became upset with her insistent approach, lost his temper, and called her a bitch. The *b-word* no female counselor will tolerate. She reported it to his probation officer, and he was asked to attend a full year of our classes.

His past history, including a conviction and jail time, compounded his situation—perhaps unfairly, in this specific instance. Doesn't it say, somewhere in the annals of the law, that prior bad acts are inadmissible, and may not be applied toward determining consequences for a new offense? But perhaps justice is indeed blind; humans will apply the law as they see fit. As a punitive measure, not as commensurate, compassionate guidance.

For the benefit of the new member, and others who came in previously, the group went through a sequence of introductions—brief confessionals—disclosing what brought everyone into the class. This continued the next class as well, where we heard from another new member who was sent to join our group because he'd set fire to a wooden stool inside a room for warmth. It did-n't help him that the room did not have a fireplace, or that he set fire to the stool in the middle of the room away from anything else that might catch fire. He carried out his act of arson without consulting any resident who could have granted him permission, or shared responsibility.

Others went through their brief stories as well, as did I: I pulled my wife's arm in an argument, Paul—got a live-in girlfriend with kids who did not like being asked to move out, Oscar—flipped out his ex-wife because she let a felon cohabit with her and his daughter, Jim—sent a text message to his stepdaughter and ex-wife while a restraining order was in force, Ken—threw a glass cup down in an argument with his wife about her family's racist attitudes toward him, kid—mom reported a hole he punched in a wall, and so on.

Our descriptions of events that brought us into class became shorter as classes progressed, almost as if they mattered less as time passed. Or we'd all become weary, of repeating our pathetic stories, of a weekly reinforcement of the memory of acts that led to the state-mandated class that we endured. It re-minded me of punishments in school of writing, on chalk boards, or in our books, *I will not sneak a kiss on a girl again*, or other embarrassing sentences, a hundred times or more as the correcting teacher fancied.

In the next class, my customary seat in the circle near Sid was taken, and Paul stated that I'd been demoted. Laughing, I took a seat next to him instead. Jamil brought news of Jerome—he'd suffered two epileptic seizures, bit a hole in his tongue, and slammed his shoulder. He was hospitalized with serious in-juries. Jerome had been diagnosed with epilepsy some time ago. The stress of his present situation evidently exacerbated his condition. Natasha, his ex-wife, was at the hospital taking care of him. Besides injuries, his hospital bills were sure to be an immense burden. Any challenges the rest of the group faced seemed insignificant in comparison.

There were a good few new guys in class, and Sid busied himself with roll-call and payments collection. I spoke to the group about news on BBC Online that domestic violence cases had climbed 320% in Alabama due largely to the massive oil spill and consequent loss of livelihoods in the Gulf of Mexico. Po-lice calls had increased by as much as 216% in Louisiana. A month prior to my arrest for DV, I too had quit a stressful job in another town in Wariduna, and returned home to derision, from my spouse, about my inability to hold onto jobs. The coincidence and correlation was significant, the group agreed. Sid appeared busy in his tasks and did not comment.

Don, one of the newbies, had engaged in a scuffle with his wife of twen-ty-seven years, but had taken the blame because his wife was a heart patient. **Chuck** enrolled himself. No police or state involvement, just various things in his life that compelled him to come seek help. The group applauded his aware-ness and his resolve to change.

Getting to my last class, I wondered aloud in the group about whether I'd like six more months of this regular gathering. And that the answer in my mind was, "Yes!" Everyone burst out laughing. I explained that I'd thought about it, and determined that it was because I felt useful in the class. Sid asked me to repeat that word—*useful*—saying it fed into feeling important, and that it made perfect sense to him. But that's just it, Sid—it's simply what we do. I had no need or drive to feel important in this class, but appreciated being useful and knowing that fact—a benefit to the group and its recognition, as opposed to benefit to the individual ego. But I let it go; it was my last class after all.

Sergei, the third newbie that day, came to us from Russia. He married a girl in Dilbut, and had come over to be with her. Five months into his stay here, they fell into a loud argument, during which he hit a wall, causing some visible damage on it. Someone called the police, leading to his arrest. The cop had the temerity to apologize, informing him that it's criminal damage and DV. Sergei tried communicating with the cop, in his broken English, to the best of his ability. He told us, similarly, "Cop—think, think, think, say *have* to arrest you." He spent only two hours in the station, and was prohibited from speaking with or seeing his wife for two whole days. He stayed in a hotel for the two days before getting back home.

Sergei also met his wife over the web. He'd asked her to come over to Russia, but she studied here, and got him to come over to Wariduna and the city of Dilbut. All of us felt quite sorry for Sergei.

We discussed Don's problem next. Don had volunteered to throw his wife's small dog—a pug—through the window because it peed on his clothes on the bed. This led to the argument and scuffle with his wife. Sid attempted to apply his *belief-rule-action-results-change* loop to Don's matter, changing contents in each of the boxes to suit Don's dynamically varying inputs, with little success. Psychoanalysis, at best an inexact science, and at worst, Freudian, wasn't something the group members took to easily. From past experience, I ventured that the situation may be the result of Don and his wife not having any children, his wife loving the pug like a child, but not disciplining it accordingly, since the dog faced no consequences out of the home. Sid pointed out that the best solution could be positive reinforcement, providing practical tips, which was generally accepted.

Sid got on Jamil's case this day, about his beliefs—Jamil was black—wanting him to admit that he *believed* that his ex-wife should listen to him. Jamil resisted, insisting that he just liked to talk, say such things; I helped out by pointing to his evident gregarious nature, that he could be fulfilling his need for affection, to be liked. Sid got off Jamil's case. Winning over the group with his attempts to apply the BRARC loop just wasn't working that day.

Before the end of class, I made a confession that I inherited my father's anger, but also adopted many of his principles, one of which was to always work to leave a place better than one finds it. That summed up the twenty-six weeks I spent with the group.

• • •

Graduation involved receiving a course completion certificate with comments from every participant. I thanked them for their camaraderie, parting comments, and wishes from those who knew me:

It was a pleasure to have your feedback. I wish you the best of luck.—Jerome

I can't wait to read 'the book.' Thanks for all your input!—Paul

Good luck.—CT

Good luck with your marriage.—T

Good luck.— AM

I'm really gonna miss you, I love your insight. Hit me up whenever.—Jamil

Top of the World—C

Congrats & good luck!—A

Don't come back.—M

Keep up the good work! You're a 'seeker.' That is an adventurous lifestyle.—Sid

Good luck. Stay clean.—J

Good job, dude.—D

Good job :-)—F

I thought Sid meant that I was a trouble-seeker; his second comment seemed to confirm it. Yes, Sid, I have been an adventurer all my life. What other way of life could there be?

• • •

My exit meeting with Sid was scheduled for 2:30 p.m. the next week, but overlapped, due to a scheduling conflict, with Paul's exit chat, also with Sid. I used the additional time to fill out a final form indicating what I learned in class, how I took responsibility for what brought me into the program, how I would avoid such dangers in the future, what had changed in my approach, and how the program may be improved, etc.. I didn't think that anything much had changed in me, but awaited Sid's verdict.

Sid did remember my situation despite the number of people passing through the program. I spoke with him about recognizing my own disturbed state and the impact it had on my children and wife. And about voluntarily taking classes in a community program for Parental Anger Management, and getting help from friends and well-wishers. He pointed out that anyone could tell I wasn't a violent man.

For my part, I expressed deep disappointment with my spouse—her actions being rather common with spouses of entrepreneurs, for most of such families eventually do go through breakups. And that this, to me, showed a lack of strength and will-power, an inability of spouses to empathize with the struggles and challenges entrepreneurs faced. I admitted, nevertheless, that my own spouse may have faced a difficult situation as well, one that she could not resolve.

Sid pointed out that my spouse's choice of an affair was out of place. I said that her distinct lack of faith, of trust, of loyalty to me as an entrepreneur as well as a good human being, hurt me. But most troubling was the utter lack of any remorse in her, and continuation of her old ways of wanton social contact, lacking propriety, with impunity. Clearly, none of these aspects could be addressed by any class, he agreed.

I spoke with him of my resolute stance with respect to my children, and my determination to resolve, unequivocally, any legal challenge my spouse might bring. He cautioned me about statements I might make to my spouse in closing.

A Family Torn Apart

The mother of my children—I couldn't bear to call her wife or spouse any more—would assure you that all the classes I attended changed nothing in me. That wouldn't be entirely accurate, for I'd now begun to commiserate and sympathize with men more than ever before. A pendulum having swung to the benefit of women in society, and toward punitive actions against men, women seemed bent upon taking any and all advantage they could from that swing. I had a clear understanding of it, due in large part to the classes and to tales of woe from many others.

You could say that my re-education by the state hardened my heart against relational injustice. That exposure toughened an aspect my mother often cautioned me about—a *Nishkalanka Hridayam*, an unblemished and soft heart, unsuited to the task of dealing with cold and selfish entities—and my children's mother realized this soon enough.

She moved out of our home, by her choice and under no compulsion, into our other house two months after my classes were done. And took many of our valuables from the home—gold jewelry the children received as gifts—with her, which escaped my notice then.

A new routine began for all of us. While my children stayed with me in our primary home, one paid for in full from earnings in my first start-up, their mother stayed a street away in our second home, on her own, with the privacy and freedom she desired. She came and left as she pleased, in the early morning to help our children with breakfast or lunch preparations before school, and in the evening for dinner and homework, which allowed me some time to myself. With no corporate employment feasible in view of my arrest, and the subsequent criminal record, I focused on being a driver, the occasional cook, and the primary parent for my children. The DV program counselor's words of caution remained in my mind; I limited communication with their mother only to that needed to care for our children.

Disagreements arose on occasion, particularly with respect to making sure the children consumed nutritious food—their mother often packed only chicken nuggets for their lunch—or when they made demands that both parents did not see eye-to-eye on. During heated disagreements, she sang her now common refrain, "I only need to call the prosecutor once, and you'll be gone." Though this seemed disrespectful, I learned to see it as utterances from a frustrated human who could not be expected to rise above such behavior.

Nevertheless, to ensure that it did not go any further, I informed Dilbut cops and Lauren that such interactions continued in my household. They could offer no advice or assistance in the matter other than to caution me to not fall afoul of their laws again.

Not only did the children feel their mother's absence troubling, our time together and happiness in play was greatly diminished by their mother's demand that I stay away from the second home. That house was to be *her* place. I heeded this demand more because my friend John, who posted my bail, cautioned me that the kids' mother could fabricate new allegations against me if I accessed the place where she lived alone. Fear of such manipulation of the system, and the knowledge that others had successfully done that, now determined decisions that impacted the happiness of my children.

The strange family dynamics limited my time with our children to the commute to school and back, and occasional homework assignments or weekend outings. I'd even taken to retiring to the farthest corner of my own home when their mother came to visit so I could avoid communicating with her. When discussions became heated or loud, I'd walk away from the situation—as the DV classes recommended—and then have to hear her say, "Look at him running away." What sort of a shallow human was I coping with? This surely wasn't a healthy or sustainable domestic situation—change was necessary, and I knew that I would have to be the one to bring it about. But how could I change things without further traumatizing my children?

Lauren, maybe? A demand for a mediator was a recurring theme recently. Lauren seemed amenable to mediating between two emotional Indian domestic partners. I broached this topic with the children's mother, that the state made family counselors available at no charge, and that she was a nice person to talk to. It took an enormous effort to convince her that mediation with such a counselor could be helpful. Lauren had indicated that counseling discussions required both participants to voluntarily request the service. I persuaded the children's mother to call and arrange a first discussion session with her. Having gone through classes with the state, I kept my expectations low.

The first chat passed uneventfully. She found a quiet audience in a state counselor and a troubled husband. Both listened to her long-winded outpouring of pain and sadness in not finding much affection and love in our marriage. This was true enough. We'd been through a rocky, up and down relationship in the eighteen years that I'd known her. Life hadn't been easy at all—looking after two little kids while holding a full-time job, and a husband engaged in high technology entrepreneurship who did not find much time for family or his wife, who did not make things any easier.

Yet, as many others had asked her in the past, in their attempts to help, did that mean life for her was agonizing or insufferable in any way? My mother asked her, in early 2009, when she questioned her with the typical, "Don't I need a life too?" in a face-to-face discussion about these marital troubles, "What other life are you talking of, daughter-in-law? Don't you have a good husband, two beautiful children, a spacious house, good employment, and all that you need to keep the family going?" This question brought only silence from her, or claims that she endured an abusive husband, one who emotionally distanced her, who did not give her love, and who often seemed angry with or suspicious of her.

Much of the hour with Lauren was spent in her drawn-out explanations of how difficult and painful her life was, and of how I gave no support or love. Lauren listened with a few remarks and questions, while I stayed largely silent this first session, keeping continuance of these sessions in mind.

The next session was my turn, and I let her have it. From 2007, ever since her affair with a co-worker, whom she continued to contact through that year and the next that I knew of, I had tried my utmost to see things from her point of view. I'd listened to the same story from her at all intervention discussions we participated in. John and Parvathi attempted to help in '07, when I did everything under the sun, guided by Parvathi, to make her happy, including purchasing a second home that she now arrogated to herself. Quite frankly, her story stank. There wasn't anything I could see as true or honorable in this person's actions and statements, and I wasn't sure that trying to keep her happy, for the sake of the children, would be the right thing to do any more. I opened my heart in that session, and let loose with every feeling, frustration, disappointment, and all my attempts to free myself from her clutches that I could remember—and there were many such.

I let loose in a manner I'd never before done, to good effect, and to the utter surprise of Lauren, who previously knew me only as an emotional and gentle person. I think I did not care to listen to the children's mother ranting and raving about herself, and her pain, while being utterly thoughtless about the pain and anguish so many others around her suffered. Not any more, not after the devastation caused to my family. Her actions reminded me of how she tormented her first husband, and accused him of committing unspeakable violence—a disturbing story for another day—and of how I'd been a pawn in her manipulation at that point in time. My audience remained speechless in that session.

Lauren could see the signs clearly enough. In the next session, when our discussion began to heat up again, she asked the both of us, "How would you like to meet with me separately? Or, perhaps, not at all?" For a family counselor to say this—I cannot do anything to help you—seemed beyond the ordinary, but then the situation was not in any way typical. Our discord stretched the extent of Lauren's capacity to resolve disagreements. She dealt with the typical misguided youth, or adult with habits that needed management, not with strong, self-willed individuals, confident in their identities, but vastly different in their goals and attitudes in life. Any interest Lauren professed in learning Indian culture took a remote seat in the back of her mind. She knew that she faced an intractable and irremediable problem, of counseling warring individuals from rather different sections of a complex cultural melting pot.

Perhaps the extent of emotional expression in our joint sessions was too much for Lauren, who hails from a culture where emotions are considered aspects of human interaction to control and suppress. Freudian psychoanalysis, and counseling education based upon it, could surely bring that thinking into a society that employs such categorizing methods more than empathy and compassion. I thought that she was too quick to give up, that she really did not care to help any more than her employment and role required her to. But she may simply have been confirming the inevitable in this family. We parted ways with Lauren and counseling for good after that session.

The possible failure of a second attempt at a family troubled me greatly. Not because that might reflect upon me, but because I'd seen the pain caused in my son, who grew largely without a father, back in the country I originated from. His mother had asked this one thing of me, never to take her son away from her, as I left that turmoil to seek a future elsewhere. I did abide by that request. Yet, when my son grew into adulthood, he summarized my actions thus: "You may have thought that you did a noble thing, by heeding my mother's request, but I grew up without a father." He was right. I had indeed wronged him, though between the choices of rearing a son as a single parent, and of the presence of extended family near him who could help out, the latter seemed the wiser approach. And he'd grown up with his mother, grandparents, and other family members nearby.

How could I let the same—the loss of a father—happen to the two little ones in my care here? I resolved to do everything in my capacity to be with them, to be the father they need me to be, particularly in a land where there could be no extended family to nurture them. I made a promise, to myself, not to disrupt their lives any more than had already occurred. A promise that I feared I might not be able to keep; there was clearly nothing I could do about their mother's conduct.

· · ·

But mine wasn't the only Indian family in trouble. A friend who played volleyball with me called and asked me to meet with another, also in our volleyball group, going through a difficult legal situation then. **Giddu Jacob**'s wife **Guddy** had served him divorce papers. They had two little children, which made their matter that much more difficult.

This wasn't the first mention of trouble there; I had heard that matters weren't in good shape with him earlier. Having quit playing volleyball, I wasn't

in regular contact with these friends, and hence had not known about his recent predicament. With legal papers served, he clearly needed help. My friend
knew of my familiarity with litigation and asked for my involvement. I invited
Giddu over to my home that evening.

Giddu was a dark, slender, balding young man a good few inches shorter
and years younger than me. I remembered him as a jovial clown on the volleyball court—and as one of the pair that helped me get back home when my foot
dislocated at play. He appeared less than jovial this evening when he came by.

Offering him some refreshments, I asked him to be as free and frank as he
felt comfortable being, and inquired as to the circumstances of his legal action.
He spoke of recent events first, which, over the past couple of weeks, began
with an altercation with his wife Guddy. She'd cut off cable television service
at their home, objecting to his parents watching TV programs with the volume
set high, since it disturbed her sleep. She worked nights, slept during the day,
and found that the television didn't permit her much needed rest. Her in-laws,
visiting from India, needed television for entertainment. They failed to respect
her requests to keep it turned low. Discovering that she had cut cable TV service without warning, he fell into an angry argument with her resulting in her
calling the Dilbut police.

When cops arrived, they found him carrying his son, comforting the little
child, and Guddy quite emotional, striving to convince them that he had been
abusive, and had slapped her silly. Finding no such evidence of violence perpetrated, in the home or on her person, the Dilbut cops cautioned her against
making false statements, and declined to file her complaint. Given the extent
to which she escalated the matter, Giddu left his home accompanied by his
parents, but without his children, and moved to an apartment. A prudent step
for him in such troubling circumstances, I agreed.

Staying away from home, in an unfurnished apartment along with his elderly parents, and without his children, clearly disturbed Giddu. He told me of
how his parents came around to where he slept, late at night, to reassure themselves that he was alright, that he wasn't emotionally disturbed or perhaps even
suicidal. It hurt him a great deal to know that his visiting parents observed him
go through humiliation and pain in such severe marital discord. Though I
could understand his hurt and humiliation, I couldn't grasp how it could ex-
tend to making him suicidal. Surely there was more, yet to be known, underlying his marital discord.

What seemed to cause Giddu the most hurt was having to stay away from
his kids who couldn't be expected to comprehend these events. He did meet
with his daughter, who was my daughter's age, and with his little son twice the
past week. His daughter relayed to him explanations Guddy gave the children,
for his absence from their home, that were quite unflattering to him. That reminded me of statements my children's mother offered my son and daughter

the day I was held in jail—that I'll be allowed to come back home only when I learned to behave.

But the first order of business—if it could be called that—was to deal with his legal matter. Giddu was evidently troubled by it, for it asked for all the usual things—the house, money, custody of children, etc.—in the adversarial, one-sided manner common in such actions. Advising him to conduct research on the lawyer who filed the papers, and any subsequent legal events associated with the case, I promised to meet with him the next morning, and saw him off somewhat reassured.

Getting To Root Causes

Giddu owned a curio shop in a local mall, and sold a colorful variety of trinkets, items for home decoration, small pieces of jewelry, and even some specialty clothes, all imported from vendors and craftspeople in Southeast Asia. He hailed from the same Indian state I originated from. It was therefore quite easy, culturally, to identify with him and the woes of his family. He belonged to the Catholic Christian faith, while I identified with none despite being born and raised in a devout Hindu family. He did not seem overly religious, though his shop did include items of overt expression of Christianity—crosses, statuettes, and such—which perhaps gave his customers comfort in their belief that those of a familiar religious mindset will not fleece them. His shop smelled distinctly of Indian incense.

Giddu was busy with a few customers when I visited him at the shop, and asked that I wait in his storage and office room in the back. The room contained an old sofa I sat on, an office desk with a computer and printer, and an office chair in a corner, with the rest of the space occupied by storage shelves and boxes. He came into the storage area a while later, and apologized for my wait. He was rather animated, pacing along the long room as he spoke.

"She really tried to screw me!" he blurted out. "When I checked online for case details and proceedings, I saw that she tried to have me slapped with a protective order—twice—but failed."

"Restraining orders are common in divorce cases here, Giddu," I reassured him. "It's nothing unusual. You should be pleased that her protective order pleadings have been dismissed."

"How can she claim to need protection from me? How can she demand that I stay away from my home and children?"

"It may not have been her at all. Lawyers do this as the first step in divorces to gain leverage in negotiations. It's unimportant. Dismissed twice, it cannot be asked for again—tell me, how did all this begin? Can't be just a disagreement between her and your parents."

Giddu poured his heart out, interrupted occasionally by customers dropping into his shop, as I spent all morning listening. His troubles began when they first moved from the northeast of the country to Wariduna, when his wife accepted a new nursing job offer. She stayed with a married couple from India, whom they'd known before coming to America, and developed some intimacy with her hosts, the husband in particular. This was some time after the birth of their second child, a tot of two years then. While he ran a business in the northeast, similar to one he owned now, and took care of their children, she began to look to a new friendship, a possible romance.

When the family moved down to join her, he discovered her daily communication with this other fellow, and raised strong objections to what he saw as an affair in progress. Giddu confessed to me—that he'd slapped his wife repeatedly with a slipper, a grave insult in any culture, when he discovered her affair. In the social intervention that followed, with friends from the same part of the world, they apologized to each other and resolved to carry on together to make the best of the circumstances for their family. He spoke about regular prayer meetings held in his home by a local prayer leader and wife, that he assumed was of some help to Guddy and therefore tolerated, though he had no desire that such people visit them for this purpose.

This occurred a few years before their discord escalated to his current legal predicament. In recent months, he discovered the continued communication, between his wife and her male friend, which, in this instance, was conducted through a fake female email account. He chanced upon one such email message on his home computer screen. With suspicions aroused, he asked to meet with her and the other individual to dredge this matter out. After the male friend vociferously disclaimed any such communication, and left their discussion at his home, his wife informed him that it was indeed the other person, her male friend, sending such messages to her.

That led to an argument, and a turning-point in his relationship with her, for he saw, in lies by all involved and in her actions and speech, a lack of respect for him that could not be bridged. And now, forced to leave his home and children with his visiting parents, he faced a difficult legal battle.

I remarked on striking similarities in his experiences—including the blatant communication between consenting adults pursuing an affair, physical or emotional, sharing my stories along the way—which helped him relax. Much like myself, he was determined to make things better for his children, which meant the legal battle he faced was best avoided entirely. I knew that a greater challenge lay in renewing mutual respect between the separated partners.

There had to be a way to show his wife that he meant business—effective legal business—without actually joining the battle, without financial commitment that could weaken his already precarious position. I asked him to obtain permission from Dilbut cops to visit his home, where a complaint and divorce action arose, to retrieve his business and personal belongings. And to ask that they accompany him—in what is called a 'civil accompaniment'—in accomplishing this without incident. At this event, I instructed Giddu to document everything through photographs—to make sure that all family possessions remained in place and were not disposed of by her unbeknownst to him—a task to be done diligently in her presence.

He accomplished this simple task marvelously, for I heard about it through the social grapevine—that she had been taken aback when the cops contacted her, and then accompanied him to obtain his items, while he photographed everything. The grapevine was not too long: Guddy, Parvathi, my children's mother, and I. This human chain gave me an indirect channel to convey strategic information through.

And convey such information I did, in vocal conversations over the phone with Giddu, enthusiastically discussing his preparations for the oncoming legal battle that I joined in. I knew that my children's mother would listen to these conversations avidly, and pass it on to the rest of the social group. I overheard such a conversation between Parvathi and her, where she informed Parvathi that I, with my prior legal experience and victories, had joined this upcoming battle wholeheartedly.

Yet, it was important that we prepare ourselves. Giddu conducted an online search for divorce lawyers, and we met with one—he insisted that I meet with him too—for an initial consultation. The lawyer we approached appeared more experienced and capable as compared with the divorce attorney his wife worked with. A lawyer's language and construction of legal complaints are often dependable indicators of litigation experience and skill. Her lawyer appeared to me to be a cheap one.

With pressure mounting, I heard from Giddu that she desired to talk about a settlement with a family friend present—not at his request at all—which was what we expected. After this meeting held at his shop, one that I required and trusted him to manage on his own, he called me in great cheer to convey that she had dropped the divorce filing at the urging of their family friend. And that her lawyer too was pleased, agreeing that resolutions out of court were the best for her family. I cautioned him nevertheless that this was only a minor battle won. The war that began with disrespect and distrust, and continued for many years, remained to be resolved.

To address his family situation effectively, I desired alternative perspectives on the sequence of events, and asked John, Parvathi's husband, if he knew anything about it. He had been only peripherally involved, but appeared to be convinced that Giddu was gay! Not the happy sort of gay. And that this had been the cause of his wife's discontent all along. With two children in their family, this was hard to believe.

I wanted to get this straight from the horse's mouth—and asked Giddu if I could speak with his wife along with the family friend who mediated most recently. With his approval, I spoke with his wife over the phone, and met with her in person at their family friends' place. The messages that came from all of them remained the same, that he tended to like men more than women. Guddy detailed all her findings from when she married him to me.

I confronted him with this, teasing him gently about many pink storage boxes in his shop, and various multicolored clothes and jackets that he placed for sale within. He was vehement in his denial that he was gay as I labored to explain to him that it's simply genetic, a difference in how some of us are constituted, quite common all over the world, and not something to be troubled about.

There clearly was something a good bit more feminine about him. He appeared more artistic, expressive, intelligent, generally neat in his habits, and his curio shop undoubtedly could not be mistaken for a man-cave.

He was quite the successful entrepreneur, negotiating all his agreements with marketplaces and retail conventions, and seemed to possess an aptitude for working harder than I would have expected him to. But I chalked it all to his sense of responsibility—for he had, on his own, elevated the station of his family. He overcame limitations of a father who drank a lot more than he showed responsibility toward children, helped all his sisters gain their education, and married them off himself. I could see many things in him reflecting qualities I too worked hard to develop.

Yet, a bit of input I received—from his mother, as she and her husband prepared to return to India—troubled me, for she blurted out to me, "But he won't sleep with his wife!" I assured his mother that things would eventually work out—or so I hoped. Perhaps he was just not happy with his wife any more. She was a big girl, something he disliked.

But it wasn't just that. He'd discovered another aspect of his wife, long hidden, revealed when communication between them became argumentative and disrespectful: the foul language she used, the words and phrases that came out of her in a state of uncontrolled anger and frustration. It was coarse, and vulgar, of the lowest form he'd ever came across; he called it *low class* and dreaded it. That put things in an entirely new and difficult perspective.

His situation was similar enough to mine, except that he had to collect his children to spend time with them. His unfurnished apartment was rather drab, and I often asked him to bring his children over to my home to play. As he learned more about my own predicament, he engaged in an intervention effort, holding a good few discussions with my children's mother to help resolve the impasse we faced.

But try as anyone might, hearts and minds hardened over years, and divergent in their directions, do not easily come together, and I was not looking to change things in my marriage any more. I appreciated that he tried to help—as I did with his situation. Things are more complicated in such lives than can be expressed in a few pages, or changed with a few discussions and compromises.

Nevertheless, accommodation seemed the best way to go. I spoke often with him about catering to his wife's wishes and aspirations. She was eager to vacate the house they lived in, purchased at the peak of the market, and now at only half its purchase price in market value. This was a good opportunity for them to do something together, to make a decision for a change in their family's direction that they both could be happy with. I asked her to let him, as the husband of the family and a businessman, lead this task of finding a new home that they could all move to. He pursued this with some eagerness, and did find a couple of good houses to move to, away from the neighborhood where his family had descended into a bad social situation. But try as we might, she was not amenable to his selections. Nor was he comfortable with her choices—in part because of a realtor she favored, his cousin's wife, who didn't seem to care much for his expectations.

I had the misfortune of seeing this cousin once at his shop, where this fellow was strong-arming him to choose from one of the homes his wife had located, which he had no interest in pursuing. When I interjected in that matter, this relative aggressively challenged me, "WHO ARE YOU? WHO ARE YOU TO SPEAK FOR HIM? I am his cousin, his family. Who are you?" I rose from the computer chair in his office that I was seated on, and asked him to meet me out in the street, where I could show him who I was more freely. Suffice it to say that the arrogance and this urgency of self-interest shown by such family members roused the demons in me, and I found it necessary to quell the insistence shown by this aggressive individual.

Instead, I walked out of Giddu's shop, pointing out to him that with characters like this cousin and the realtor wife involved in his family affairs, he could find his ability to get along with Guddy much diminished. His cousin's wife telephoned him, threatening to complain to the Dilbut cops for having intimidated her husband, calling him names and cussing him out roundly.

Guddy eventually selected and bought a home in the same neighborhood where her social network existed, and did so through this realtor wife who, on a few occasions, offended Giddu despite being family. He gladly signed all papers she needed him to so as to have no association whatsoever with this new place of hers. Though she seemed overtly to desire that he move to this new home, it was obvious that he harbored no desire to move to a place she'd acquired without his willing participation in the decision.

All our investigations into home buying, sharing of costs and capital, and low mortgage interest rates at that point in time, planted a seed in my mind about my predicament as well. I suggested that my children's mother refinance our second home that she now claimed for herself, and that she do so without me so I'd have no legal connection to that home—which was what she desired, that the place be *hers* and hers alone. I initiated a refinancing arrangement with a mortgage loan company, withdrawing from the loan application at an advanced stage so she could continue with the process.

Though the loan institution insisted on having me as a co-signor, I chose to sign away my claim to the original capital invested into the second home, amounting to $50,000/-, and more in loan-closing fees, so my children's mother would now not only have her own home, but also gain the $50,000/- that she demanded, taken out from the family, all to herself. My good friend Giddu negotiated this for me, for I could no longer speak with my children's mother.

He cautioned me repeatedly against it, advising me that I should also get a release from the kids' mother disclaiming her ownership of the home that the children and I stayed in. But this I did not pursue for reasons I cannot explain—perhaps because I've never really considered any of these possessions as my own, but rather thought of them as belonging to the family, the next generation. I've never, ever, carried anything from any place that I have departed from other than the clothes on my back and meager personal items.

A good American friend, Sandra, a travel business entrepreneur, who shared office space with me years ago, expressed this sentiment succinctly and with finality once, "A coffin has no pockets." She was, at that point, considerably closer to that final state we all get to eventually.

Nevertheless, was it wise to sign away a house, and the substantial capital invested in it, to the children's mother? Will she permit others legal authority, over this gift to my children, in the future? I couldn't know the many implications of this action, but hoped that the underlying good intentions would prevent further conflict. Was I again falling into the trap of idealistic thoughts, expectations, and actions?

Another in Distress

Giddu coming to me for assistance, and the activities we engaged in to-gether had, in an unusual way, substituted for the camaraderie and commiseration I engaged in with court-mandated classes. Identifying with difficulties he experienced, I helped him in any manner I could, including with fixing his shop computer, a far easier task than fixing the domestic discord he and his family had fallen into.

Try as I might, in many joint discussions with his wife Guddy, I could not bridge the gulf between them, or get them to work together as a family instead of the individualistic pursuits they engaged in. Guddy insisted on taking the children to a Sunday church service that Giddu detested, for it was organized by a group where his social humiliation would be a constant reminder. She also worked nights, as a nurse, which paid her well, but gave her little time to take care of children in holiday activities. That responsibility fell upon him. She wasn't keen to change her routine either. He, for his part, took on a second job working late nights, which he claimed was needed to augment his income from shop activities. There was little to do together as family. Not that either of them had much desire for such activities anyway.

She planned to bring her parents over to stay with her and help with taking care of her children. These in-laws did not respect him much, and he detested them too. These complexities of their family life were beyond that which any external participant could address in discussions with either of them.

Nevertheless, he found solace in similarities in our respective situations, and appeared to take to my own inability to address my children's mother by name. He adopted my words to refer to his wife as well, calling her a '*Kutti-galude Amma*,' which, in our shared mother tongue, translated to the mother of the children. We had other terms for these spouses, of course, '*Aa Pennuh*,' or 'that woman,' a term I used often, and '*Pishachuh*,' roughly translated as 'demon-ghost' that he preferred. We joked about our respective kids' mothers and their selfish pursuits, and laughed about our woes, our predicaments, and our woeful selves.

· · ·

A young man worked part time in Giddu's shop. He was a quiet, less than sociable individual, of Indian ethnicity, who preferred not to mingle much with customers, but nevertheless generated great sales numbers for him. Polite and unobtrusive, he seemed to blend in as one of the pieces of furniture in Giddu's office. An older woman, small, good-looking, and motherly in demeanor, presumably related to this young employee, also came by on occasion. They'd leave the shop together after the young employee's work was done.

He introduced her to me as a friend he met though the prior owner of this shop that he now owned. She worked in another shop at the marketplace where he organized his seasonal sales stall. Over time, he shared with me her troubling tale of domestic discord, for I'd drop in occasionally to find her sitting in the back office of the shop, engaged in earnest conversation with him, and often in tears.

Monty—her nickname for a longer Indian name—married when she was barely nineteen years of age and just beginning college. After marriage, she abandoned her educational pursuits, devoting her life to her husband and his tyrannical mother as was often the case with Indian families. Her husband completed his master's degree in America and worked for more than two decades in the Information Technology industry. They had two sons, **Param**, the elder son who worked part-time in the shop, and a younger boy in the 9th grade at a local high school.

Some years ago, Monty's husband cultivated an extramarital affair with a Caucasian American divorcee, known to the family, who often visited them at their house. This began as friendly assistance on her husband's part when the other woman passed through challenges in her divorce circumstances. Both Monty and her husband attempted to intervene and help. Their involvement led to continued interactions between Monty's husband and this damsel in distress. Monty soon determined that this relationship between her husband and the other woman had grown into an affair. She nevertheless kept a brave face for the sake of her family, tolerating his untoward behavior for a long time.

The situation had now become intolerable because her husband, unemployed for over two years in an ongoing economic recession, spent more time with the other woman than at home with family. To make matters worse, they had invested in a couple of additional homes that were now in peril of repossession by banks because they'd missed payments on mortgage loans. To sell these homes before the banks took over them, her husband took to staying alone at one of these places, coming home to visit his family infrequently. That he engineered a measure of privacy and freedom by this move didn't escape Monty.

All of this caused great stress in their family. Her son Param lost any respect he had for his father and desired only that he stay away. The younger boy, who was attached to his father and alike him in many respects, was torn between his parents. He acted out by not eating, or crying incessantly late into the night.

Monty's husband would on occasion take the younger boy away with him to help him ready the other homes to be sold. He was adept at such handiwork and trained his younger son to be so as well. These trips out helped the child, but the absence of his father at home hurt him. He fell behind in classes and homework, while his elder brother Param, in college for a difficult Mathematics degree, often wasted his time at home playing on an XBOX gaming device for hours at a time.

Monty did most of the chores at home and worked in a sales role at the marketplace to help augment the family's income from welfare payments collected by her husband. So Monty cried, and did so often. A simple girl, who sacrificed college education at nineteen, and devoted her life to family, now watched helplessly as her family disintegrated.

To Giddu and me, Monty was the antithesis of our errant spouses, in devotion to husband and family, and in her love for her children much beyond herself. Though many tried to intervene in her marital situation, and help change her husband's individualistic path toward a more family-oriented approach, there had been no change in him. I had also been approached, by the friend who brought Giddu to me, to talk to Monty's husband about possible assignments, for I too persevered in the IT field and worked on start-up efforts of my own. I spoke with her husband, before I came to know her, and quickly reached the conclusion, in a single and brief conversation, that he'd have a hard time finding a job or partnership. Hence we knew what Monty was dealing with at home.

When visiting with Giddu and Monty at the marketplace one fall day, I observed Monty's employer admonish her about her diffident approach to her family's situation. But Monty held faith in traditional ways, and hoped that God would help change her circumstances. It helped her to talk these things over with Giddu. I took note that he was glad to talk with her, and always ready to help her in any manner he could. She was a great cook, and often brought Indian gourmet preparations for her son, that he that I sometimes got to share in as well. I visited his shop more often then.

He called me one such evening and asked that I drop in at his shop as soon as I could. At the shop, I found Monty inconsolable, crying buckets, and engaged in vigorous argument with him at the same time. She'd been served divorce papers handwritten by her husband and submitted to court. He had the outrageous temerity to come hand her the papers himself. She was beside herself with grief, unable to comprehend that her husband of more than twenty-one years, the father of her two growing boys, someone she loved dearly and who cared deeply for her, could precipitate such a terrible event in her life.

In her simple mind, her husband and family formed the edifices to which she bound herself and her life. A realization that these entities of her devotion were now turning against her was quite beyond her understanding. It wasn't that she hadn't encountered such an event in the past—she did go through a difficult breakup of her brother and his wife back in India—but that it was happening to her—that was far too much for her to bear. Giddu was upset too, trying to get her to calm down enough to respond to his queries rationally. All I could do then was listen to anguish pouring out from another distressed soul.

Monty's explanation of what transpired was excruciatingly painful to hear. She insisted that a priest cast a black magic spell on her husband when he visited India many years ago. She recounted her husband's earnest explanation that the priest informed him that his association with her family had been most inauspicious, which led to the appearance of a mark of ill omen on his body. A 'Keel ka nishaan' in her language from a northwest state of India, a mark of a nail on his chest. This mark and the bad omen would dissipate only if he eliminated bad influences, that led to such a mark on himself, from his life. And, that he had held this thought in his mind for long, deciding only now to act upon it, for the bad omen resulted in much grief in his life as their present circumstances attested.

Monty and her family were Hindu and from an orthodox sub-division of this way of life. Given the simplicity of folks in the region she was raised in, such beliefs, in bad omens, black marks, and magic, were quite common. Giddu couldn't bear to listen to this any more, and yelled, "*Gaon se aayi ho kya?*" in her language—which was—"Did you come from a village? And, are you so uneducated as to believe such horse manure?" Monty sniffled. She insisted such things come true, that one cannot dismiss them as mere superstition. What was most painful to me was that in view of the unmistakable selfishness of her husband's actions, precipitating a split convenient to himself, she sought justification, for his conduct, to exonerate him.

It reminded me of how my children's mother continued to eulogize Bert Burgess, her source of affection and intimacy, despite admitting that he too shared responsibility for her affair and the consequent split in my family. Monty blamed everything and everyone else—her mother-in-law, the black magic priest, even herself—and refused to see what was glaringly obvious. It was the awe-inspiring power of blind faith, and infatuation, in deluding oneself, in overcoming all rational thought.

Monty's situation was clearly more difficult than others we'd come across. She was neither pragmatic, nor equipped with the knowledge and experience needed to deal with matters confronting her. That, and their rather impoverished circumstances, explained the handwritten, self-authored divorce papers her husband served upon her.

More of what she faced was revealed upon a careful reading of these papers the next day, at Monty's place, with her friend and Giddu's prior business partner participating. The split, were she to agree to it as specified in the papers served, could leave her with no means for survival in the country. It would require that she leave America, and return to India to live with her aging parents. It would also give her husband control of the children and family assets he desired, and give him the freedom to pursue any romantic partnership he wanted.

The patent unfairness of what the divorce filing proposed seemed to shock Monty. But it wasn't surprising to me or her friend Pamela who lived just a few houses down from Monty's place. Pamela, also Caucasian, taller and bigger, and a very good friend to her, did not like Monty's husband much. He reciprocated this sentiment, blaming Monty for heeding the '*gori*—white female—instead of him.

The divorce filing called for an effective response. Monty needed to face a battle for survival, and for the welfare of her children who depended on her more than her husband. Her friend Pamela had some experience with such matters, having gone through two divorces in the past herself. She promised to go through each itemized demand in the papers served, and provide opposing facts and details, in Monty's favor, in accordance with the law to the extent she knew it.

With little to no financial resources available, Monty's response would have to be crafted without legal assistance and filed in court herself. She'd have to request that her response be served by the court, which I knew meant delivery to her husband by the court's process servers, who often were on-duty police officers.

We worked the next day diligently on facts and details compiled by Pamela, with Monty's tearful help, and Monty and I headed out to the Superior Court where we filled in her response form. We made sure to demand, respectfully, anything and everything state law permitted. We requested a listing and valuation of all assets held jointly by her and her husband, which included two apartments in India that he failed to mention in his filing. We asked for their financial assets to be frozen, so Monty could hold money needed for her family's expenses, and for custody of the children until final determination by the court. I added a handwritten request to the court to allow Monty more time, of a month, toward preparing a comprehensive response to add to the one presently filed, citing financial and employment limitations along with childcare as reasons. We accomplished all this by paying just the court fees of $240/-, which, to Monty, was a month's grocery money.

The handwritten, cogent plea to the court was not because Monty needed time. It was essentially a message to her husband that Monty now had help, and could meet any legal challenge head on. No longer could he assume this was a village girl he or his mother could run roughshod over, who had only the *gori* to help her. No, the cavalry had arrived to respond in a similar yet stronger manner than that with which the attack on a helpless damsel had begun.

Monty was frightened by the divorce papers that had been served not only because the papers comprised a legal action, but also because they came from her husband. She knew her husband to be quite clever in such matters, having watched him win a civil action in the past when a partner defrauded him in a construction deal.

Besides, despite her dutiful conduct toward her mother-in-law, including massaging her legs on command, and being at her beck and call whenever she visited them in America, Monty could not endear herself to this dominant parent and be recognized by her as a good 'bahu,' a beloved daughter-in-law. She knew her husband remained under his mother's control, doing most everything with her approval. There was no doubt that this in-law did not like her much; help from that quarter could not be forthcoming.

But backed into a corner, with the survival of her family threatened, Monty, like any of even the most docile herd animals, saw the need to point her horns and effectively resist. It was her good fortune, perhaps resulting from her gregarious nature and interactions, that she found Giddu, Pamela, and me, with at least three divorces and experience from many lawsuits under our collective belts, beside her as she went through this process.

A Battle Joined

In conversations about reconciliation, Monty spoke of an elderly man she and her husband knew from their ethnic community, who she thought could help resolve the conflict she faced. This seemed a good time to request his assistance to put an end to the divisive legal battle faced by the family. Monty promised to contact him and ask him to intervene. There was no social grapevine for us to employ here.

Meanwhile, she remained fearful about what her husband might do upon receiving her response to the divorce petition. She had experienced some violence from him, one instance in particular observed by her elder son Param, when an argument escalated to her raising the topic of his other woman. He had slapped her then, in an angry and uncontrolled reaction, and walked out of the house. The matter had not gone any further then.

In view of recent developments, we recommended that she call local law-enforcement and ask of them what steps might be taken, which she did do. A female Dilbut cop came by her place, and learning of these details of her situation, supported by Pamela as well, she advised that Monty petition for a protective order, to deny her husband access to their home, to ensure there could be no opportunity for actions leading to further harm.

Monty was reluctant to apply for a protective order against her husband, for it was, to her, strong action against him in this battle. It was something she did not wish to do with her future and the future of her children in the balance. Yet Giddu and I worked to convince her of such action being common in any divorce proceeding, citing the example of his wife's attempts when she filed for a divorce. And that given incidents of violence, witnessed by her son, there was a good chance of such an order being granted. After much convincing, by her friend Pamela as well, she resolved to petition the court for a protective order.

Monty wrote and filed this action in court herself, and obtained a hearing the same afternoon. I heard of the petition results from Giddu. He praised Monty and Pamela, who appeared at the hearing with Param, and overcame a judge's reluctance to grant the plea without a police report accompanying it. It was Monty's resolute engagement in the process that resulted in the protective order being granted.

This was a big step forward for Monty, an uneducated, traditional girl, who stood up for herself and obtained what was needed from the system on her own. I thought this was a turning point for Param as well, for he must recognize a determined mother standing up, for what was right, against a family bully. Now her husband could not saunter in anytime he desired into their home, partake of food prepared by her, and walk out with their younger son. A phone call to arrange his visit would be a first necessary step; Monty regained a measure of control over her household.

She nevertheless prepared her husband's favorite dishes and took them along with her younger son when she'd go over to drop him. This was the same interaction Guddy continued with Giddu, in giving him food prepared and packed neatly, when he collected his kids. Monty continued to maintain the family bond she shared with her husband, which he surely noticed. I feared he might perceive that as her weakness, and cautioned Monty against showing excessive concern for his well-being, particularly since an adversarial process had begun.

Some days later, Monty conveyed to Giddu and I that her husband received the legal reply she'd filed, and had remarked about the handwritten request, for additional time, which had also been granted. She worried about how hard he took the protective order which was in place. In the past, she explained to us, her husband had engaged in civil litigation against an ex-business partner, and had won a settlement. But he was not familiar with failure in court proceedings. He dismissed the efforts of the elderly family friend, who tried to intervene at Monty's request, refusing to speak with him. Though he now was careful in speech and interactions with her, she was afraid the worst was yet to come.

Giddu and I worked to bolster her courage, chatting with her often about being prepared for next steps in her battle. Monty did mention that the family had about $40,000/- saved in cash in a bank account, and a few gold coins deposited there for safe keeping. These assets could be secured with assistance from a lawyer who could subpoena bank records, and file court documents requiring that liquid assets be shared equally by both for survival purposes. When Monty vacillated, complaining in character, "*Mei yeh sub kaise karoongi?*"—how will I do all this—I ventured to express anger that she appeared so weak and needlessly fearful. We pushed her to research family lawyers, in the local area, that she and Pamela could call and choose from.

Motivated, she found a local lawyer, Biff Dibble, and asked that I accompany her to a meeting with him to see if he would be a good choice. Though Biff Dibble was rather insensitive in his comments, as for instance suggesting that Monty date me—an available individual given my spouse had in effect separated from me—to find love again, he did promise to get the necessary steps done, including discovery demands and a hearing to secure and divide the liquid assets between the parties, in short order. He agreed to do all this for a lump sum payment of $3000/- for legal fees and expenses, following which she could decide on a continuance of the lawsuit. That, and small initial install-ment payments, seemed quite reasonable and helpful, and I gave her a thumbs up for this lawyer.

Monty and Giddu often came by my place, where they'd sometimes see my children's mother in the evenings helping the children with their activities. Though Monty greeted her courteously, and did speak with her on occasion, she realized and respected that the impasse that existed in my life could not be addressed by any other than the actors themselves, and did not intervene in any way. Perhaps that was her humble and unobtrusive presence, which mani-fested in her son Param too, or reticence in view of the dire situation she her-self faced. My spouse showed them none of the hospitality customary in our culture, and more often than not ignored their presence. We expected nothing else from her in any case.

My daughter, on the other hand, enjoyed having Giddu's kids over, while my son, older and bordering on becoming a teen, did not care much either way. Monty's children, a good few years older than these kids, couldn't relate to them much.

The increase in social contact seemed beneficial generally. A plan was hatched to conduct a Thanksgiving gathering at Giddu's place. He appeared in-tent upon making it happen, promising to get his wife to agree, and to work with him on it, which I thought to be a positive development for him. Every-one was invited; we knew some of our family members would most definitely not come.

• • •

At home, I faced varying difficulties as the impasse continued. One evening, seated thoughtfully in solitude in the family room, I was asked to re-veal my thoughts. My son, who often had to know everything that was going on, was the curious questioner. I told him he wouldn't like my thoughts, but re-alized what he really didn't like was that I was seated on his video game playing couch, which prevented him from playing his favorite games. Games I disap-proved of.

"Can you go think someplace else?" demanded my son. "What are you thinking?"

"I don't approve of you and your sister going to social gatherings your mother and Parvathi aunty arrange," I replied.

That riled my son. "Why? You disapprove of anything we do."

"I don't think that social gathering, at Parvathi auntie's, is a good influence on you," I explained. "She—Parvathi aunty—has advised your mother for more than five years now. That hasn't brought out anything good."

"Why?" he persisted.

"I think many there, and Parvathi aunty, are materialistic, status conscious, and uneducated."

"You are materialistic!" retorted my son. "You are status conscious! You are uneducated!" That was his typical response to any criticism from me, especially when it involved him, or his mother.

When it came to his mother, and my objections to company she kept, my children rose to her defense with unreasoning aggression—and I spoke firmly with my son, denied him TV privileges for the night, and sent him to his room. Why did they so often take her side? Was it because I invoked the criticism? She clearly bonded more with them since my attention was focused on business efforts.

Also, to be fair, Parvathi had been a great help with the crisis my family went through, often taking good care of my children. Yet she and John enjoyed reveling in their roles as the local host and hostess. They held parties for a small social group, and planned and arranged community activities with religious overtones for this predominantly Christian gathering. I avoided these parties when possible, given my own multicultural preferences and unaffiliated spirituality, but my children's mother took them to these events anyway.

My disagreement with my son, and firmness with him, led him to complain to his mother as she bathed him—yes, even when he'd grown to almost be a teen—"I hate him. I wish he were dead." To which his mother gave her typical response, "He is your Dad. That we cannot change. Just walk away from him." Dime wisdom from the intellectually penniless.

Their conversations were loud and the bathroom door open, so they knew I could hear everything that was said. But for the very first time, I heard something that troubled me greatly. "I'll buy you a PS3 if you come over to *my* house," said his mother. "I don't buy anything nice in my house because you are not there." Bribing a child— so it seemed to me—to change a family situation, to suit herself, seemed beyond extraordinary. Immature guidance I could understand and tolerate, but bribes? How far would this go? And what next? Accusations of abuse of the children, planted in their minds by her that could then be brought against me in a court of law? My son would never do such a thing, despite any disciplinary action I might resort to, but I wasn't so sure about my daughter, well under her mother's influence, who was far too young to know any better.

I shared these concerns with Giddu one afternoon at his shop—that he wasn't far off the mark in his revulsion at the language used by his spouse—to hurt, to accomplish their ends, anything was fair game for our spouses. My son's teacher's words came to me again, "They can be vicious... Be careful." I had not given that bit of advice as much consideration as I should have.

My daughter was less prone to such material inducements. I asked her if she experienced problems with her mother that required resolution, but she said she did not want me to intervene. It was never an easy discussion between the adults in the home, and I felt the children understood that rather too well.

How could I help my children under such circumstances? How could I mitigate the manipulation practiced by a mother on such young minds? Could I approach the state's child protective services for help, to provide recommendations on parenting to the mother? Wariduna's CPS was said to pay little attention to requests for help, and often fall behind in its mandated duties. How could I resort to them for help, to guide a parent? To correct one recklessly conveying her prejudices and lack of comprehension to children, building disrespect in them for their other parent?

Do our children not need a father's discipline and guidance, and a mother's gentle care simultaneously? Do they not need to see adults working together, guiding them firmly? Are my children now destined to become the typical results of a broken home, lost, lacking in identity, and without clear purpose in their lives? Or can I turn this on its head, and help them build strength and resilience, in this great adversity the family faced?

Once, in an argument where the kids' mother had gone so far as to insult my late father, I recall being so troubled that I conveyed to her, in writing, "*Do not disrespect a deceased person, my father, and memories of him, to serve your purposes. Do not teach my children such disrespect. This behavior is not welcome in this house. You do not know, and will never know, the esteem and affection that both I and my mother have had, and still have, for that great man.*" This brought out an acknowledgment from her that what she'd said was hurtful, but she twisted that against me to say that just as it had hurt me, names I call my son could hurt him too. I did inherit my father's anger, and his habit of sometimes letting frustration show in descriptions such as *moron*, or *insolent boy*, but there it ended. She on the other hand called my father, a man she'd never met, an *abuser*, because of his strict military discipline that I could not conform to, which I had mistakenly shared with this slippery shrew. I could see glimpses of what my son's school teacher meant about viciousness.

But the condition of Monty's children was much more severe. Param seemed listless, lacking the necessary help with his difficult maths course. He often engaged in video games to while away his time. He did play basketball whenever he had the chance, with a local team, but blamed his father for not giving him encouragement and support to achieve more along that path. Param appeared to have only such thoughts—hoop dreams—and no other worthy goals, Giddu said to me one day. Nevertheless, he was quite a capable worker who gave him some of the best hours of work and sales he could expect at his shop.

Monty, who had not progressed beyond her first year of college, seemed quite concerned, but lacked any thought as to how to help him. Her younger child had begun asking her about the legal action ongoing between her and his father—who evidently keyed him up. She did not know how to deal with that either, and could tell him only that it was his father who started it.

I offered to help Param with his math challenges, if I could, and found it beyond my capabilities. Instead, I resolved to help him face employment better—for he seemed good at managing things at Giddu's shop—and asked Monty to push him to ask for help on his résumé. I too reminded him of the need for a résumé whenever I met him at Giddu's shop. He did eventually send me a note asking for tips. I sent him my older son's résumé, prepared for him as he began a hunt for jobs and internships in India, as an example. Param filled in his information into the template, and I helped polish it into a one-page version any reasonable employer could appreciate.

With Giddu as a reference, now armed with a strong résumé he too could be proud of, I encouraged him to begin applying to assignments in larger stores, and banks given his skill at math, even before he finished his degree. We could do little to help Monty's younger child, who, with greater attachment to his father, was now more disturbed than ever before, and was struggling with his school work.

I talked with Giddu often about his kids too, about ensuring they continued to respect their mother despite all that transpired in the family. This was something I approached with near religious zeal. The sins of the parents must not become punishment for innocents, their growing children. Still, of all the battles faced, this was the hardest, for it required self-control beyond my capabilities. And yet this was the battle I knew must be joined, and must be won—a battle that could perhaps bring adversarial adults together in common purpose.

This goes against much of the understanding and social practices prevalent in the global society we all live in: a sense of entitlement to pursue happiness individually, a default acceptance of trickle-down benefits, and a dominance of concerns of an individual self above family or the larger community. But isn't this worth striving for, worth sacrificing oneself for? And it also goes against the prevalent litigious habit in society, of seeking a measure of satisfaction for oneself to mitigate or avoid conflict.

What of innumerable examples throughout history that point to a self-sacrificing path as the greater good? And what of the fabled adjudicating example of Solomon, where a true parent would rather see a child thrive than see the child torn between individuals claiming parenthood?

Giddu, fortunately for his children, was of a like mind on these matters, and did appreciate my thoughts. Yet he spoke with sadness about his children not being able to enjoy an active social life, other than getting to play occasionally with my children and other kids nearby. And about the hardships of his transformed existence.

Small Victories and Celebrations

Monty found the numerous documents and letters from her lawyer exhausting, and often asked me to review such material that came by. Discovery requests to her husband produced many documents of interest, such as bank statements, and income tax returns, but information about two apartments they owned in India remained to be disclosed. The income tax returns showed large sums of money paid nearly every year to a religious entity back in India, '*Amma Ki Dwara.*' She did not remember such large payments made, regularly, as indicated in their income tax filings.

I cheered her up, pointing to these questionable items of information that could be used effectively against her husband in any court hearing, and suggested she query him about these transactions if she were to talk with him. He couldn't fail to recognize the damaging impact of irregularities in his income tax returns, or of his non-disclosure of property holdings, in a judicial proceeding requiring that all his transactions be revealed.

These discoveries could not only have him at a disadvantage in divorce proceedings, they could also pose him further problems in the possibility of investigations by tax authorities—once his statements, under oath, got on the record. That raised her mood a great deal. I suspected that much of this would find its way back to her husband either directly through her, or through their younger son who sought to know more about these legal proceedings. While she may not have realized it then, all this was in fact aimed at getting her husband to drop the legal action between them.

Thanksgiving week arrived soon thereafter. Guddy called us for assistance with the barbecue stove they stored in the backyard. With just a day remaining, and Giddu unable to figure out why it wouldn't light, I was called in to help. Though I had no prior experience with such stoves, he and I went over to his wife's place to inspect and clean the stove as best as we could.

The regulator appeared to be the prime suspect, for I couldn't blow any air through it. We decided on a dangerous experiment of punching a hole through it to test everything else. A hole permitting air flow in both directions through the device did not solve the problem. The hose was the final thing to replace, and we now also needed a new regulator. I headed over to a local store, while Giddu headed elsewhere to obtain food items to prepare in the afternoon. Suffice it to say we did get replacement parts, but given the state of disrepair of the stove, we borrowed a neighbor's stove the next day, and moved it over to her place.

For the first time, in a while, I saw Giddu and his wife working together in the kitchen, readying food for the guests expected that evening. They cooked the food, and I helped as well. The social gathering comprised four families with some missing spouses: them and their children, me and my children, Monty and her younger child, and our common friend, who'd brought their conflict to my attention, with his family. It was a motley mixture of folks, and a lively gathering, where I saw Monty's younger child for the first time, a taciturn young boy with a strong frame and the largest workman's hands I've ever seen in a child. It was calming to see our hosts working happily together. Their children were, needless to say, the happiest that evening.

•   •   •

It was around that point in time that I received a disturbing voice mail message on my mobile phone. I called in for messages, after finding three missed calls from my children's mother on the call record, and heard the following:

Indistinguishable noises of the phone being knocked about, and silence, with what sounded like breathing.

"aaOhhhhhhhhhhh!" came a throaty scream in her voice.

A pause, and then her sharp, short intake of breath.

Followed by a lusty, ecstatic laugh from her, "He…he…hea…"

"I'll say this, that went fast…" she said, her voice indistinct, fading at the end.

"Yyeeahh…" agreed a male voice.

More sounds in a short period of silence.

"Ohhhhhhhh!" the male exploded.

A pause, and the male exclaimed, "OH!" There were sounds of a scuffle, and something falling, ending the recording.

From the kids' mother's mobile phone she carried on her person, to mine, in the middle of the work day, immediately following two other quick calls terminated with no messages, this recording seemed suspicious to say the least. Clearly, her phone had been through quite some bumping and grinding that day. The message had been received in her lunch hour, and I couldn't believe what I had listened to. But I had at least two others I could approach to provide opinions on what it comprised. With Giddu away on an errand in the city, I had Monty listen to the recording. She looked at me with concern after listening to it repeatedly.

"You do realize what this is, don't you?" she asked.

I nodded, and we spoke no more.

When Giddu returned that afternoon, Monty and I met him at his shop and had him listen to it as well. After listening to it thrice, he busied himself with things he had been doing in the shop and did not say a word. Under pressure from us both, he blurted, "You know they are having sex, don't you?" It seemed we all had the same impression, and couldn't think of anything else as an innocent explanation for the recording. I guess I didn't care to think of any other explanation for the outrageous event, and informed my friends that I'd report it to the authorities as an instance of extreme harassment.

Giddu was concerned such a step could lead to an escalation in the conflict in my family, and a legal action, but I was determined to get local law-enforcement's take on this unwanted contact that truly caused me much distress. I gave it a few days, knowing he would no doubt work to elicit an explanation from my children's mother. The weak explanation that came along—that the phone had been in her work coat, and could have turned on during an ordinary office conversation—wasn't convincing to any of us. I had reviewed this possibility a good few times in my mind before dismissing it.

Calling the Dilbut police on their non-emergency line, I requested a meeting to furnish them with this evidence of unwanted contact and harassment. I was prepared for inaction on their part, and in fact had accepted that result, in my mind, as a better outcome, one that would not cause the family more distress and damage than had already occurred. Nevertheless, I did desire to obtain their opinion of the recording, and to document its occurrence.

A Dilbut cop, almost as tall as me, appearing to be twice my girth, presumably due to his protective vest and diet, came in to the interview room. He played and listened to the recording on my phone a good few times. He then smiled and agreed that it was damning, and sounded much like a lusty ruckus. But he could not agree that it was intentional, or that it constituted harassment, since no protective order existed. He also conveyed his judgment that my desire, at present, was perhaps not to get the children's mother in any trouble.

I wondered if I had been too transparent in my conversation with him. I spoke instead of difficulties my children went through in the current situation, and tears flowed as I talked about their confusion and unhappiness. Unmanly of me, crying in the presence of a tougher man, complaining about a wayward wife who indulged in activities harmful to the family—those were my thoughts then, but they remained unexpressed.

I told him about my children's mother's repeated threat, "Just one call to the prosecutor and you'll be gone," asserting that I considered it prosecutorial misconduct, and asked for identification of the officer she referred to. I spoke with him about my arrest record becoming a long-term sentence for me, since corporate employment would be impossible upon a background check. He said it would be taken away from my record in five years. I wondered if he knew whether anyone in the industry would hire someone unemployed in his field of expertise for five years. I suppose my thoughts and speech reflected only the pain in my heart and mind, not a desire to have the mother prosecuted.

His skill in reading my mind correctly, and the circumstances narrated, did not escape my notice. Perhaps Dilbut had awakened to the complexity of my situation, given the number of interactions with them, and assigned an experienced cop to service my request. His evaluation of my state of mind, confirmed by my statements, probably also convinced him that there was no danger to the children's mother or her unknown partner in her recorded act. A fruitful exercise in applying knowledge of the theory of mind on this cop's part.

I desired that they comprehend the reality of my circumstances, which they had given little or no consideration to when arresting me, and the eventual consequences of their actions. But all he offered was that I could petition their court and obtain a protective order that could then permit cops to act if any such further harassment came along. He wished me luck, and escorted me out of the station when I left. They could offer little else—how could I have expected them to?

· · ·

In a highly litigious society, where everyone risks being sued for actions outside their purview or authority, law-enforcement, prosecution counsel, and courts work carefully within defined boundaries. I pen these thoughts, Priyavani, so you may view your predicament from this perspective, perhaps comprehend your own situation better, and determine what you can do, independent of the typical legal advice, to help change your family's difficult circumstances. The police do what they are required to—stop bad folks, and protect the public. At times, they too misbehave, or employ excessive force, and find ways to conceal such actions.

And human factors built into the system compel them to go after big game, after that which has more impact on their careers and that of their superiors. They go for sure convictions, where they can readily demonstrate that laws have been broken, and go as far as they can to portray facts in a manner favorable to winning convictions, notwithstanding the need to rise above the matter, or to recognize other perspectives of the situations they come across.

You fell into the system's machinery probably because of your many instances of contact with them, where they couldn't identify the one you pointed an accusatory finger to as their potential target. I too had many complex interactions with cops here in Dilbut—and the circumstances, my own behavior, and effective emotional displays by my children's mother made me the bad guy they could arrest and prosecute with relative ease. Besides, they are conditioned to be on the lookout for violent domestic males.

I guess cops in New York were similarly on the lookout for circumstances involving exploited domestic help. It is inconceivable that Veer Batata or others in the US Department of State had any political, pecuniary, or personal reason to charge and prosecute you. They employed a grand jury of citizens assembled for the purpose, who indicted you solely on the basis of sound evidence available to support charges against you. It is, nevertheless, true, that once you fell into the machinery, you were sure to be indicted.

Was it not far too soon for you to celebrate the easy dismissal of your first indictment, and for your father to then assert, "It was all lies!" to the media? Indictments are *not* handed down, commonly, for any corrupt purpose or falsified information in a nation of laws. We strive to maintain a convincing semblance of having followed laws here, and I am sure it is not just a semblance, but indeed reality, in your situation.

What could one expect a judge to do, when presented with your indictment contested with diplomatic immunity granted before it was handed down, but dismiss it? The urgent and intense political pressure from your country, to have you granted full diplomatic immunity in place of work-related consular immunity, couldn't be ignored. Nor could such a request be refused, given that such action could appear rather vindictive. Hence that was granted first, and your indictment handed to you afterward. This was done with full knowledge in the system, and all involved, that you would hence be allowed to leave, just as in a number of other such incidents here. But this isn't the old wild west, Priyavani. Actions begun against a law-breaking individual aren't brushed under a carpet, or shelved in cold-case files, when such an individual flees the legal system and its jurisdiction.

You spoke about a maid, her drunken driver husband, and their children as those America received instead of yourself. How do you expect America to justify their presence here without a case against you that requires their testimony? The laws here require that they be deported back to India if your prosecution is abandoned. You must understand this. And, with Seeta's national identity now denied by her country, combined with the court order from India demanding her non-bailable arrest, you surely do understand that it is inconceivable for her to be deported to face certain persecution. Seeta's future, her status here, and your prosecution are inextricably linked at present.

What then could you have expected of Veer Batata, but a reconvening of a grand jury to reinstate an indictment on a person with no immunity here? What Batata, a man of the law, has done here is only within the law, based upon known, verifiable evidence, in keeping with what he needs to do to protect a victim and her family. A family the system came in contact with, one that has evidently been victimized in a manner unacceptable to people everywhere. This is in accordance with the American spirit of justice: we welcome those who fight injustice, who take risks to fight such oppression, and combat those who harm others and attempt to circumvent justice and fairness.

The justice, or more aptly, legal system is by no means efficient or perfect here. One in four incarcerated, a fourth of all humans in jail in the world, are here in America[4]. We have privatized incarceration and private illegal immigrant detention in the nation, a conflict of social and business interest by any other description. But I think the system is aligned acceptably with the ideals of the nation's constitutional framework. It is unbiased, mostly, and is not vindictive.

The humanity of any procedures followed and serving the cause of justice are quite distinct matters that such a legal system isn't designed to address on its own. I'd hope that is where humans come in. But how often do we find people courageous enough to bend laws, go above and beyond, and employ established systems and human tendencies to serve justice?

Knowing this, what do you think you might do, as an ordinary person, to change your family's circumstances? But you cannot speak any more of your continued prosecution by America, or of anything related to events that led to it. You have been restricted under a gag order issued by none other than the Foreign Secretary of your own country.

I do not know if it is unusual—for a civil servant of a democratic country to be expressly ordered to not communicate facts, thoughts, and feelings about a personal circumstance and related prosecution faced; it seems so to me. I suppose this could fall into a category of matters requiring diplomatic silence, given that the Indian government was involved in this debacle. Why do you think you have been deprived of the freedom to express yourself in this painful ordeal? Is it possible that your country may have been embarrassed, and may be further inconvenienced, by statements you or your father may make? Could you, perhaps, be on the wrong side of this matter?

Can you see, Priyavani, that you and your father, and those in your government who worked with you on your predicament, have led to much confusion in the minds of well-meaning, simple people in both countries? I think you have highlighted a cultural gulf between two great democracies of the world. I must write what I comprehend to bridge this most unfortunate, untimely chasm in solidarity between countries that stand for unity, integrity, and justice. More importantly, the innocents harmed by actions of manipulative individuals and oppressive systems need a voice. I hope my thoughts and words serve that purpose.

I can see questions rising, in anger, in your mind, "Who are you? Who are you to speak for me, or for others I deal with?" That would be no different from the questions asked by my friend Giddu's self-serving cousin. Yet, I can claim to be more patient now than when I faced him and invited him out onto the street. I am but an ordinary man, some years older than you, with more

---

4   Chris Jordan, "Turning Powerful Stats Into Art," TED February 2008 presentation

empathy and compassion than the ordinary. And one who has lived and experienced many aspects of both democracies and cultures. These words are meant only to help, with no desire or intention to be judgmental, as were the words to my children's mother when the family began to split despite all my efforts to save it.

I promised my children's mother that I would persevere to bring out the truth, either in legal action in the courts of America, or in the court of public opinion. She too, like you, has broken laws of this country, rules of common morality, and, in my mind, the simple mores of community and humanity. Whether she answers to these charges or not, I would like my children to know the truth when they are old enough to comprehend what transpired. Their mother has spoken of confusion in their minds caused by my behavior in our home. I've promised to set the record straight.

They must know how much their father strove to mitigate harm and bring normality back to their lives. And of how their father stood by them through deprivation, impoverishment, and periods of untold suffering. I am certain they'll question me when they are grown. They may associate difficulties in their lives with the absence of normality in their childhood years. But I do not wish to see them make excuses for their conduct, and blame others for what they go through. I hope they learn from good examples in their own lives, from truthful guidance offered by parents and mentors.

The cycle of selfishness and violence upon innocents must not perpetuate. I cannot bear to see my children become typical products of a broken home. But as you do know, Priyavani, little that occurs is for us to determine. I have realized that all I can do is work to mitigate damage, understand the truth from all perspectives, and convey it in an effective and harmless manner.

Trials and Tribulations

By the time Thanksgiving came along, Monty had been through ups and downs of family circumstance beyond anything she had ever experienced. After handing her the first set of legal papers demanding a divorce, her husband had informed her that he was going to Canada, where his friend lived, to seek software jobs there. Noting and investigating the number that appeared on the home phone's display, when he called their younger son, she discovered that he had instead moved to Atlanta in Georgia, close to where his love-interest, who had caused much discord in her family, moved to the previous year. This troubled her a great deal, but a legal response and related other activities kept her mind off this deception.

He returned in a month or so to face her response filed on her own, and the protective order she had demanded and won in a court hearing. With a lawyer now assisting her, and key discoveries made of misuse of family finances, she had everything she needed to expose his questionable activities in any legal proceeding. A court hearing was scheduled for mid-December.

Giddu, Pamela, and I ensured that Monty made her demands quite clear: unrestricted access to their bank accounts, half of any of her family's liquid assets, and at least one of the apartments in India in her name. Information about these apartments owned remained to be provided by her husband. Upon receiving her response, and discovery requests, he too hired a lawyer. The two lawyers talked and agreed upon matters to be decided in the first court hearing.

She was concerned that he too had hired a lawyer—this could only mean further depletion of the family's resources. But it also indicated diminished confidence on his part in facing the legal challenge ahead. She often repeated her fear that he was skillful in legal matters. I worked to reassure her that the tables were turned in this situation, for he was the defrauding party, and therefore the law will side with her. I hoped she conveyed to him, through her son, her thoughts about questionable aspects of his financial activities.

At the first court hearing, Monty won everything she asked for. The judge ordered that $20,000/- be withdrawn, from cash assets in the family's bank account, and given to her. She was granted possession of one-half of the gold coins that were in a safety deposit box in the bank. Custody of her younger child was given to her as well, with her husband granted visitation rights twice a week. The judge went so far as to order him to give Monty and her young child at least half of anything he earned, through unemployment benefits or any other source. This could help her pay the mortgage on the home the family lived in, and minimize the burden upon her own meager earnings through minimum-wage work.

She promptly pursued her husband, compelling him to withdraw money from the bank, and obtained the $20,000/- that would keep her family afloat. At the bank, upon inspecting the safety deposit box, she found their gold coins missing. He offered no explanation for their absence. That caused Monty much anguish, for she was attached to gold, and those coins were a gift from him. But all of her jewelry was in the safe deposit box, except, again, for a gift her husband gave her. And there was no mention or information about their apartments in India, so additional discovery ordered by the court remained to be completed.

But it is what Monty did after her complete victory that caught us all by surprise. She kept a portion of the $20,000/- with herself, to pay off Biff Dibble, and to support her family for some months, and returned the rest, more than one-half the amount, to her husband. We were all shocked. I recall Giddu yelling at her, "*Paagal ho kya?*"—are you mad—but she explained that she had never dealt with matters of finance in her life, and always trusted her husband in such aspects.

She let her teenage son, who was clearly in much discomfort due to the battle in the family, stay with her husband despite being granted full custody. She said her son was disturbed and sad, and perhaps this—living with his father with whom he identified most—would cheer him up, and help him do better at school. Monty also had the restraining order against her husband dismissed, and said she was thinking of dropping the battle for assets entirely.

Not having obtained any information regarding the apartments in India, which property was identified to her as a safety net for her and her children, I objected vigorously to her plans to drop everything. Yet, it was important that Giddu and I did not always insist upon the *right* things being done by her. A different path taken by her gave us a reason to withdraw gracefully from her complicated family matter. Monty was well in charge of her future now, and I was secretly quite pleased at the transformation in her. I made sure she saw disapproval from us instead. Giddu was certainly livid, asserting that she too was a '*thanded*' like his wife, one who always followed her own wishes despite all wise counsel. I knew his show of anger too was an act, a necessary one given Monty's actions.

• • •

Christmas holidays came along, and since we had gathered for Thanksgiving, no social event had been arranged. I made sure to put a couple of additional presents for Giddu's kids under the tree in my place. My children insisted on seeing that old tree every year. It was of no use explaining to them that this symbolic conifer tree with shiny things hanging on branches came about as a tradition from snowy and cold locations in the world, where icicles form on conifer branches and reflect daylight. And that in dry and arid Wariduna, a Saguaro cactus with a few raised hands and holes in its trunk for cactus wrens might make more sense. They looked for the usual goodies under the tree, and did not care for much else.

This was the first year when presents appeared under my tree for Giddu's kids. They'd become quite close to my daughter and loved to visit. They seemed none the worse for all the confusion in their family, spending time with their father whenever he could pick them up.

There had been an argument between Giddu and Guddy, on which Christmas programs at church or in other social settings his kids would attend, for he detested the small social network that she preferred, a network that labeled him unkindly. He complained about this vigorously to me. The act of complaining dissipated his angst at the situation and there was no flare-up. Getting angry, and expressing it, does replace any thoughts of getting even. He had also received large boxes of gifts for his kids, from friends and relatives far away, which gladdened him a great deal.

One early January evening, Guddy called me to ask if I knew where Giddu was. She expected him to collect their kids, but he had not done so, and she couldn't reach him on his numbers. Promising to find him and let her know, I called his other friend, who had introduced him to me, and Monty, with no results from either. I drove by his shop, finding the mall closed for the night, and then stopped by his apartment without finding any trace of him.

Guddy became quite concerned by this time—she had not been friendly with him after the Christmas argument—and began calling all of her other friends. Monty offered to ride with me as we searched for him, which took us around the various stores in the neighborhood, and even the local cinema theater complexes, without success.

An hour later, as we rode back after our fruitless search, she connected with him on his mobile phone—he said that he'd decided to treat himself to a movie because it was his birthday, and no one here had paid his special day much attention. He walked to the theater complex nearby, which explained why we found his car parked at his apartment.

I suspected it was Guddy who hadn't cared to give his one special day any notice, but said nothing, promising to remember this day the next year. Clearly, his wife ignoring his birthday had hurt him—though he wouldn't admit it. Monty and I made sure to let him know how concerned she was, but he dismissed it as nothing but show.

Giddu began to talk about changing his life. He found the hard work, in his store at the mall and stalls at the marketplace, as well as the second job he sometimes went to in the night, tiring and lacking in prospects. He began to explore a possible sale of his shop. I hoped instead that he would look into expanding his business, growing his shop into a chain of stores, for he did have a loyal customer base that continued to give him sales year after year. But a disappointment with a key product—a woman's handbag with changeable outer covers—converted into a home-party-only item, by its original creators and patent holders, had been difficult for him to bear. It was his highest revenue earner.

Giddu himself was quite creative in generating ideas for trinkets to be made in India or China. I felt that he could patent some of his creations, and develop them into product lines himself. But he hadn't been able to make such a transition in his entrepreneurial efforts. He was exhausted by his many trials and tribulations, with the ongoing challenges of his work, and with making a life alone.

When reminded of his duty to his kids, to ensure they grew with the love and presence of both parents, he dodged the matter, and said he'd be amenable to any decision he'd have to make. He loved his children more than anything, and thought Guddy might agree to the children leaving with him if such change came about in his situation.

His arguments did make sense. He believed that his business, of trinkets procured from India and China and sold for low prices here in America, could soon diminish in profitability, given the price inflation of such goods, which ranged from 20% to 30% every year. He estimated a life of less than three years for this business without significant change in the model employed.

Besides, diminishing profitability could only be counteracted by matched increase in revenues through growth and diversification. And he simply did not have the energy or inner motivation to grow this business he had run for so many years. There also appeared to be increased competition in retail activities of this sort that he had seen at retail expositions. I therefore suggested reversing his business model, and procuring luxury items labeled American in bulk here, selling them to the growing middle class in India that seemed to be rapidly improving in its ability to spend.

Giddu sought business opportunities in India as a change in his life to look forward to. Moreover, his kids could gain a new, family-based, enriching social environment there, in the company of their many nephews and nieces, that they could benefit from.

It was hard to argue against his thoughts about returning to his country of origin. Not only would it be a sea change in his work and social environment, and that of his kids, in a desirable and beneficial way, the school system his children would enter into ranked among the best in the world, a level above the public secondary education system in America. Giddu, Monty's husband, and many others I knew here locally, who did quite well in life, came from that educational and cultural environment. The boost it could give his children was un-deniable. A change of place could offer him an opportunity to restart his life, move away from hurt and humiliation he suffered in America, and reconnect with family and friends in India.

Yet both Giddu and I knew his wife Guddy would not, under any circum-stance, relocate to India, for a nurse's employment there is one that is meagerly compensated, and minimally respected, as compared with similar jobs in America. She could easily afford a home on her own here, and had indeed demonstrated that capacity in buying her new house. There was no conceivable way she could be swayed to change her path again, which meant his kids could lose the constant presence of one parent if he did relocate to India. I remained concerned about the possibility of reigniting the conflict between them by Giddu's new direction.

Giddu increased his efforts to sell his business. I noticed that he began training a girl, the daughter of a potential buyer, in dealing with customers at his store. He seemed confident that Guddy would let him take their children to India—he had been their primary caretaker for long and managed them far bet-ter—and proceeded to obtain their dual citizenship identifications from the In-dian embassy. He began looking into good schools for the children to begin their education there, and accordingly located a safe place to stay in, close to schools of his choice. His planning for this global relocation was efficient and comprehensive.

Neither Monty, nor I, or his friend who connected him with me, could do or say anything to change his mind. He was determined to bring about this change he saw as beneficial to the kids and himself, a change that would give his wife a measure of freedom she seemed to desire.

I visited Guddy's place one evening to give her kids a gift my daughter wanted me to, and to chat with her about his plans. It was their dinner time; she invited me to join in with them, which offer, I suspect, was more out of pity for a single father. She'd made fresh *parathas*—Indian layered bread in the form of a thick crepe—and *sabzi*s, various sautéed spicy vegetable prepara-tions. I sat down with her children to enjoy dinner, marveling at Giddu's miss-ing out on all this wonderful food.

Perhaps that explained why he was deeply into cooking these days, com-peting with her to feed their children well. She seemed unconcerned about his plans that could split the family and leave her alone in America. She thought he would not pursue such plans with determination, and even if he did, that he would not succeed. She didn't seem to mind that he could in fact attempt to make such a transition. Though she did not oppose his plans, it was clear she also did not support him in his difficult endeavor.

Changing Circumstances and Lives

The collapse of capital markets and the housing market bubble hurt everyone. Some, who purchased their dream homes at the peak of the market, saw their home prices drop to nearly one-half of what they paid. Many jumped into additional home purchases when prices dropped, as potential nest eggs that could grow, and watched the capital they put into such investments evaporate, as home prices dropped far below loans taken to pay for them. Many were forced to abandon such investments and write off their capital losses.

And many single income families, upon losing the only job held by a family member, in the recession that accompanied the market collapse, were forced to walk away from their homes to smaller apartments to avoid having to file for bankruptcy. In financial ruin, some were forced to apply for bankruptcy protection as well.

Others found creative ways to stay in their own homes by having relatives purchase these houses placed on the market. Such properties were often sold at lower prices, in agreement with banks, to achieve quick, 'short' sales. Guddy took advantage of this procedure, a short sale of their first home, and purchased a new home at a price lower than their first. Giddu, who did not participate in this transaction, had no plans of joining her in her new home, and prepared instead to relocate back to India. A feeling that the much lauded *American dream* had become a ruinous nightmare was widespread. The financial strain combined with job losses put many immigrant families in additional peril of devastating breakups.

Some families, burdened with loans for homes now priced much below their purchase prices, considered 'walking out' of their homes despite their ability to make monthly mortgage payments. I remember a couple of such families calling me for my thoughts about this path. I could only recommend that they seek legal counsel for clarification. It occurred to me that banks could investigate their financial situation, and sue them to recover loan amount losses incurred in such foreclosures.

The argument for these banks was simple. If clients who took out mortgage loans had the ability to pay, how could it be permissible for them to walk away from their loan obligations? But some said laws prohibited banks from moving against families who did walk away from loans on homes much devalued by a market in recession. I wasn't so sure. I felt that at a minimum, banks might report such write-offs in their loan losses as gains by defaulting home-owners, as virtual earnings through breach of contract, and hence cautioned families considering such a move.

Those who argued most vigorously that laws protected such acts, of walking away from homes and loan obligations, predictably, were real estate brokers such as Giddu's cousin's wife. They seemed to bask in the warmth of fires that burned families, in the large flow of business in home sales resulting from the agonized departure of those who could no longer afford their loans for such homes. I wondered if they ever thought about the human cost of the profit they made from the suffering of so many. But they'd probably argue that if folks did choose to walk away from their dream homes, why should they not be the ones assisting in that pathway?

It wasn't clear why laws would protect borrowers defaulting on loan obligations, and not shelter lenders equally. Perhaps the rampant speculation fueled by banks offering loans with little or no down-payment, and sub-prime interest rates, had something to do with it. The very idea of long-term mortgage loans offered by banks is rather confusing. The risk in such contracts appears to be borne almost entirely by the borrowers. Banks are assured of steady streams of returns on money loaned, regardless of vagaries in the economy, while multitudes of borrowers suffer in the ups and downs of the market.

A loan that helps a borrower buy a home for his family appears more a roof over the lending bank's money, and its assured appreciation, than a roof over the borrowing family. Is it fair for any financial entity, leveraging deposited money, to isolate itself from all risk, forcing such risk upon the many who borrow from such entity? Perhaps boundaries of propriety are blurred, or crossed, when banks offer unusual inducements to attract borrowers.

These economic systems, and the laws governing them, are surely beyond comprehension for ordinary Americans. Little did anyone know that methods for profiteering in financial markets had advanced to massive transactions of 'collateralized debt obligations,' and 'credit default swaps,' which are complex derivative contracts. In these exotic transactions, the latter fed off the *failure* of the former, while the former fed off the hyperactive sub-prime mortgage loan and housing market, which, in turn, enticed simple consumers. Very many Americans hence rushed to buy homes, artificially inflating market prices. This unsustainable rise eventually led to the market collapse, and the ensuing chaos and immeasurable suffering. It was all quite according to the laws and regulations of the land, of course, but inscrutable to simple and gullible folks.

· · ·

Monty's husband, who had invested in two more homes besides the one the family lived in, now struggled to maintain these homes until he could sell them without incurring a loss. In a losing battle against unpredictable market forces, he was forced to abandon both these investments to repossession by banks. His filing for a divorce from Monty could have been a path to avoiding financial ruin for her, for her husband insisted on holding on to the investment homes, draining meager family finances. He continued to make the bare minimum monthly mortgage payments required to maintain ownership of these houses. Giddu and I did point this out to her that she should rid herself of such a financial drain as soon as possible if the divorce were to go ahead.

Her surprising and comprehensive victory at the first court hearing changed circumstances in ways none of us could have anticipated. Her husband returned home to stay together as a family once again. We learned of this development only after he'd been home for more than a week, when she came by Giddu's shop unexpectedly. She looked happy, and explained to us that her husband had decided to let the investment homes be repossessed. It made sense for him to stay with the family now.

Monty explained further, after our expressions of surprise and happiness for her at this turn of events, that she discussed dropping the divorce case with her husband after the hearing victory. And he agreed to do so as well. She'd also discussed the matter of continued financial drain due to their investment homes, and he agreed, at his uneducated wife's earnest request on financial management, to let the houses go, and avoid further monetary damage to the family. Giddu and I could hardly believe this transformation in her situation—and remained silent, listening to her as she continued.

There had to be a downside to these astonishing developments—or so we thought—and indeed there was one. Biff Dibble continued his discovery filings, and sent her regular invoices for services, even though the legal matter had been terminated by the parties concerned! We speculated that Dibble saw an opportunity, having found that the family had a bank account with a balance of $40,000/-, to extract as much money out of them as he could while she remained a client. Perhaps he was disappointed that she'd made effective use of his offer to provide his services, all the way to a first hearing, for only $3000/-. What can a capitalist do, but capitalize on obvious opportunities?

Monty couldn't understand Dibble's approach to the matter, which she felt was inhumane, and asked for my assistance. Unable to intervene in her relationship with her lawyer, having no direct connection with the legal matter or with either of them, I asked her to get her husband to help in the matter, given his experience in legal matters. She thought that could work, and Giddu supported it enthusiastically as well. This was a lump sum lawyer who truly disappointed. I hoped Monty's husband could thwart his avarice.

Giddu and I stayed well away from questions regarding the depth of Monty's renewed relationship with her husband. I hoped she would be careful, and go slow. But he did let slip a few days later that she had once again been inti-

mate with her husband. That is how many are, with little or no training in social deception, in the land we all came from. We trust far too readily. We are
taken advantage of, and exploited, rather too easily. Was it just weakness, or excess trust in others, often misplaced? In Monty's case, perhaps, she had no
choice but to submit, for this was, in her mind, her destined pathway. But
couldn't she have played—just for a while—hard to get?

She had shown more strength in her mind and approach in the past year
than she probably had all her prior marital life. Couldn't she have built upon
that, and made him work harder at winning her trust and affection? I stayed
away from discussing anything relating to her marriage from that point on. Her
simple approach to life included trusting her husband and long-term life partner implicitly. She did demonstrate this after her victory at the first hearing, in
her actions of returning more than half of the money she obtained, and having the restraining order dismissed. Perhaps that too could be strength.

• • •

Giddu and Monty also avoided discussing my marital situation with me after having listened to the voice recording from my children's mother. We never
talked about it again. To this day, and I do still have the recording with me, I
haven't been able to comprehend it. Not just the act, or the apparent loose behavior indicated, but the tone, the lack of any propriety in her voice, her expressions, her conduct generally, which I *had* noticed earlier. It took just a few
utterances from her, in a social environment she had become very comfortable
with, for us to observe her individual sense of freedom in behavior. This was
quite alien to the society and culture we knew: lustful voices, squeals, and sug-
gestive sounds in lax interaction with males around. I'd never seen such behavior in all my years of life, in any context other than the sexually intimate, not
even in western countries, where there is said to be a lot more freedom in expression.

I had not seen such behavior from her in any social gathering we attended
together either. This evidenced a glaring difference in social conduct and deception—between the children's mother and me—that could never, ever, be
bridged. *Susheelam*, good habits, and *Othukkam*, roughly translated from my
native tongue as propriety with comity, seemed entirely missing in this girl who
befriended and manipulated me to her ends. How could I *not* have seen this
then, almost two decades ago? But that story remains to be told.

This recording, of her intimate act with another, confirmed my suspicions
about her, over the years, that I could not mask very well. *Samskarashoonyaruh*, which translated to those with a total absence of good social
habits and culture, was the term my mother employed in describing such folks.
I was done with her; Giddu and Monty knew it well. Nevertheless, she re-

mained my children's mother. Their happiness depended on normality main-
tained under these tough circumstances. I needed strength for this, and a measure of self-control I'd never had to exercise before. There wasn't anything my
friends could do to help.

Giddu meanwhile completed preparations to leave for India. He sold his
shop to another entrepreneur who had prior experience in retail himself. The
new owner was happy with what he and his daughter saw in the shop over a
week they spent learning its operations. They planned to grow it further by
opening another branch, in a mall on the other side of the metropolis, closer
to where they lived. This was, therefore, a promising transition for Giddu's
business. He filled the days remaining, before his departure, with helping the
new owner iron out problems with suppliers, shop operations, and personnel.

Accustomed to visiting him at his shop in the late afternoons, both I and
my daughter now missed Giddu and his kids. And with his shop no longer a
convenient meeting place, though we couldn't have guessed it at that time,
Monty and I would also lose touch after his departure. Giddu for his part was
quite excited about his relocation, remaining busy until his departure day arrived. We arranged a couple of social gatherings with friends to bid him and
his kids farewell. He called me from the airport, before the long flight out of
the country, to say goodbye again. I couldn't help but feel a deep sense of
loss—of a friend moving away to a distant location, and of a small social network that kept me occupied and my children entertained and happy.

But Giddu's excitement and happiness, at the promising change in his circumstances and that of his children, had been infectious. I felt great relief and
happiness that he regained his sense of purpose, and motivation in life, despite
the distinctly Indian-American nightmare he had gone through.

Once in India, Giddu settled down quickly into a suburb of New Delhi,
and enrolled his kids in a reputed school in the area. Though the fee for their
education was unusually high, $5,000/- annually, he assured me he'd be able to
take care of this on his own, as his business ventures moved to profitability.
He invested in modern saunas for the newly wealthy middle class in India.
Sauna visits had become a rapidly increasing trend there. With a partner, he
opened two such facilities in the city. The services of a skilled marketing professional helped him popularize his saunas and the brand.

Giddu also brought over domestic help, from the state he and I were born
and raised in, who stayed with him and helped care for his children while he
focused on building his business. He made sure to tell me of the facilities he
arranged for that elderly lady who'd cook and help maintain the home: a good
bed, a little table, and a new flat screen TV for the family including the lady. I
felt confident he would have a reasonably good home situation, now that he
did not have to do the cooking and maintenance in his residence. I worried
more about how his children would take to the tough school curriculum in In-

dia. He mentioned that he'd hired a part-time tutor who helped his children meet their school's expectations.

He also indicated that Guddy planned to visit the kids later that summer. I pleaded with him to let her stay at his new place with the children, rather than have her stay in a hotel as he preferred. He dismissed the idea. He insisted that the *Kuttigalude Amma* could come and visit, and take the children out, but would not be welcome into his new residence. Giddu was concerned that she'd corrupt the minds of neighbors he befriended. Nevertheless, I knew he would have her stay at his place with their two kids, which is just what he did. I gathered from a later conversation with him that her visit had gone well. I did not ask him for details. That should remain between him and his *Kuttigalude Amma.*

· · ·

Yes, Priyavani, the first thing Giddu did when he settled in a new place with his children, was to find help for them, for chores and food preparation, and for tutoring. That must not surprise you at all, for there are innumerable middle-class homes with domestic help in the land we all originate from.

I grew up among domestic help of all sorts. I remember two others helping the large family I lived with as a child, Chellamma, and Naaniyamma, and most of all, that I was raised in part by Naaniyamma. We shared a few secrets: Naaniyamma did not reveal the perpetrator of mischief around the large home, and I gave her the five paise or so, extracted from my mother, so she could buy *beedies*—hand-rolled mini-cigarettes—that she smoked. I recall my family treating domestic help *as* family. They shared our living space, our food, our celebrations, and sometimes our sorrows as well.

After settling in America, I returned once to this old home, and Naaniyamma came over to visit. I seated her, my part-time mother, on a chair, and kneeling next to her, holding her withered hands, inquired as to her health and her children. My cousin, a woman older than myself and one who stayed in my childhood home, charged into the room, exclaiming, "*Heyyyyeh! Yendha ethuh?*"—what's this?—when she saw her on a chair. I have never felt as much embarrassment and anguish as I did then. Naaniyamma for her part only smiled and rose from the chair. I insisted she remain on it, and we continued our chat oblivious of that cousin's presence. Many in the family ignored her uncensored expulsions and uncivil behavior anyway.

Growing up, away from my ancestral home, in military camps with my father more than three decades ago, we had a *lashkar*, a militiaman employed at home, stay in a servant's annex behind our quarters. A remnant from colonial rule, no doubt.

Our *lashkar* was my constant companion on school-free days. He taught me to fashion catapults from tree branch junctions, shoe leather, and bicycle inner tubes. He taught me to ride a bicycle too, in his own inimitable way, launching me on my bicycle from the top of a small hill to roll on as far as I could before falling. In this unique training, my bicycle once met a streetlamp pole head on, and stopped dead in its tracks, while I carried on beyond the pole, and flew for a distance. I also learned from him a curious thing, that one can mix sugar into a spicy soup—*Sambhar*—and yet enjoy it, so such experiments became a hobby. It is not far from the truth to say our *lashkar* widened my boyhood horizons.

My family dealt with him with benign neglect. We knew he really wasn't all that dependable. We laughed when recounting the tale of burglars at our quarters. The first one to run from the home was our *lashkar*, and then the burglars, who saw my father awake and observing them from inside the home. Our *lashkar* stayed with us as a stray family member, tolerated with empathy and compassion. How else can a country teeming with people working as domestic servants include them, but by accepting them as part of the family and community, by treating them kindly? Is that not taught first in one's upbringing, or in a training institute for the nation's Civil Servants?

Giddu and I talked about this topic a lot. As one who worked with his hands, and worked hard, he respected those capable of manual labor. Curiously, his choice, in organizing his stall in the marketplace, was Dora, a woman who, with her husband, ran a shop adjacent to his shop in the mall. Dora was from Mexico, and was a strong girl who enjoyed physical labor. Giddu sang her praises, of her ability to handle heavy equipment efficiently. It wasn't hard to see that he respected people for all the right reasons, and was certain to treat them as he wished to be treated.

The good old Golden Rule, as is said here in America, but not the one that says, "The one with the gold makes the rules," which guides the trickle-down, stratified, devotedly materialistic society of the present.

Freedom

Society doesn't want free men. Society wants conditioned men.
Men who march in step.
— Henri Charrière [*Papillon, The Magnificent Rebel*]

After Giddu's departure from the country, and Monty's husband getting back to their home, our small social network withered. He did call occasionally. I learned of how his kids fared at their new school, and how his business in India inched to profitability, but there wasn't much else to talk about. He gained his freedom from the nightmare that descended upon him in America, and seemed to thrive in India. After Guddy visited him and their kids at his new location, he indicated that she desired the kids back in America for the next school year. This gave cause for concern, about repeated disruption of their school and social lives, and I hoped she wouldn't insist on that direction.

He also informed me of Monty's state, for with her husband back home, I exercised the utmost caution in any interaction with her. I stopped calling altogether, and she too reduced external interactions, focusing mainly on her family. The last I heard about her from Giddu, her husband succeeded in stopping her lawyer Dibble's incessant invoices, and both their children were doing well. Param continued his part-time employment at Giddu's shop now under new management. In time, he stopped calling as well.

A year passed in this silence. You could say we had all found a measure of peace in our lives: Monty with her family back together, and legal troubles at an end, Giddu with his kids and far away from his *Kuttigalude Amma*, and I with my children and my *Kuttigalude Amma* at her own place, though she continued to invade my home whenever she wished to. That rankled some, but how could I deny my children the presence of their mother in their lives? That was essential to their nurture, just as their presence in my life gave me a sense of purpose.

But that didn't mean there was no stress in my little family. My daughter desired to live with her mother and let me know this often, while my son did not wish such a change. Yet I knew that some change was necessary to minimize any possibility of further conflict.

Lack of any corporate employment for me wrecked the family's financial freedom. Paying a high annual fee, amounting to $16,000/-, for private education for my children, became a burden their mother bore on her own. She planned a change to a public school to divert this money to her new savings account. Unable to determine alternative arrangements to pay my children's private school fees, I offered them the option of going to the public school their mother enrolled them in, or to the private school they'd attended until then; I'd pay their school fees through any employment I could find. My son leaned toward the new school his mother insisted upon, while my daughter desired to stay on in the private school.

With a good friend's assistance, I did land an assignment, related to my profession, in a city a few hundred miles away. A job with the least responsibility one could assume, in my field of engineering, which helped me escape the typical background check. In this aspect, and in the failure of my marriage, I felt much like Kevin Spacey's character in *American Beauty.* Though occupied full time in editing and completing a second engineering book, I accepted this new job, away from my home state, before my kids' new school year began.

Moving away from home and leaving my children behind, in the clutches of a person I could no longer trust, was one of the hardest things I've ever done in life. They took to it easily enough, moving in with their mother, forming a good school-going routine to the new school that was not much out of the way on their mother's work commute. I missed them terribly. I made sure to converse with them over a video connection daily. And they visited our home every day just to check on the stray cat who had, with her kittens, adopted the home, and who had stayed with us, her kittens having departed to claim territories of their own.

I filled the additional time now available with tasks that remained on my second technical book, and worked furiously. My life thus took a strange, unexpected turn, quite the opposite of Giddu's path. I'd always emphasized being with children as the most important thing a responsible parent could do. He did just that, and changed his circumstances for the better. I gained freedom from my troubles, but of a sort that held little meaning or happiness for me. I wondered if this change in my life held any significant benefit.

A few months into this nomadic existence, messages from my children became increasingly plaintive. Queries of—"Dad, when are you coming home?" changed into, "Dad, please come this Friday!" from both my children. They missed me as much as I missed them.

My work on the second engineering book had finished. Book chapters and related material had been readied for submission by a co-editor, a professor at an international university working on it with me. My continuance in the minimal-responsibility job had also become untenable. Though I did ask for and obtain tentative proposals for alternate assignments in the company I worked in, my heart was not in that path.

A transition to another job with higher responsibilities ran into typical difficulties in any entrenched, political, fringe organization of a large company. The folks there may also have run a background check on me, and found its red flags. Truth be told, I'd grown rather tired of the jerking around, bullying, and plain mistreatment by senior employees in the organization, who enjoyed treating temporary folks like myself much as pieces of old furniture they liked to toss around. Many other such workers in the group assured me that this treatment was the norm in the organization. I harbored no desire to engage in another battle against such conduct; my time to leave had come. I'd been looking forward to getting back home in any case.

But trouble doesn't easily let go of those who let go of it. In my last two weeks, I was asked to meet with the company's lawyers because someone indicated, through his management chain, that I had voiced concerns about this company infringing on my intellectual property. Though I made it expressly clear that I'd conveyed no such concerns, the company lawyers insisted upon meeting with me.

I sought to identify the individual who relayed such rumors. I then provided them with as much material as I could gather, from my records, on this fellow. These records evidenced that it was he who engaged in such conduct, and blamed me instead in an apparent attempt to endear himself to upper echelons in the company.

I expressed disgust at being subjected to such an inquisition, but gave them what they demanded of me, a written statement declaring that I did not have any concerns of the sort they had been intimated of. Affronted by having to meet with such corporate lawyers, and their human resources people, I opened up and gave them evidentiary information about the ill-treatment their employees inflicted upon temporary folks like me.

Predictably, though their investigations did result in a retraction of sorts, of the statement made by the brown-nosing employee, and in confirmation of the facts I provided them with, they took no action against any of their permanent employees. I hadn't expected them to, nor desired any punitive action on their part. I'd prepared to leave, wanting nothing more, but that just wasn't how things worked out.

• • •

The sense of freedom I felt in escaping that corporate environment was immense. I could see, vividly, that corporate America didn't want free thinkers, rebels, those who fight injustice and abuse—I was informed by one of the permanent employees in the group that I spoke up once too often—no, they like to see men who march in step. Men who follow orders. Men who can be sent wherever they wished to send them to. Men who trudge on, without any complaint, in the suffocating working conditions they create and perpetuate. It is not free men they seek, but men who live in fear, who do not give them cause for fear.

A plantation owner mentality is not one to recede on its own from exploitative minds and systems easily. If anyone were to hint at the possibility of holding them accountable, they would forthwith require irrefutable assurances that they would not be hauled before judicial authority to explain their conduct. Why is there so much fear in their minds, if not because of their own guilt? No ordinary circumstance, or grievance from a humble worker, could change their behavior or the culture inbred within their companies and institutions. Such change requires an amendment to their governing constitution, which could take an act of God, or a dictum from someone at the top of their long-established pecking order. It was quite an education for me in just a few short months.

But I had rebelled against such practices, exploitative work environments little different from sweatshops or cheap assembly lines, more than a decade ago, and ventured independently, which led to my acquisition of some of my own intellectual property. The very same intellectual property they were now worried about. Few escape these oppressive, unfair practices prevalent in the industry. No lawman here can be expected to risk his career fighting for the oppressed and disadvantaged in this pecking order. Such a fight impacts profitability in a culture where profit is king. It felt good to be free, of the fear and insecurity, of the oppression and constant unhappiness.

• • •

But wasn't that just what the children's mother always complained about? That she found life to be oppressive with me around? That I hadn't been of much help with the family, pursuing an entrepreneurial path, subjecting the family to much difficulty and unhappiness?

Yet that was a decision made after an attempt at commuting to work to another state—which paid well, but wasn't a sustainable path, lasting only a few months—and I thought we made a joint decision to forge ahead with my first start-up business effort. Perhaps I was wrong. Perhaps I should have learned to be a man who marched in step. So others around me would be comfortable and unafraid, no matter the cost exacted from my own life. Could that have been a better pathway for my family? Had I subdued my yearning for freedom from bondage?

But what did she have to complain about now—had she not won her freedom, freedom from me as she desired, through her own deliberate actions, supported by all her helpful, sympathetic workplace friends? Or was this a hollow victory for her, with naught to celebrate?

On my return, I spent a weekend with the children, going to a movie show, eating out at places nearby, and buying things for them which they enjoyed. A fancy new bicycle for my son, and a full set of crafts tools and duct-tape rolls for my daughter. She'd learned, all on her own, to create wallets and purses, with duct-tape, by following instructions on YouTube. My children returned to their mother's on Sunday night to get up early for school, since they had become acquainted with doing so there.

They desired to continue that routine to minimize disruption to their school activities. Much as I wished to, I couldn't ask that they change their routine again and stay with me. It was decided: they'd stay at their mother's and come by every day they could to spend time with their father. They came early in the morning on their way to school the following Monday and every weekday, but stayed at their mother's the next weekend.

And so changed our arrangement again—the children's mother now had effective custody of our children. They came by on weekday mornings for a few minutes before school, and sometimes on weekends if they had the time to do so. They had a few activities in the week—piano classes for both, and advanced swimming for my daughter—that occupied them in addition to their school homework. I now saw them only when they could come to see me.

My only companion who remained in the house was our feral cat, named Lucy by my daughter, who often saw the children off to their mother's house on the next street, but always returned to her territory that included my home.

The house all to herself, $50,000/-, custody of the children, and freedom from me—my children's mother gained all that she demanded. Would that ensure her happiness and, consequently, the happiness of my children? The insatiable nature of human desires doesn't much allow for peace. My son, keyed by his mother, began talking about how he'd like it if his mother obtained a *legal divorce* from me, so she and I could *both* move on with our lives. She now wished that I legitimize her illegitimate, immoral actions! After being heckled a number of times, I reminded him that the matter was not for children to resolve, that she could gain what she desired only if she left us, the family, in peace.

I'd promised to bring out the truth of our circumstances in a court of law or in the court of public opinion. But I was also willing to give her what she demanded if she left the three of us, our little family, to our lives, and did not subject my children to boyfriends or possible step-fathers. Such distortion of the lives of my children was not a demand I could willingly grant.

She has always been free to leave—but not free to subject our children to confusing experiences. It wasn't my decision alone. My children had no desire for a step-father or a boyfriend in their lives. But in a land where everyone is free to do most anything, how could I shield them from her manipulation, from such influences brought into their lives? What would prevent her from diminishing their attention and respect for their father, now that the children lived with her? How could I depend on a person I could not trust to carefully vet any new influence brought into the kids' lives? Would she honor the promise made, that she wished only that the children grow strong and secure with guidance from us both? Or would she corrupt that promise as well, pursue a path of her convenience, and bring in a boyfriend into their lives, gradually alienating their father from them?

Is it safe to trust a parent, who seeks freedom that splits a family, to do the right thing for children, to not diminish the bond children share with the parent who gives up custody? I can imagine the discomfort my children may go through—if their mother did permit access to their residence to her partners—how may the children address such a person cohabiting with a woman who is separated but stays married? Recalling Sid the counselor's words, how could one look upon such an action by an adult, a parent or a partner, seeking physical and emotional satisfaction, imposing an undue influence upon the minds and into the lives of children who do not deserve such influence? And how may innocents view the explicit intimate contact that these adults display in the residence? Besides, how could I be certain that such a person is not a pedophile or a sociopath? My heart cringes at these thoughts.

Would such a boyfriend attempt to endear himself to my children through material inducements, through gifts not approved of by me? Would their mother compel them to lie to me, about such activities in their residence, through fear instilled in them that I might react with strength upon discovery, and change the way of life they've settled into? What form of child abuse would it be, if she persuaded the children to deceive their father? How can any man be so devoid of self-respect as to occupy a home gifted to my children and family, invading the lives of the children? But in a "free country," such a man would most likely argue that he is free to do as he pleases; gifts, in his mind, may have no more significance than their material use.

Why does society allow for such freedom, such deviation from tradition, from acceptable social norms? Is there no honor in promises made anymore? I knew my troubles here were by no means over, that I'd face greater challenges with her choice of a way of life for the children. Did I relinquish parental control, and become a hapless spectator in how my children's lives might be changed by their mother? Or did I provide their mother just enough leeway, to reveal her true nature, to manipulate the children now under her control?

• • •

Eastern or Western, the *Samskarashoonyaruh*, those without good culture and habits innate and nurtured in them, contain a cavernous vacuum in their selves that pulls them inexorably toward easy ways of life. Insidious religious or cultural conversion, and persistent social stratification, employs this weakness with economic and intellectual poverty effectively. I saw this clearly in my children's mother. She readily took to the freedoms and wanton ways of life prevalent in present society. That's just how she trapped me into a relationship in the first place. And she did so with utter disregard to her marriage as she pursued me relentlessly, free from any social constraint. I fell for her ready displays of affection, her offers to help, and her unrestrained revelations of private details—for which I too must share in shame and blame.

Restraint and circumspection, even with respect to children, seem absent in her newfound way of life. Never once did she talk to me, in any depth, about my son from my first marriage. That concern was simply not something she could care to contemplate. She often cut corners when she traveled, on roads, and in life.

But children too are empty vessels as they grow their identities and character, looking to their parents and mentors for examples to emulate. Having given up custody of my children to their mother, for what I thought was their benefit, had I put them into an environment where the very habits I would caution them against were encouraged and commonplace? Instead of simplicity and thrift, and devotion to family my late father taught me through his example, had I now put my children into a life where everything was allowed, as long as it made them happy?

Will they learn that infidelity and adultery, or convenient and pleasure-seeking ways of life, are quite normal and acceptable, since everyone deserves to be happy and comfortable? Will such thoughts become the foundation of their developing character and identities? It cannot be easy for them to separate convenience from truth. They could come to view their mother's actions as necessary and beneficial, and their father's explanations and guidance as that of someone not well aligned with the times. They may even believe their mother was justified in her actions that split the family. How will they discern what values to adopt within themselves? How will they learn of consequences for ways of life lacking in discipline and commitment?

The Eastern culture of my clan and community within which I grew up to adulthood in talked of "*Naanoom Maanoom*," translating roughly as a deep sense of shame and like regard for others. Social stigma was a direct consequence of actions against accepted social norms. Here in America, on the other hand, I recall words from a DV counselor, that their intervention wasn't a shame or blame effort. The culture of the present in which my children grew seemed to show little regard for social stigma or shame in pursuit of easy, convenient ways of life.

I remained troubled about a clash of cultures in my children that could delay their development of strong identities. With them lured into the undisciplined and profligate ways of life that their mother and her new boyfriends practised, would I be compelled to do the unimaginable, disengage from them to prevent this conflict in their minds? My son queried me on occasion about disparate guidance from his parents that left him more than a little confused.

Will they understand and accept what I do, with a clear understanding of our difficult circumstances, and resolve their doubts? Will I succeed in bringing them back to me with truth, love, and reason, through non-violent ways, or must I steel myself for a battle through an impersonal legal system? How can I best guide them, help build their character, identities, and culture, under such diverse influences? What will their cultural values and habits become?

* * *

Despite my efforts at bringing my children closer, my son in India and the young ones here in America, my grown son remained distant from his step-siblings. He wasn't comfortable interacting with his step- brother and sister, children of a family formed after his father and mother separated. I could not object to his stance; such things are not part of one's typical experience, but not alien to our culture or to my ancestral family in India.

My aunt lived with a step-daughter in the childhood home I grew in. This step-daughter, the elder cousin who objected to my regard for my part-time nanny, lost her mother at a very young age. My paternal grandfather abandoned his wife and five children to live with another woman, while my father and his siblings struggled to finish their schooling in abject poverty. They grew up with their single mother to learn the value of hard work and discipline, and to support and rebuild the family and their home.

Two generations later, events took the opposite course; my so-called life partner and children abandoned me, the father of the family, leaving me only our feral pet Lucy for comfort in the home they grew in. Nevertheless, I empathized with my grown son's discomfort. And, I did not wish that his siblings encounter similar experiences.

It just doesn't seem right, to expose children to domestic discord that they can do without, so adults can practise any sort of freedom they profess to believe in. All for physical and emotional satisfaction, and convenience, which could nevertheless gravely impact young ones unable to speak in opposition. I learned from my son, from his pain, that I had not given this aspect of life enough consideration. And I sure won't be making the same mistake with my two little children here in America.

* * *

But the law in America, that wonderful human institution, will not agree, for everyone here is *free*. Free to do anything and everything they desire to, with their right to individual pursuits of happiness they believe themselves to be endowed with from up above. Oh—the law is supreme, "...'Cause I am the law! You can't beat the law!" said the bewhiskered little big man of the law, in his southern, Georgian accent, to Idgy Threadgood in *Fried Green Tomatoes*, my all-time favorite. Yet, what is the law, but ways and means convenient to, and agreed upon by, a majority or those that control the majority? Can laws mandate ethical conduct? Can a free mob adhere to principles or conform to disciplined lives?

No, sir, I shall make no attempt to beat any law; I shall work only to bring out the truth. And in doing so, in my atypical ways, I will hope the ancient wisdom, *Satyameva Jayate*, that it is only truth that wins, stays true in my humble circumstances. For I cannot agree—laws and heavenly dicta or not—this is the nurture of my children, the strengthening of their identities, and the inculcation of values that no true parent can let go of. Where laws cannot help, I must do what I can.

Who could be more compatible with them in nature but their true parent, one who fathered, loved, and carried them through their early years? Who but I could best take my children through their rites of passage into adulthood, rites learned and developed through culture and the innumerable experiences of this uncommon father?

I can neither conceive, nor agree, that a substitute male from a disparate way of life, a live-in boyfriend for a woman's indulgence of her physical and emotional needs and wants, can better guide my children toward moral and spiritual maturity. I cannot agree that such arrangements of convenience, immoral by any religious or social norms, can nurture and guide children into living ethical and happy lives, otherworldly entitlement and earthly institutions notwithstanding. How can any exercise of social freedom infringe upon the birthright of children, their natural, biologically inalienable right to be protected and guided by their true father?

The Fallacy of Subjugation

One early Spring day, just a few weeks ago, I was out jogging with my son—he jogged, and I rode his bicycle to accompany him—and on the way back from the local library, a car blocked a small street we were about to cross. The car looked familiar and the driver even more so. It was Monty! She saw us jogging, driving along, and turned into the side street to stop and talk.

We hadn't communicated since Giddu left America, and it felt great to see her again. Pointing to my son, she marveled at his growth in the two years that had passed. I introduced her to him formally. She conveyed that Param had landed a good job as an agent for an insurance or mortgage company—I do not recall which—and within a few months, was absorbed as a full-time employee. Monty continued with her part time work to augment the family's income. Her family stayed together.

I did not ask her how things had progressed between her and her husband, though she volunteered that nothing had changed—but I could see that she seemed happy. She had visited her parents in India, and had also met with Giddu there. His children stayed with him in India. They had not been compelled to return to America as his wife Guddy contemplated doing. It was heartwarming to learn about the lives of my good friends and that they did well. I saw Monty again another day, on the same road we jogged along, and offered her lemons, from the tree in my backyard, that gave me a bumper crop this season. She declined, saying someone else had given her lemons earlier.

Everything had changed for Monty, despite her dismissive down-playing. She never desired to stand up to her husband and oppose things he wished to do. No, she had never even conceived of speaking against his thoughts and actions. But she had indeed stood up against injustice and selfish behavior, after tolerating it for long, and set an example her children could learn from. She brought out the steel in her heart and mind, tempered by trying circumstances, and guided her strong-willed husband away, from arguably foolish pursuits, toward maintaining the integrity of the family.

A source of inner strength and compassion, she'd seen to the best interests of her children, navigating them through a ruinous financial situation to where one of them found promising employment, and the other continued his growth with both parents nurturing him. She succeeded in her devotion to her family and her duty to children, despite the most challenging circumstances a girl with only high-school education could have faced. She would not admit it, but she had found renewed courage, and a measure of peace, however small.

· · ·

I hoped, after meeting Monty, that my children's mother could also find the measure of peace, in her life, that Monty had won for herself. Instead of the house, the $50,000/-, custody of the children, and freedom from me that she had demanded and gained over time. Her mind at ease more than material in hand, and such peace without myself in the picture, naturally. She too could then set an example for our children, a worthy one—instead of coercing them to adapt to her wanton ways of life.

But how can she ever find peace while she continued her attempts to manipulate me through our children? She had my children ask me to be permitted to travel internationally—to India—with the same tired excuse used for years that their grandfather was dying. I refused, given that they'd planned another trip this summer to see their aunt Binita. Also, travel all the way to India isn't by any means easy or safe. The venom that came at me for this denial, through my daughter and my son, exceeded anything I'd seen previously. "You will pay for what you've done," said my daughter in a text message, along with other angry expressions. "She will take you to court," said my son. These could not have originated from anyone other than their mother, or in response to her histrionics. They revealed, to me, a distinct lack of understanding and calm in their mother's mind.

A lawsuit will be nothing but a battle of attrition, and protracted violence, with a life-changing impact in our circumstances. A battle with her could be interesting, for her fraudulent actions will then face intense legal scrutiny. When she came back to the country, prompted by her long-held desire to marry me, she claimed that her previous marriage had been legally terminated. But I have, to this day, not seen any documentation to indicate that she did indeed obtain a divorce, from her first husband back in India, prior to marrying me.

Besides, her father had a lawyer in their home town, *Ididabad*, prepare a letter of questionable legality stating that a marriage dissolution agreement sufficed in place of a legal, court-approved, divorce in India. I accordingly executed a dissolution agreement with my first wife in India, and then married this person who returned to America, for this purpose, on a tourist visa. We then applied for her permanent residency on the basis of this marriage, absent legal divorces from family court in India, supported only by a statement of an unknown lawyer in that nation. And green cards came through for both of us. But misgivings remained in my mind about the legality of these procedures.

Later, when I applied for citizenship in America, she lied about her prior marriage in my application. That, conveyed to immigration authorities, could have led to denial of my citizenship—yet that was resolved in an embarrassing but constructive manner. How can any applicant be responsible for a blatant lie by a spouse? Nevertheless, it is clearly on the record that false information provided by her was rectified upon a government investigation. These matters will no doubt come to light in any lawsuit between us.

• • •

I look forward to bringing out the truth, of this manipulation and deceit carried out by her and her father, and prove that I became an unwitting participant in an illegal partnership. Here, Priyavani, is a parallel—between your situation and actions, and mine—where you and your father resemble my children's mother and her father. Her actions, like yours, are not in accordance with the letter or spirit of the law in America or in India. Your deeds have been exposed, and you stand accused of matters the state can prosecute. My children's mother and her father, having succeeded in their willful subversion of this nation's laws, remain to be held to account in this legal system. I explained to my children that I shouldn't lie for their mother's benefit anymore.

And, like Seeta, I will not be signing any more documentation she may want me to. She can call her *one-call* Dilbut prosecutor for such help. But I digress. Perhaps facing the deceptive actions of the past, the parental alienation pursued in the present, and their consequences, will be the only path to closure and peace for her. Or a path to her judgment day. Only the truth of our lives revealed may set us all free from our constraints.

• • •

The patriarchal model of a controlling and benevolent father of a family, a drive to subjugate one's individual self to such authority, and life in fear of retribution to come, is a concept alien to my childhood learning. I hail from a matriarchal and nurturing culture, one where a family is led by a mother, while a father provides for and protects the family. Yet, the father is often portrayed as the decision maker, perhaps to satisfy male ego. But it is the mother who rules the roost, and family decisions are invariably made together. This learning is reinforced through mythological stories, portrayed in artistic dances and enactments on festive occasions, and through widespread publications, as well as personal examples in families. I miss that gentle cultural inculcation.

Giddu hailed from the same region of India, though he learned through religious teaching, in local Catholic schools and churches, that may have been patriarchal. I envisioned him as a considerate and respectful partner in his relationship with his wife. But, by his own admission, faced with her dalliance, he reacted with rough physicality that must have eroded any remaining respect. Though that was only an uncontrolled overreaction on his part, it no doubt reflected a desire to subjugate her behavior to his rules.

As events over the years proved to us, Giddu, Monty, and me, such methods of control do not lead to lasting transformation, but instead to increased efforts toward circumvention. Monty's husband's efforts at subjugating her to his will and direction for the family, Giddu's efforts to rectify his wife's conduct, and my own attempts to keep my family together by sheer will—none worked. Life has a curious way of dismissing such insignificant thoughts and efforts, that may well be incompatible with human nature, rather effectively.

Nor is the strongest of natural instincts, to protect and nurture our progeny, easily subjugated. It is this instinct that compels us to act against our self--interest and do what is best for children: as Guddy did in permitting her little children to go with Giddu as far away as India, or as Monty demonstrated in letting her younger son stay with his father despite custody granted in her favor. We instinctively know what is best for our children. Conscious, self-centered thought, on the other hand, often tends to go against such instincts.

I admire Monty's strength and devotion to family, to her husband and children, which they must now comprehend well. As I admire the mother of my son in India, one who shunned remarriage and devoted herself to bringing him up. My son grew to respect and love her far more than he respects me, his father. Though it is true he grew largely without me by his side, I hope he comes to see that this tough circumstance gave him the opportunity to grow stronger, out of his father's shadow, and to grow more responsible to family.

My son here in America grows stronger and more responsible to himself and family every day, learning without my regular assistance. I now do see that it is not necessary for me to be in his life at all times, to enforce rules, to inculcate discipline in him. It is not by my efforts that my children learn, and grow their skills and knowledge, but by their own. There is little need for rules, regulations, laws, or any enforcement within a true family. Compassion, empathy, and patience are, perhaps, all that is needed.

Some argue otherwise, that well-defined rules and expectations provide a framework for conduct and activity in any family, and that without this framework, predictable and measurable success cannot be found. But is a family governed with codified laws, and strong enforcement, suppressing internal freedom of expression and action, a safer, richer, and stronger family? Is human thought and conduct best developed through extrinsic constraints and force? Is the appalling statistic, of one in four in jail in the world here in America, evidence of the success of our system of laws and law-enforcement? Yet, laws are indispensable in large, diverse populations.

It is hard to envision force as the solution to inculcate discipline and maturity, to build a rich culture, and to grow a peaceful society. We may do better through devotion to our children, to the nurture, growth, learning, and critical thinking of future generations.

. . .

And you, Priyavani, must see how the efforts of those in your home country, who helped you with Seeta's complaint, amounted to extreme subjugation. Can there be a rational explanation for Seeta's status in America rendered illegal? Or for an Indian court, without any jurisdiction in New York, to issue a non-bailable arrest warrant for her? And all this for raising concerns with you about conditions of employment and life in America under your contract with her?

Was it a fearful overreaction because another like you, from your country, was sued in America by a domestic help whom he employed, and compelled to pay a large settlement to end the matter? Or because yet another was sued, with the case tried in her absence given her failure to appear, and a judgment of $1,460,000/- entered against her?

When your embassy wrote to the American State Department to assert that Seeta sought to subvert American *and* Indian laws, there was surely more to your matter than could be readily seen. It is not the first time a branch of the Indian government manipulated rules to favor you. A prior event resulted in the punitive dismissal of another civil servant in India who protested against the preferential treatment that you were given. Though that dismissed civil servant eventually won a favorable ruling in his matter from the Supreme Court of India, it is clear that representatives of the Indian government take extraordinary measures to accommodate you. Why do they do so?

Nevertheless, efforts to subjugate Seeta and her family have failed in America. Instead, you have been ordered to remain silent by your government, which favored you in the past. Will that harm attempts to enter into a civil compromise with Seeta? Will you persevere, with political force and influence, to brush aside reinstated allegations against you?

Did your father not declare to the Indian media that the Saudis, or possibly Rahul Gandhi, a leading young politician, could accomplish this for you? Presumptuous on his part, and insistence on the *old* way, no? How did you fall so far from favor, from the unusual preference your government showed you? How will you rise above this circumstance?

. . .

Giddu too made a similar declaration, albeit in the negative, when his prior social network pressured him to forgive his wife's dalliance and return home. He declared then that he would not do so even if a Pope of the Catholic Church himself made such a request. Not even the highest recognized authority in his religion or any other—male, naturally—could subjugate his freedom of thought and action. But the anguish his children felt could melt his heart and perhaps change his direction—with sincere support from Guddy.

Hence my focus on children, Priyavani, and the best possible outcome for them. I hope you too will think similarly. I'd heard this once, from a Dilbut cop, surprisingly, "You cannot go wrong if you keep the best interests of your children at heart." A belief I do identify with well. I wish my children's mother had stuck to the earnest declarations she'd made, after admitting her extramarital dalliance, that all she wished to do was to take good care of the children from that point on. But neither I nor my children can depend upon her promises.

So—I'll work at subjugating my fears, hopes, and ambitions, my self and my ego, to the needs and interests of my children. They are my purpose, my motivation, my joy, and my legacy. They are the principal reason for my continued existence. Without them, I'll find no meaning, no value to ascribe to my life. What greater purpose could there be for a simple living being in the vast timelessness of the universe?

Just as life is that which creates, nourishes, and protects all life, consciousness is the light of life, the self, that learns, integrates, and enlightens other selves. My children are my consciousness. My responsibility is to guide them into lives better, happier, and more fulfilling than mine. And I have lived a life more interesting than most, one that occupies me, and one that I am grateful for.

I will live on and contribute to society and life through my children. They are the greatest of gifts I leave to the world, as I leave it in time to rejoin nature. I am, only because they need me to be; the subjugation of my self to them and their lives is but my humanity.

Small Measures of Peace

I learned so much from Lucy, the feral cat mother, who adopted us and our home. I learned from her, and her alone, that in Wariduna's dry air, bedeviled by static electricity, it is good to brush your body against walls and other items in the house often. This helps dissipate the charge accumulated, and lessens static shocks. I learned this watching her rub her fur all over the place rather than just on us. It is a habit I have now adopted zealously despite not having as much fur as she does.

Did I tell you about how she came to live with us? Not in any detail? Let me do that now, before I tire of penning my many stories. Lucy is important to my little family. She is family too, and taught us much about being family. So much so that my daughter and I have begun to write a book about her, about what she taught us.

Cleaning my backyard, many years ago, I happened upon a young black cat watching me. It was standing on the gravel spread along the side of my house. With no pet collar visible on the cat, I walked around and looked for a broom to shoo it away. Back with the broom, I proceeded to make loud noises, but the cat stayed in place, standing between me and a lawn-mower lying beside the house.

Looking more carefully, I saw three tiny heads poking out from behind the mower. This was a new mother looking for a place to raise her young! What could I do, now knowing the reason for her resolute presence in my yard? I went into the kitchen and came out with a bowl of milk, for the kittens and the cat, that I laid beside the boundary wall.

My children, quite small in those days, were the first to notice the presence of the cat. They brought it to my attention, and now were most pleased by the turn of events. Needless to say, replenishment of the bowl of milk became our daily family activity. Over time, their mother also involved herself in this pursuit. She insisted that milk could be bad for the kittens, and replaced it with kitten chow. This changed things somewhat. We now began to cater to their needs specifically, buying whatever was required. Looking after them now became a chore to plan for. The kids named the mother cat Lucy, and her kittens, Black Panther, Brave Heart, and Recluse.

As the kittens grew bigger and more active, we worried about the possibility of their continued multiplication in the neighborhood, and discovered that Dilbut had a program in place to mitigate just this problem. This involved catching them, neutering and spaying, and then releasing them into the territories they adopted. They called this catch-and-release or CNR. Clearly a better program than another I'd heard of, one that involved bringing in hawks to hunt the many feral cats in the local Riparian Reserve nearby.

While this—distorting their bodies for our convenience—was much against my own nature, and something I'd fought when it came to doing so for our pet dog who died some years ago, I could not object where feral cats were the concern. My children and their mother took over the CNR activity. Lucy and her kittens passed through this traumatic journey, seeming none the worse for the experience, missing just a tiny bit of their left ear tips to indicate that they had been so treated.

The kittens grew quickly, and became a common fixture on our backyard walls and in the patio. They had distinct behaviors: Black Panther was a male loner, staying away from the pack, Brave Heart was active and frolicked, and Recluse was a scaredy cat who stayed close to her mother. A complication in territorial ownership arose when another feral cat, a *Russian Blue* with her own small litter, also came into our yard. Lucy, a *Ragdoll*, sometimes engaged in hissing matches with the new mother named Trixie by the kids, but let her use the front yard as her domain and a place to raise her kids, while she and Black Panther, Brave Heart, and Recluse stayed in our backyard. In time, Lucy's kids grew to require territories of their own.

Black Panther was the first to leave. Brave Heart stayed on for some months more, and left thereafter, while Recluse remained with her mother in the backyard. Meanwhile, Trixie's kids also grew, and having journeyed through the CNR program, dispersed, until only Trixie, Lucy, and Recluse remained.

My kids observed these aspects of feline nature with keen interest, and prayed that all their now adopted pets wouldn't leave. Recluse was eventually persuaded—by her mother's not-so-subtle physical inducements—to leave to find her own territory. Though both Lucy and Trixie, the two cat mothers who successfully raised their kids in our home, stayed, in time, Trixie, who appeared to weaken, also disappeared, which the kids and I grieved over for a while. But Lucy remained with us, and showed signs of a desire to venture into the house. She appeared to want to be a house pet, to stay indoors when it suited her, and leave to roam the neighborhood when she so chose.

And so, Lucy, her parental duties in life complete, moved in with us. After a few scratches she inflicted on us at first, she learned on her own to keep her claws retracted when swiping at us, if we ventured too close, and eventually learned not to swipe at us at all. She soon selected a few favorite lounging locations, explored the beds and little enclosures my daughter arranged for her, and chose the kids' bunk bed's upper bed as her own.

She also learned to do her excretion outside, and to ask us to open doors for her, and climb our apple tree in the backyard to get onto our balcony. I fixed a cat door section to the balcony's sliding glass door, and she learned, with much coaching and coaxing in this instance, to push through the magnetic flap to get in or out.

But most of all, she learned to be a companion to my daughter, who often declared, at times of stress or anguish, that Lucy was her only friend in the world. In her evident affection for us, and in caring for her too, Lucy greatly comforted my children. As is the *Ragdoll's* nature, she followed us on walks in the neighborhood, and would run after my son when he'd run back to his mother's after dinner with me. But she always did come back home, as did my children, if only to see her.

· · ·

I wonder how Guddy, my good friend Giddu's wife, fares these days. I heard from him a year and a half ago that she visited them in India, stayed a few days, and returned to America. And from Monty, recently, that she had not insisted upon the children getting back to America after their first year in India with their father. That was truly good to hear, that her kids' education was not disrupted again—it can only mean their children are doing well at school in India. That too is a surprise, and a most pleasant one.

Giddu may hence be doing quite well in his new businesses. While that isn't a surprise to me, it must be so for her, for she'd said to me, before he left America for good, that he'd return, tail between his legs, in a few short months. She was evidently wrong in assumptions about him and his ability to restart life and business anew, in India, with his kids in tow.

It may be that she found him and their children happier than they had been here. Their happiness may have persuaded her to let her children live and grow without her always by their side. Perhaps she sees him now in a new light, as a successful entrepreneur and a devoted parent. Or she knew this all along, and only spoke negatively about him due to frustration caused by their circumstances. Yet her sacrifice, of a life without her children here in America, must, despite its unhappiness, bring her a measure of comfort and peace in the newfound happiness in her children's lives.

Monty surely must be happier now than when I first met her. Not only is her husband back home with the full family, her son Param now holds a good job, earning for the family and for himself, gaining his father's respect once again. Her younger son must also be doing well at school, now that his father, who no doubt helps him with his school work, is with all of them.

She spoke of health troubles her friend Pamela was going through when she stopped to chat some weeks ago. And that Pamela continued her relationship with the auto mechanic who cared for her. It is of course common for a girl to convey gossip, but Monty's continued concern for others, her friend

Pamela in particular, reveals her state of mind. It tells, perhaps, that she is no more subject to her husband's likes and dislikes, for he had not liked the *gori* at all. Perhaps her husband accepts her now with minimal restrictions or demands. And she finds the time and attention to inquire after Pamela, to be concerned about others, now that her own troubles are greatly diminished.

Will I and my children find peace in an ever-changing world? Things are not always as they seem. I cannot know of the situation at their mother's—is she bringing a boyfriend or two to the home? Do they intrude on my children and their time together as family? Do my children deserve to have to adapt to such experiences? Does their mother respect boundaries of what the children may be subjected to? I try to not let these questions disturb whatever peace I find in my heart and mind.

But if I am to determine that their mother has been changing and distorting their lives in ways I would not wish for them, this peace will be overcome. I make this promise—to my children as much as to myself—that if their mother abuses the freedom of her own place with the children in it, gained solely from hopes for the benefit for my children, I will change these circumstances, and bring them back to our home, even against their wishes if need be. That is a battle I must fight, and fight to win. Their mother's needs and wants cannot become an imposition that begins to diminish their bond with me, their father.

I'll readily admit to this difference: I cannot agree to my children subjected to influence by step-fathers or boyfriends as long as I am alive, and in their lives. How can one trust such males, who have little regard for cultural norms, in the world of today? Is that really what's best for children, or is it better for them to learn from examples of devotion, commitment, and responsibility? What right permits anyone to distort the lives of children in this manner? This—adult pursuit of happiness at the expense of children—may be the difference, in a trickle-down society, from societies of old where one's focus stays on duties and responsibilities to one's children, family, and community.

Oh, I have thought about this popular, convenient idea often—no more than an excuse, that children will be happier in two happy homes than in one—and discarded it every time. To compel them to accept and adapt to such fast-and-loose ways of life is a crime, not a kindness. It may be convenient in a society where families fragment so readily, or in communities where individualistic pursuits are far too common and may not be discouraged. But this is not something I can adapt to, or cooperate with.

Fragmented parts of a family do not sum up to the same as an integral family in the development of children. The whole is indeed greater than the sum of the parts here. I have known the pain and suffering brought about by such behavior, forced fragmentation of families, in the generation before me, and in my own life. Peace isn't brought about by such ways, nor is a community strengthened by such practices.

• • •

Is peace found through inaction, through disengagement? Is that path, of walking away from confrontation, a non-violent, better pathway? Why are we compelled to intervene, if non-participation will be more peaceful?

Yogis, it is said, act with the body, mind, and intelligence without attachment. The ancients advocate pathways of action and learning, and life pursuits combining these activities to suit one's nature, albeit without expectation of reward or material benefit. To them, purification of thought, of the mind, of the essence of ourselves we call the soul, is the principal goal.

Yet, is that not an individualistic pursuit? A pursuit that distances one from all that is around oneself? How useful can one's purification of thought be, if not propagated to those who may be helped by such purity? Of what use is wisdom and enlightenment I gain for myself, if it does not translate to betterment in the lives of my children, of those around me who are full of consternation? How can I know that the enlightenment in any aspect of life comprehended is indeed valid, if I do not apply it? How can anything I learn be useful, if not engaged in developing and growing a consciousness greater than myself?

No, peace isn't gained through detachment from emotions, or through disengagement from the varied aspects and challenges of life. Purposeful action, and active engagement in the material world, is necessary, perhaps without any demand for satisfaction or self-benefit.

There is hardly any peace to be gained in my heart and mind as I watch my children distanced from me by a spouse who reinvents a new family life for them, one that could readily be termed immoral and sinful by the church she professes to conform to. Their mother, in her relentless pursuit of a *life* for herself, cannot be expected to remain true to her promise of caring only about the children. No, she'll be diminishing and harming my children and their right to develop and learn from me in a growing entity, the family they were born into. But she will, of course, lay blame upon me instead. No peace can be found in passive non-intervention under these circumstances.

I understand the need to act; bringing about peace and keeping it, sustaining order in the disorderly world, does need both thought and action. In scientific parlance, analysis and experimentation, theory and practice, are necessary together to comprehend truth. All natural phenomena, down to the thermodynamic behavior of molecular matter, demonstrate this simple precept. But my thoughts alone cannot be the reason to act. I must respond only to the actions of a willing, armed adversary, or to the anguish of the innocent.

And what of myself, my feelings, my happiness? Why am I often dismissive of myself in evaluating circumstances I must think and act through? I think the ancients left us clues to grasp this aspect of our conscious conduct. Happiness, sadness, feelings, and emotions in general, are states of mind. It is how one relates to and thinks about any circumstance one faces that determines what state of mind one moves into. If comprehended well, this realization makes one's mind independent of material gain or loss.

Practicing thought and action without expectation of material benefit, or fear of loss, reinforces this equanimity of the mind. That is not to say one's mind becomes as calm as the ocean, for strong winds and currents do whip up turbulence in any ocean on its surface. Calm lies deep within, nevertheless, as it does in a human mind that is an ocean of memories, thoughts, and knowledge. Thus, for someone as emotional as me, as prone to stormy temper, it helps not to take myself too seriously, to dissolve my ego, and to find happiness in meaningful gain for others, sharing in their joy.

Yet, it is this very effort, of building a greater consciousness of family and community, in which one is but a small part and therefore unassuming, that is shredded by those who work toward self-benefit. Little wonder then that less forgiving societies, and groups functioning under strict codes of conduct and discipline, punish such infidelity, and adultery, with extreme severity. Misery and unrest from such selfish conduct spreads and destabilizes civil society, disintegrating the social fabric.

Such punishment isn't by any means unnatural—societies of ants and their capital punishment for strays comes to mind—though Sid, the intervention counselor, deemed their behavior instinctive and not regulated by discipline. Nature must surely have found such discipline to be of great value to the survival of these societies, be it instinctive or contemplative. Strays and their self-orientation are of little benefit to the family or the community.

Severe punishment and related harsh social practices against selfish conduct are no doubt abhorrent in the present day. Hence our system of "due process." Yet, how civilized is the practice of forcible vaginal and anal cavity search, of a woman and a diplomat, of a representative from a culture that greets strangers respectfully without bodily contact?

Social deception and infidelity are just as natural as kinship and loyalty. They are often mechanisms of competitive gain, and of necessary social relief. But the protection and nurture of the young—this is where fidelity and loyalty to family, to community, to a consciousness greater than oneself, is the humility most needed.

Nevertheless, it is fallacious to subjugate free human thought and will by norms, codes of conduct, and laws—no greater consciousness can grow and last through such extrinsic inducement. Where enforced laws regulate conduct, individuals conforming to such regulation, and some bypassing them, thrive, while many are compelled to defeat such restrictions and control. Where a greater consciousness of a cohesive growing group, *a more perfect union* as in the preamble to the American constitution, guides individuals, thought and action often go toward strengthening this consciousness that shelters and nurtures. Here, individualism as well as ego dissipates.

What social fabric, and consciousness, shall we aspire to? What is our hidden web of dark matter, the unseen but influential gravity of which maintains dynamic social galaxies whole, and prevents our systems from flying apart?

• • •

I wonder about my many classmates in the state's re-education program. And about Sid, with a private side-business of psychological consulting, and Lauren, who counseled the state's youth and families. I did leave Lauren a voice message, and sent her an email message to follow up, but haven't heard back from her. The state may be keeping her busy with all those they put through their process. And Sid did seem to siphon off one or two of those who passed through class into his private consulting, so he must do well in the perennial stream of DV intervention program candidates.

Does anybody from the state follow through to see how the lives of those they dealt with continued? Perhaps it's only those the state considers *victims* that it is concerned about.

From recent findings on child protective services in Wariduna, and from a lack of response from Lauren, I'd say they do not care. They follow the law, and processes set in accordance with the law. Theirs is not to question why, or to know of how they do.

When this book is published, I look forward to following up with my classmates. Some did leave their contact numbers on my DV course completion certificate. Paul, who expressed much interest in the book, I recall, seemed to be in better shape after our twenty-six weeks of classes. Levi transferred out of state, and thus out of our sessions; it is hard to imagine things could have improved much for him. Ken seemed fine, but Lopez, with his newfound beliefs, Jerome, whose ex-wife knew and controlled his state of mind, and the kid, who was nineteen…

In the five years since the State of Wariduna took me through its criminal prosecution and DV re-education, my two start-up efforts have effectively ended. I haven't found any corporate employment, nor have I been able to generate any business revenues. An immigrant accepted into the country as an *outstanding researcher*, with only a master's degree, is now effectively branded a criminal. An entrepreneur who contributed as much in annual state taxes as the average hourly wage worker earns in a whole year, prior to the events that led to the state's actions, now generates little tax revenue for Wariduna. Nor am I motivated to do so. Any new effort I engage in will probably not be in this state. But I did co-author two engineering texts in an emerging area of the electronics industry in these five years, receiving sample copies of the second book most recently. And events motivated me also to pen this book, and to leave these years well behind.

Is it fair to say that I've spent the past many years impoverished by unemployment? That my children and I have suffered, and yet suffer, unjust, and lifelong punishment? Recalling my good intervention counselor Sid's words, relating to sexual gratification, with a partner who could or did not agree to it, what can one call the state's actions, of intruding into my home, engineered by my so-called life-partner for self-benefit, and humbling me to its full satisfaction, reducing my family to its present circumstances, when my cultural and personal differences did not, and could not condone any of its actions? And more tellingly, when the situation, and those involved, did not merit such irreversible steps as arrest, booking, and criminal prosecution?

Did circumstances and the state's actions decimate my capacity to provide for and be an effective father to my children? Did this add fuel to their mother's efforts to alienate them from me? How can I now protect and shelter them, without the resources or even the access to do so?

But I have employed the time for introspection, for reflection upon life and learning, and do write about both. In such pursuits, I have found the clear comprehension I sought, and peace in some small measure. This, to me, has not been any blessing in disguise—as Paul, my DV classmate, called his saga—but prolonged, indescribable suffering which led, strangely enough, to self-realization. Or that is what I think—while Sid, the state's counselor, will assert that it serves to enhance my sense of self worth in my devastated life.

Epilogue

Humility is not thinking less of yourself; it is thinking of your-self less.

— C. S. Lewis

Sheriff Waspoia, who looks much like Pappy O'Daniel in *O Brother Where Art Thou*, was on TV yesterday night. An inmate in the Cluckear jail in the larger metropolis had killed his cellmate. This killer was an inmate awaiting trial for stabbing his twelve-year-old half-brother to death while watching TV. He'd said that he—"Just felt like killing." This second murder, only a few weeks after the first, was committed with a small pencil as a stabbing implement, a plastic bag, and peanut butter. He stabbed his cellmate of three weeks with the pencil in his eyes, stuffed the plastic bag down his throat, and smeared peanut butter over him. A reporter was attempting to get any answers she could from the big man of the law in Wariduna.

"Sheriff, wasn't this inmate known to be extremely dangerous?" asked the reporter. "Why wasn't he put in a cell by himself?"

"I have four hundred inmates in Cluckear waiting to be tried," replied Waspoia. "For murder. I can't give them all their own rooms."

"How did the perpetrator get his weapon?"

"He used a pencil—a half pencil," clarified the man of the law. "It was I who cut the pencils in half some time back, you know? Now they are small... just this long." Waspoia uses his thick, sausage-like fingers to show how long. "But he stabbed the other guy through the eye into his..." his voice faded into a mumble.

"Sheriff, can you tell us how the victim was killed?"

"He stuffed a plastic meal bag down the other guy's throat. I am thinking of changing that, you know? Maybe make them paper bags."

Always about you, Sheriff Waspoia, even when discussing ways to avoid tragedies. Yes, we know you work to get re-elected, that you use every bit of public face time to showcase your so-called virtues. Not one thought about screening violent inmates better, about preventing violence. Can you, Waspoia, comprehend that it may be the intention to kill that finds a way? Which must therefore be identified, and addressed, as the reporter asked you? Or do your thoughts dwell upon incremental ideas that occur to you, reacting to events in your facilities? You are past eighty after all…

. . .

Does the *swing of the pendulum*, as Sid called it, or *the ninety seven thrown under the bus, to catch the two or three bad ones*, help? Or does it create a punitive state, a prison state? Does the State of Wariduna find its extreme reactions and force an effective way to keep society peaceful, and the social fabric strong? Why does one dread the future, knowing this state's inadequate attention to troubled children, in its lax child protective services, and its lack of empathy for the least endowed and the most oppressed? And Sheriff Waspoia's many posse raids on immigrants they call illegals and undesirables?

Yet, he was re-elected in recent years, and continues his questionable activities despite impeachment efforts, and pressure through lawsuits, against abusive practices, from the federal government. Perhaps the rich and the powerful back their valiant Sheriff Waspoia, for he does their bidding while doing his job. *He marches in step*. And ensures that the riffraff are kept away, or processed and locked up.

The well-endowed surely take good care of their children. Why would they look to see how well child protective services conducts its work with children of the least fortunate in society? The rich can pay for any and all goods and services they may need in their well-ordered society. They risk only their children's catching *affluenza*. Why would they care about the lives of the least fortunate, who survive by helping each other so their children can have a better future?

Is there more vindictiveness than compassion, more righteousness than wisdom, in such actions by the powerful, who carry merrily on in their authoritarian ways, swinging pendulums and rolling buses over the ordinary? Isn't there something inhumane about passing laws adverse to immigrants, and those that are not quite the same as some good books require, in a land that is a melting-pot of immigrants from every possible culture in the world? Yet, in a state where a head governess wags a crooked, wrinkled forefinger at the head of the country, at a president with enough audacity to speak of hope, and encourages legislation that goes against inclusiveness, perhaps one cannot expect much else.

But it isn't just Wariduna that's troubled. Much of America has grieved over numerous instances of violence, upon innocents, in the decade and a half since the massacre at Columbine[5]. Based on the Supreme Court's interpretation of an amendment to the American constitution, one that allows militia members to bear arms, this right to own and use deadly weapons is vested in

---

5   http://en.wikipedia.org/wiki/Columbine_High_School_massacre

the common public. A right defended vigorously by gun rights lobbies of the country. Guns are hence all too common, and the speed and force with which law-enforcement respond to perceived threats far too often involve guns.

There have been eighteen shooting incidents involving cops in Wariduna in the first four months of 2014. Many deaths resulted from these events, including that of a police officer. A homeless camper, living in hills around Albuquerque, fell to police bullets, though he was complying with police commands, as seen in a video recording by cops of this event on the 16th of March, 2014.

Why are lobbies so powerful that change in the easy availability and use of guns is so hard to bring about? Why do our movies, and video games, display and promote the use of weapons more violent, and more effective in causing death and destruction, when society grieves over tragedies that repeat again and again?

Why is our social consciousness so fragmented that decisions, to mitigate proliferation of weapons of extreme violence, or to change anachronistic government and law-enforcement methods and systems, cannot be made by democratic thought and action? Have we hardened our framework of governance into a sacralized idol that no common citizen or process may now readily transform? Have we corrupted its true purpose, of determination *by the people alone*, into what appears to have become determination by a select few?

•   •   •

My daughter promised to come in the evening after school today. And to work with me, over the weekend, on some projects—a toy for Lucy that hadn't been put together for the past three months, and some spring-cleaning in the house. She reminded me again that weeds needed plucking, and the backyard grass needs mowing. Yes, my dear daughter, I know…she ran upstairs to visit with Lucy, who slept on her bunk bed.

My son dropped in as well; he had a few minutes to spare before going to school with their mother. He, like his sister, ignored slices of crisp red apple I arranged in a floral pattern on a plate for them, and grabbed the vitamin gummy candy I'd have out for them in the mornings before school.

"Dad, how are you paying bills these days?" asked my son.

"I saved enough from the contract assignment last year…replaced the water heater and softener from that. Paid two thousand."

"What about utility bills, Dad?"

"I'm changing automatic payment for bills to my new account. I don't use the old family account for anything, you know?" I saw that he'd brought along an envelope for me to look at.

"Are you going to get a job, Dad?"

That reminded me of Ulysses Everett McGill's children accusing him, "But you ain't bonafide, daddy!"—in the Hollywood narration of a man's trials and tribulations, *O Brother Where Art Thou*. Children like to see their sources of security in safe financial and social situations. They like to see parents who march in step too, perhaps.

I had tried to explain to my children that having gained a record of the less admirable sort now, I could find only odd jobs, or do something on my own. They were right, nevertheless. I was indeed not *bonafide*. But could this also be an opportunity, to display fortitude, and to be a source of inner strength for them?

I am no Ulysses Everett McGill, sent to some penal farm for practicing law without a license. But wait just a minute! Did I not assist my friends with their legal matters? Nevertheless, parallels between my story and that of 'Everett' are tenuous at best. I harbor no thought whatsoever of winning back a needy female, one engaged in a relentless pursuit of dalliances and a *life*. I hope only to save my children from the alienating influence of their manipulative mother.

Silence and my reverie did not help me escape my son's questions.

"Dad, Mom's thinking of cutting you off from that account."

His evident concern brings a smile to my heart, and a long reply.

"Oh she'll do whatever it is that she feels like doing, son. And I'm sure her workplace supports her, helping her deplete the account, just as they helped her create an injury report in '09... They all seem to think they're doing the right thing. Don't worry about it, Dad has more than enough money to last a few years. Another contract will come by soon. Or my books will make some money."

"Your books won't sell, Dad. The textbooks aren't selling well, are they?"

I frowned, for this was from his mother; he couldn't discover this.

"Engineering books are boring, yes. But books about life can be fun and popular—sometimes. Don't you read some?"

"I play video games, Dad. They teach me all about life."

That shut me up—he knew it would. Not only did I not like their video games, I knew the dangers of repetitive physical activity with such computers and electronic entertainment machines. My eyes, back, and wrists could attest to that.

He went upstairs to get his sister—his mother had sent him a text message that she was in the driveway—and they left for school. I looked forward to seeing him in the evening. My daughter promised to come too, which'll be a treat. We'll eat dinner together, just Dad and kids. With no thought of their mother, who opposed so many things I cautioned them about—video games, email accounts, mobile phones, and unrestricted internet access far too early in life.

But this is America, and kids have to be able to withstand peer pressure.

All the more reason for a father, one who can discipline himself and be a disciplinarian, to be close to his children, to counterbalance extraneous influences. Will my resolve to stay close to them succeed? Will they appreciate a father who disciplines them, when they live with a mother who bribes and appeases them with material rewards and absence of restraint?

• • •

Betrayal. Disloyalty. Infidelity. We think of these terms nowadays with aversion, for they are negative expressions, and are associated with extremes of thought and conduct in society. We like words such as forgiveness, tolerance, understanding, and compassion much more. Yet such aesthetic preference does not absolve behavior and actions that merit negative descriptions. A penchant for such euphemisms reveals a desire to evade responsibility, to circumvent that strong, unpleasant emotion—shame—within ourselves that can guide us to making amends. Shame and anger are natural. Without these emotions, and recognition of conduct that evokes them, one's consciousness remains incomplete, and identity unbalanced.

It is said that a lie requires a thousand more to cover it; is betrayal any different? But what is betrayal? Is amorous love for another, when committed by one's promises, betrayal of love? That is readily overcome by a claim that one could not find the love sought with a partner one committed to. Isn't it healthy to correct a mistake? Wouldn't that benefit everyone in the long run? No, betrayal is a denial of one's conscience, a suppression of all natural feelings of shame, remorse, and trepidation, in pursuit of selfish actions, with consequences far beyond the deterioration or termination of a relationship.

A dalliance my children's mother engaged in wasn't betrayal as such; her willful denial of every attempt I made to rebuild the relationship, for the happiness of the children and the extended family, *was* betrayal. The adversarial stance she assumed, with the state in sympathetic cahoots with her, turned into betrayal as she compounded my situation, by her failure to counter the state's so-called evidence with truth, and, with no shame, demanded material benefits from me, burdened as I was by my legal predicament. Perhaps the most egregious of her cascading actions is the betrayal of family, and alienation of children from their father.

The control she gained over the minds and lives of my children may be convenient to her and materially beneficial under this legal system. Yet, are her efforts to diminish the bonds of my children with their father forgivable, tolerable, and understandable acts? Especially when this—*the role of a father watching over children as they grow, one I could not fulfill in my first marriage*—was her promise to me? Or is it betrayal of her conscience, of the least bit of exercise of parental responsibility?

Is her imposition of a substitute male into the lives of my children, to occupy their minds and time, to change and diminish their need for their father, an act worthy of compassion? Or is this how deadbeat dads are made in society today—and will that blame also fall upon fathers, as the term implies?

Women, give your men a break! They are not the mindless brutes you may imagine them to be. They too have empathy, compassion, and a deep desire to be true to their purpose, their families. In their single-mindedness, they are less capable than you, and frustrated and misguided by manipulation.

You have a natural gift of bonding—with your children, with family, and others—this capability, fueled by your human physiology, the hormone Oxytocin that glows in you as you engage in becoming mothers, gives you a far greater ability to hold families and communities together. But it also lends you the ability to be socially deceptive, to lie when it is beneficial to you, your group, and your family. And this—but not only this—may be unfair to men, who are often attacked mindlessly by society and its systems deeply repulsed by violence that is but a symptom of maladies within itself. Will you attack symptoms in addressing the root causes of social agonies? Will you cleverly manipulate and brutalize the very beings who want to protect you, your children, and your families?

Without you, beautiful women, there can be no world at all, for you are mothers, you are creators and nurturers. But if you turn against men, against creation itself, if you manipulate and lie to suit your needs and wants, with no thought of harm that may come about, what will become of the world? If you feel no shame, no remorse, and do not manifest nobility of character, what will children you nurture learn from you?

How will you make a team, a strong family, if you compete with, and not complement the opposite sex? You must know that you complete men, just as much as they complement and complete you. Only together, in body, mind, and soul, can you form a whole, a creative union.

A man without a cause is soon lost, as is a woman without an anchor. You must indeed be rulers of the family and the household. Only you can soften the blows that pendulums of transient systems land upon the men you do love for their rough simplicity and devotion. You, mothers, must set examples to follow, and rule a gentler world. Why, you ask? Brutish and simple men may be, deceive and win them you will with feminine wiles, yet hold them you will only if they respect you.

•　•　•

My good friend Garth McDonald, who helped me find a temporary assignment last year, often meets with me to share pizza laden with salty anchovies. He vowed never to speak with me if I voted for a woman politician whom I talked about over a meal. I was all for another change in our nation's leadership, one that I hoped would be far more gentle and compassionate, and yet decisive and strong. But Garth has strong reservations about this lawyer and ex-senator who seems to be a clear choice in the next presidential election. Perhaps I'll abstain from voting as I do in political matters of the great State of Wariduna. Not very civic of me, but it is hard to be civic-minded in a state that shows little or no civility to its less fortunate residents.

My son and daughter came by in the evening. I busied myself with dinner preparation, while my son played on his PS3, a TV game device—something permitted minimally—and my daughter played with Lucy upstairs.

"Dad, have you been following what Russia has been doing in Ukraine?" asked my son.

"Sure, they annexed Crimea. Very efficiently too. The Ukrainian soldiers offered no resistance."

"How could Russia do this, Dad? Especially nowadays?"

"They've had a strong presence in Sevastopol, the Crimean city where their Black Sea naval fleet is based. Sort of like how we are in Qatar or Okinawa. When events in Ukraine pushed out the president friendly to Russia, they wanted to keep their only warm-water port."

"But isn't that wrong? Isn't that occupying another country?"

"Sure it is. It's annexation, illegal by international law. But they did it cleverly."

"How did they do it, Dad?"

"They'd already gained public support in Crimea, which is 70% Russian. Their meddling with the secret services, to help the old president stay in power, failed in Kiev. So they moved into Crimea by arming local militias helping them. They supported these forces with soldiers who couldn't be recognized as Russian. Faced with certain defeat, the Crimean soldiers loyal to Ukraine just did not resist. They then held a sham of a referendum, voted in mainly by ethnic Russians who wanted to join Russia. The results were shown to the world as a popular majority decision."

"But shouldn't the world stop it? Shouldn't they be forced to return Crimea to Ukraine?"

"Sure we should. Every country should respect borders set for themselves and their neighbors. But who will enforce international law? And Putin has high approval ratings in Russia. The people there are with him."

"NATO—can't NATO invade Crimea and repel Russian forces?"

"I don't know—I don't think so. Ukraine is not part of NATO. Not even a part of the European Union which they were thinking of joining. So NATO does not have the authority to help. But they may be able to if Ukraine asks. The country is near economic collapse."

"Will there be a war? That would be very dangerous…wouldn't it, Dad?"

"No, I don't think NATO will go to war with Russia. That would be dangerous as you say. But no one is going to use any nuclear weapons. All we may do is put financial sanctions in place, and try to isolate Russia. Like we did with Cuba, maybe, but that was an island nearby and an easy blockade."

"So what's to prevent Russia from taking even more land, from Ukraine, and then others? From parts of the old Soviet Union?"

"I don't know, son. They can only push so far before we are forced to do something—perhaps even send in ground troops to help prevent countries being taken over, if that ever happens. I think we've been indecisive in conflicts, such as in Syria, where the Russians blocked our efforts."

"Syria is in civil war, isn't it, Dad?"

"Millions are undergoing unimaginable suffering in Syria. I think we had a responsibility to act decisively there, but we did not. Maybe that emboldened Russia to do what they are doing now. This has changed the global balance of power, perhaps. Sadly, we may have failed to move nations of the world toward peace. Egypt, Libya, Iraq, Syria…we may have lost leadership most needed."

"Isn't President Obama talking to President Putin? Aren't European leaders getting involved? "

"That may help, but not much. Once, in World War II, Stalin asked, 'How many divisions has the Pope?' Some leaders only respect evidence of great strength. I read that Putin has always seen America as an enemy. Would he respect an enemy who wants to talk?"

"Hmm… So what would Putin respect, Dad? Or are we headed into another Cold War?"

"That—another cold war—is what many are afraid of. That this event makes the European Union and Russia enemies, instead of partners. But leadership doesn't always have to be what we think it is. It doesn't have to be just us, or those who align with us. Maybe there is a way to accept what has happened, and move on to building better relationships."

Dinner items prepared, we sat down together after some yelling by my son to get my daughter back downstairs. My curried chicken dish, cooked Basmati rice, *Chappathis* (Indian flat wheat bread, but made with corn here), *Dhaal* (a thick lentil soup), Indian pickles, and yoghurt. It was good to see them enjoying the results of my culinary skills developed over years of living alone. I've become quite the skilled cook, making ethnic dishes—Indian, Thai, Italian—I made a mental note to try Russian *Okroshka*, a cold soup of potato, meat, and vegetables.

After dinner came the Friday TV series my son and I enjoyed together, Barracuda Pool. It has a group of angel investors, evaluating investment pitches by small business entrepreneurs, competing for deals they could make in promising ventures. We enjoyed debating the merits of various ventures. It helped my son develop a good sense of the capital markets he'll someday enter. He has learned of valuation, profitability, margins, growth, and also that small businesses generate about half the jobs in our economy. He knows that I have distanced myself from speculative capital markets entirely after two decades of exposure. I wish my daughter would watch some shows together with us. Perhaps when she's older.

• • •

Wars, death and destruction, and the untold agony of people in all parts of the world, are vividly displayed in the media and brought to our attention. But I think there is a war within America, one for the country's heart and soul. A war that can be won only by the young, because we cannot re-educate the old anymore.

What young shall we raise? Those who march in lockstep? Who learn to adapt to, and go along with, the trend of increased violence and disruption in our lives and society? Or those who can and do question authority, the ways of life, and the systems they perpetuate? Children who grow into adults with strong and clear identities, and the capacity for critical thought, who stay well-connected within a resilient social fabric? But are we not setting them up for failure, as we perpetuate violence common in our systems, our thinking, and our ways of life?

But why must our young fight the battles we create, bear punishment for our sins? Because they inherit the world we leave for them? And if they must, is it not our responsibility to guide them truthfully about pathways to misery? Education may indeed be the answer. But can it really be a one-way street? Or top-down, and trickle-down? I think we should educate ourselves and our entrenched systems, as much as we educate the young, changing our systems to better guide growing minds and correct the ills of society. And I think *we* must fight the battles for change, not our young.

It is said those in power are afraid to lose it. This is particularly true in dictatorships and hierarchies such as religious organizations. Can democracy be any different? Those voted into power, into positions of authority and influence, are, presumably, just as worried about losing their power. They work to perpetuate old systems and methods that may maintain their power and privileges.

Change, disruptive and sustainable, requires a self-transforming consciousness. With a social fabric fragmented and weakened, how do we foresee development of an integral social consciousness, much less one that can transform itself? How can such transformation happen unimpeded, if controlled by lawmakers supported by lobbies funded by those entrenched in profitable exploitation under current systems?

How can we expect our young to bring about such transformation, when they are laden with debt, of as much as a trillion dollars in the present, as they sail into the world as adults? How did learning and teaching, a natural, noble, socially critical process, that prepares our young for their lives and betterment of the world, change into a passage that burdens them with great debt?

What is it that weakens our interconnectedness with one another, our social fabric that holds us all united in purpose and destiny? Could it be the very thing we pursue, a purpose defined for us in life, seeking pleasures and treasures in pursuit of happiness?

An economic system of rampant capitalism, unshakably entrenched in the present world, has, over countless decades, only widened the gap between the rich and the poor. Some studies show that almost one-half of estimated wealth in the world is owned by 1% of the world's population in the present. Is it not this accumulation, of apparent wealth, that separates us and makes us unequal, despite overt assurances of equality? Isn't this pursuit of profit from one another, and exploitation leading to such profit, that which distances us, and pulls us apart? Is this not a self-evident truth?

Isn't sheer individualism, a relentless focus on self-benefit over that of all others, the aspect that transforms healthy competition into a winner-take-all, avaricious approach? Those who enrich themselves in such fashion feel no shame, or concern for the circumstances of those they profit from. No *nanoom, manoom*, as my mother will say succinctly.

Perhaps John Lennon, the singer, songwriter, and activist, had just the right vision, calling to mind a world in which everyone would have minimal or no possessions. Native Americans here have an old saying, "Man can no more own land than he can own air or water." They now populate a tiny fraction of the land in which they had, for centuries, roamed relatively freely. Their culture and natural wisdom remains segregated and displayed only as antique American museum curiosities. They most assuredly will not own any air or water.

Could such ownership, one's claim to excessive material resources and exclusion of others from their use, be that which renders a social fabric tenuous? Isn't our interdependence, and innate gregariousness, destroyed by this drive to acquire and hoard resources and material wealth at the expense of others? Or is that a natural, inalienable right?

I do not at all mean to malign profit. Only to ascribe diminished importance to it. Changing the words of C. S. Lewis suitably, one does not need to think less of profit, but to think of profit less, in moving toward shared resources, greater equality, and stronger social interdependence, connectivity, and consciousness. In this humility in thought and action, perhaps, we can work to mitigate the devastation we visit upon the planet, society, and all life.

Freedom, for instance, may well be overrated. Can we truly enjoy freedom without restraint? Without empathy, or compassion, for those impacted by what we believe to be our right to practise freely any way of life chosen? Can we be set free to do anything and everything we may wish to, as Jim, my inter-vention program classmate, asked, in our relentless pursuit of enjoyment, prof-it, and power? Countless innocents suffer unconscionable deprivation while puppet masters pull strings disrupting their financial security, and, often, their lives together. Do we not see this in the circumstances of the many American families bearing the brunt of the recent economic downfall?

But what of freedom of thought, you ask. Someone wise—and I do not know who, but no matter—said thoughts lead to words and actions, which lead to habits and character, and ultimately to what one may call destiny. Is it not prudent then to ensure that thoughts too are guided by ethics and truth?

Is character developed through freely permitted pursuit of pleasures and satisfaction? Temptations resisted, it is said, are a true measure of character. What, then, are temptation pursued freely? No, I think measured, qualified freedom suits us better individually, and within families, communities, and soci-eties. Changing my befuddled counselor Sid's words, I think freedom should be an earned privilege, which, when exercised, leads to enlightenment, and strengthens families as well as the social fabric.

• • •

I rejoined my children's activities from my lone reverie when my son re-minded me that it was time for them to head back to their mother's. It's so much fun to talk about things with my son. He is so curious, and surprisingly knowledgeable, for a child his age. I do recognize that he is now a teenager. Having joined the *teen species*, as we called it, he merits greater respect from his father. I can see a growing sense of responsibility in him.

Could a father be more proud of his children, of all his children? My first has grown into a confident, headstrong young man, who cares deeply for his mother who devoted herself to his upbringing. His rough edges will surely soften with the passage of time and his own learning. My little ones grow with their mother, but under my watchful eyes close by. Yet, I couldn't rid my heart of dread for their future, for they lived with a mother who could not be trust-ed to place their needs above hers.

I watched from the driveway as they ran along the sidewalk toward the next street, where their mother lived in her house, by her pool, with her mon-ey, and her boyfriends. My son had been dropping hints of a new beau, a Bert Minnows, who often plonked himself in front of the TV turned on at high volume in their home...whatever. Everyone seeks to satisfy their need for se-curity and comfort; some more so than others. Lucy bounded along the side-walk behind them. I know she'll be back later. As will my children.

• • •

I drifted back again into personal thoughts. It is when the glaciers and ice on the poles of the earth melt that ocean levels rise substantially. Global warming is sure to make ice melt away from mountains, glaciers, and the frozen geographic poles. But it is hard to see wealth melting away from those that have acquired mountains of this material resource for themselves and their near and dear ones.

Few see this acquisitiveness as poverty of the mind and intellect, as a corruption of one's soul, as the cause of social envy, tensions, and of violent conflict. As for me, I have indeed been humbled, both materially and socially. I do accept that, seeking to learn humility, to being useful to others, rather than engaging in any individual pursuit of happiness.

Did I learn anything at all? Or did my travails only suppress my optimism and gregariousness, and replace them with cynicism? I do not think so. Perhaps you, dear reader, engaged but not immersed in my story, can judge that better than I.

Some say intelligence shines not in any accumulation of knowledge, but in social and emotional capacities. A mediator, a peacemaker and problem-solver, is often more effective than the most learned scholar. I am grateful to have touched and helped more lives than I've ever been able to before.

I did lose my drive to accumulate wealth and its apparent societal success. But is that such a bad thing? I am now eager to enrich other lives rather than fill my own with material pleasures. This book is a manifestation of that desire. I think I've gained a measure of peace and learned, again, that restraint and social consciousness are of far greater value than freedom and individual pursuits of happiness.

Life with its miracles and challenges is, to me, a more humbling and enlightening journey. I think living well despite all adversity for the right reasons embodies the human spirit. I seek to learn, from fathers and mothers in my family, about being the father my children need me to be. I hope to be the friend those around me seek in their times of need. Doesn't sorrow shared diminish, and happiness shared grow? Is that not a self-evident truth learned as we become part of a family and community's consciousness?

Freedom and liberty is, as life, a journey of discovery, following human instincts and conscious choice, that I enjoy in most everything I do. And happiness—that can be found in understanding, tranquility, and true love, which I've sought all my life. But the search for true love, and finding it, is an esoteric subject and a story for another day. A day when the seas rise. More important things await. My son and daughter are coming home to stay this weekend...or are they?

• • •

www.ingramcontent.com/pod-product-compliance
Lightning Source LLC
Chambersburg PA
CBHW050119280326
41933CB00010B/1168